Seaside Dream Home

Besieged

Scenic-Preservation Mandates and Property Rights in Collision, a Case History, and Proposed Land-Use Reforms

By

T.G. Berlincourt

FRONT COVER PHOTO: View southward from Cuffey's Cove toward sea stacks offshore from Elk, California. In this telephoto view our home and three near-neighbor homes are faintly visible at right of center. Left of center is the mountaintop home of RD Beacon. Out of the scene to the left is the village of Elk.

Order this book online at www.trafford.com
or email orders@trafford.com

Most Trafford titles are also available at major online book retailers.

Printed in Victoria, BC, Canada.

ISBN: 978-1-4269-0478-3

*Our mission is to efficiently provide the world's finest, most comprehensive book publishing
service, enabling every author to experience success. To find out how to publish your book, your
way, and have it available worldwide, visit us online at www.trafford.com*

Trafford rev. 10/26/2009

North America & international
toll-free: 1 888 232 4444 (USA & Canada)
phone: 250 383 6864 ♦ fax: 812 355 4082

This book is dedicated to the lawmakers who incorporated the Fifth and Fourteenth Amendments into the United States Constitution. May the takings and equal-protection clauses of those amendments forever withstand the assaults of activist judges and bureaucrats who seek to weaken them.

Table of Contents

PREFACE

"The desire to dictate the behavior of others is such a timeless and universal attribute of our species that it must rank with the sex drive, maternal instinct, and the will to survive in terms of the likelihood of its being part of our biological heritage."

Frans de Waal, in *Good Natured: the Origins of Right and Wrong in Humans and Other Animals* (Harvard University Press)

Why in the world have I chosen to write about, and thereby relive, a most unpleasant encounter with government bureaucracies and an angry faction of villagers intent on preventing Margie and me from building our dream home on the California coast? Well, for starters, it's been therapeutic. But there's a more-rational justification. Simply stated, as undeveloped land becomes more and more scarce, the inevitable conflict between scenic-preservation mandates and fundamental property rights becomes ever more intense. And the need becomes ever more pressing for a rational and harmonious resolution of those conflicting interests. By describing our tortuous, six-year quest for a permit to build our seaside retirement home, I call attention to the conflict and point out the flaws and inequities in existing land-use laws and regulations. Along the way, I propose reform of those laws and regulations to render them consistent with the United States Constitution and fair to all concerned.

Early on I titled this book *Scenic Exaction Free-For-All*, but that was a little cryptic, and so I chose the present more-easily-understood title. Nevertheless, with a little explanation, the original title aptly describes the problem addressed in this book. What exactly had I meant by the words "Scenic Exaction" in the original title? A scenic exaction is a scenic regulatory taking by government, or stated another way, it's a use restriction placed on property by government in order to preserve scenic vistas for the benefit of the public at large. Many people believe that to be a reasonable requirement. However, an unfortunate side effect of scenic regulatory takings by government is that they often drastically reduce the affected parcel's value to its owner as well as its fair market value. With but extremely rare exception, the abused landowner receives no compensation despite the takings clause in the United States Constitution. In contrast, in an "eminent-domain taking," government actually takes possession of the property, and, in accord with the Constitution, must pay the landowner "just compensation."

And why was the expression "Free-for-All" used in the original title? According to *Webster's Encyclopedic Unabridged Dictionary of the English Language* (1989 Edition, published by Gramercy Books), a free-for-all is "a fight, argument, contest, etc., open to everyone and usually without rules." What a perfect description of the brawl into which Margie and I were swept for a period of six years.

It's of course beyond dispute that scenic preservation is highly desirable. Given that fact, however, it's reasonable to ask, "Who should bear the burden of providing it?" Under the California Coastal Act the public at large enjoys the many benefits of scenic preservation free of charge, while the burden of providing it is borne solely by coastal landowners. Unfortunately, so long as scenic concessions from coastal landowners are accessible to the state free of charge, there will be no end to the state's demands for such concessions, and there will be no end to the associated conflict. In light of the foregoing, the title of this book could equally as well have been, *Scenic Exaction, Free for All, Except for the Exactee.* (The missing hyphens are of course intentional here, and you won't find the term "exactee" in the dictionary. Nonetheless, it's an appropriate appellation for the hapless landowner.) Clearly, the Constitution's eminent-domain and equal-protection clauses require a more-equitable and more-congenial relationship between scenic-preservation mandates and property rights. This book makes the case for such a relationship not only for coastal regions, but for *all* scenic regions.

Currently, building a home on the California Coast is a lot like taking a seat on Apollo 13. You probably won't achieve all that you set out to achieve, but, when it's all over, you'll be grateful it wasn't worse. And though you'll feel compelled to talk about it afterward, you might hesitate, thinking that nothing can be more tiresome than a tale of someone else's troubles. Indeed, Jeffery Speich, Esq., who did a lot of the legal heavy lifting for us, thought so. He cautioned me that if I ever wrote about our experience I'd be inviting wrongful-death lawsuits from the survivors of readers who died of boredom. On the other hand, vicarious armchair adventurers find accounts of the trauma experienced by the Apollo 13 astronauts to be enormously fascinating. Why shouldn't they find our far-lesser, though more-prolonged, trauma at least a little entertaining? And perhaps they might even be inspired to contribute in some way to the development of that more-equitable and more-congenial relationship between scenic-preservation mandates and property rights. I should add that people who've heard a little about our experience from others often approach Margie and me to learn more about it. They want to know all the details. They care about preservation of natural scenic vistas, and they also care about property rights, and so they find the conflict between them most perplexing. And they're curious about what damages the regulatory process might have inflicted on our project, on our finances, *and* on our psyches.

One way of writing about this problem would be to critique the California Coastal Act and its derivative regulations and implementation procedures one by one in an abstract, dispassionate, and analytical fashion, devoid of examples of the abuses that occur in practice. That would surely prove hopelessly boring, perhaps fulfilling Jeff Speich's prediction, and it would undoubtedly be ineffective in bringing about the much-needed reforms. And so I've chosen instead to tell a very personal story with real-life examples of the abuses and inequities that are all too easily perpetrated by government bureaucracies under the California Coastal Act. Described in terms of the personalities involved and the fierce combat that took place, the scenic-preservation/property-rights conundrum takes on a human-interest perspective. It's then more likely to command attention *and* gain some chance of contributing to meaningful reforms, reforms that continue to foster scenic preservation but spare coastal-zone property owners the kind of turmoil that we experienced.

This account was written mostly during the spring of 2006, twelve years after Margie and I submitted our application for a permit to build our seaside retirement home in a "highly-scenic" area on the northern California Coast. It took us six years, a $200,000 lawsuit, and seventeen transcontinental round-trip air flights just to secure our building permit. The battle was all about where on our parcel we would be allowed to locate our home. We wished to build where we could take advantage of the magnificent ocean vistas offered by our parcel. The opposition sought to restrict our home to a site that would leave us with little in the way of scenic ocean vistas. As we later learned, they had an ulterior motive. In the end, like the Apollo 13 astronauts, we achieved less than we would have liked, and, like them, we're grateful it wasn't worse.

In telling our story, I've included extensive quotes of contentious discourse from both sides in the conflict. I've made no attempt to muzzle the opposition. Indeed, their views are liberally presented in their own words. Those quotes reveal a lot about human nature, in particular, the combatants' characters, their strengths and weaknesses, their virtues, their perseverance, their flaws, their eccentricities, their deceit, their scheming, and their malice. Those quotes also perpetuate their grammar, spelling, and punctuation. (Proofreaders have been instructed not to tamper with them!!!)

To wage our campaign successfully we had to keep extensive and meticulous records. Accordingly, in writing this account I've been able to mine eleven cubic feet of documentation, consisting of letters, memos, publications, reports, studies, hearing tapes, legal papers, deposition transcripts, plans, and other records. We were always careful to record in writing the substance of important discussions, whether by telephone, face-to-face, or at meetings. What are stated here as facts have been documented, whereas uncertainties, speculations, and opinions expressed here are identified as such.

Make no mistake though, this book is written from *my* perspective, and our opponents will doubtless take issue with much of it. They are, of course, at liberty to tell it from their own perspectives, for there are indeed two sides to every land-use dispute. And I grant that some readers may very well side with our opponents and therefore see as heroes those that I view as villains and scoundrels. So be it.

Although our story is particular to building on the California coast, it has more universal relevance, for anyone seeking to build, add onto, or modify a structure almost anywhere in the world ultimately comes hard up against the zoning codes and regulations, and, inevitably, the government planning and building bureaucracies. Those codes and regulations are seldom model products of rational thought, nor are they robust enough to withstand perversion by planning and building bureaucracies intent on their own agendas. And, as if that were not enough, would-be builders often have to fend off attacks by irate neighbors as well. This account of our attempts to deal with all of the above provides useful lessons on how to, and how not to, go about it. Yes, we often stumbled along the way.

At the very least, our experience can serve as a cautionary tale for anyone daring even to think about building in the California coastal zone. If you feel compelled to do so, do it with your eyes wide open. You might be lucky and avoid being ambushed, but don't count on it. There's no rational pattern. Indeed, the laws and regulations are ambiguous, and the administrators are often capricious. As a consequence (in full confirmation of the fallibility of the laws and regulations) it really matters who the elected and appointed officials are at any given time. As a result, good timing is crucial, but, unfortunately, that's difficult to achieve, a lot like trying to choose the best times to buy and sell stocks.

Laws and regulations should always be just, equitable, sensible, and, so-skillfully-constructed that they preclude perversion by those authorized to administer them. Unfortunately the California Coastal Act and its derivative regulations fail to meet those criteria. Consequently, if you insist upon equal protection of the law, you might have to wage a costly legal battle to secure it. Knowing what we encountered, you'll be better prepared to carry out your own campaign. In that sense this tale can be of assistance to would-be coastal residents.

On the other hand, anti-development zealots might applaud our saga for its value in frightening away would-be coastal residents. I don't intend it that way, but if you're cynical enough, you could, I suppose, accuse me of having joined the "California-now-that-I've-got-mine-I-don't-want-others-to-get-theirs" club. I haven't.

Without doubt, this book will offend many. Different people have divergent and strongly-held opinions regarding land use by others. At the same time they zealously guard their rights to use their own land as they wish. Is it any wonder that conflicts arise?

Finally, if I could choose but one modest reform for this book to accomplish, it would be to replace the "S" word in the California Coastal Act with plain and precise objective language. What's the "S" word? Well, it's a lot like porn. You'll know it when you see it.

CHAPTER 1
ABOUT US

You're driving south from the village of Mendocino along the rugged and spectacular California coast some 150 miles north of San Francisco. Nearing the tiny village of Elk, you round a gentle curve, and suddenly the most magnificent panorama of the Pacific coast bursts into view (Figure 1). Giant sea stacks rise above the sea. Sculpted by the relentless surf, they've assumed all manner of contorted shapes: arches, pyramids, grottos, even dinosaurs. It takes your breath away. Impulsively, you pull onto the small turnout at Cuffey's Cove and reach for your camera. The little village of Elk lies at the left nestled into the mountains. Its brightly colored homes, B&Bs, Inns, Churches, Post Office, Garage, and General Store catch your eye, but the main attraction is at the center of the scene, *those spectacular sea stacks!* You can't help but think, what a magnificent place to retire and build your dream home!

Margie and I did just that. We now live at the very center of that scene, nearly two miles south of the Cuffey's Cove turnout. Our home is perched on an eleven-acre promontory that rises 160 feet above the surf one-half mile south of Elk. That promontory offers spectacular views northward to the sea stacks, westward toward Japan, southward to Point Arena, and eastward to the mountains. By what good fortune were we able to build our home in this paradise? As recounted in the chapters that follow, the story is long and tortuous, and the paradise is imperfect, for we had to overcome some daunting obstacles.

In planning our home we naturally sought to take full advantage of the extraordinary vistas offered by our parcel. However, early on, a hostile faction of local villagers and conniving State and County officials intervened. They sought to banish our building site to a location where our views of those magnificent scenic vistas would be greatly diminished. Their stated justification was to preserve scenic vistas for the benefit of the public at large, yet the site they mandated for our home would not achieve that end. In fact, it would place our home much closer to, and hence more visible from, public view points. There it would actually block views to the ocean. That was most puzzling, and so we smelled a rat. There had to be an ulterior motive, but it would be years before we would discover what it was.

For our retirement, we'd hoped to be able to settle peacefully into a little rural village, far from the turmoil of the big cities where we'd spent our professional careers. Instead we found ourselves mired in a regulatory morass created by the California Coastal Act. Of course, we hadn't been seeking conflict. We'd already had more than enough of that in our combined 86 years of employment. But when our building plans were attacked, it became a very personal matter, and we had no choice but to stand and fight. Our counterattack would be but one small skirmish in a widespread ongoing war between scenic-preservation mandates and property rights.

After six years of intense combat, we emerged, bloodied and bruised, with a building permit. But, like the Apollo 13 astronauts, we hadn't achieved all we'd set out to accomplish. Nevertheless, we're grateful it wasn't worse. Today we cherish our beautiful home more than you can imagine, and we consider ourselves most fortunate to be living in such a magnificent setting.

Ironically, within but a few more years, trees we've planted will conceal our home completely from public view, suggesting that our skirmish with neighbors and with State and County officials need never have taken place. While all of that's now history, the larger war between scenic-preservation mandates and property rights continues to rage in the California coastal zone (and far afield as well). The issue is so contentious, and the combat so intense, because scenic preservation and property rights are both so precious. Peace will be possible only when more-sensible and more-equitable land-use laws and regulations, consistent with the United States Constitution, are adopted to mediate and assure that both concerns are respected *and* that both sides in the conflict fulfill their rightful obligations. My suggested approaches for achieving that are proposed in Chapter 3, and, hopefully, my telling of our story will help drive the debate in the direction of those suggestions. Also, knowledge of our story will help other owners of scenic property avoid some of the pitfalls we encountered.

Unfortunately, flaws in existing laws and regulations governing scenic preservation and property rights bring out the very worst in people. That caused us many sleepless nights during our prolonged battle. But now, in retrospect, the antics of our adversaries make for a good story. Their scurrilous schemes were endless and severely challenged our ability to develop countermeasures. As noted above, we smelled a rat early on. And, as you'll learn in Chapter 11, it was only very late in the game that we were able to uncover our adversaries' hidden agenda. That eventually provided us with decisive legal leverage. After you've read our story from beginning to end, I think you'll agree that property owners have every right to demand better from their government (and from their neighbors).

Fortunately, we were blessed throughout our prolonged battle with steadfast allies of exceptional competence. But, unfortunately, at the same time we were cursed with persistent and unscrupulous adversaries, some shrewd (and some not so shrewd, though very troublesome nonetheless) and some very colorful. I'll describe the backgrounds of the combatants of both persuasions as they're introduced in later chapters. In the remainder of this chapter I provide biographical information about Margie and me. That will help you understand why, when challenged, we chose to stand our ground. (Also, it's an opportunity to counter some of the rumors that circulated during the hostilities.)

Margie entered this world as Marjorie Kathleen Alkins in 1928 in Toronto, Canada, the second daughter of Herbert John Wesley Alkins and Ellen Florence Barker Alkins. John, a jeweler, had served overseas in the Canadian military during World War I. Wounds he suffered in that conflict contributed to his untimely death when Margie was but two years old. In the same war, Margie's mother, Ellen, had lost her father, a sergeant in a kilted Canadian regiment. As a widow, with but an eighth-grade education, Ellen managed to provide for her daughters through the great depression in part with the help of welfare payments and in part by taking care of foster infants in her home. Later, during World War II, she supported her daughters by working in a munitions factory.

Ellen instilled a desire for education in her daughters, and both proved to be outstanding students. Margie was captivated by Latin and Greek languages and history. She was Riverdale Collegiate High School valedictorian, and, although slight of build, she won a letter in intramural sports. Her high school graduation photo caused some controversy. As sweet, naïve, and innocent as she was, the school authorities deemed the photo "inappropriate." In proper 1940s Toronto, that was the closest the staid school administrators could come to uttering the words "too sexy." A second, carefully choreographed photography session yielded a suitable photo. With essential merit-based scholarship aid, Margie entered the University of Toronto. She graduated with first class honors.

Preceded by a sister and a brother, I was born in 1925 in Fremont, Ohio, the son of Weldon Burnett Berlincourt and Gladys Ora Gibbs Berlincourt. Both of my parents were raised on farms and had brief exposure to college. Both taught school for a few years. My father then served in the army artillery in Europe in World War I and later entered a hardware store partnership. Although I was aware that times were difficult during the great depression, my childhood was relatively carefree. My parents also instilled in their children a high regard for education. My mother, sister, and brother were all high-school valedictorians. I had to settle for salutatorian, but played first-chair trumpet in the high school band, concert orchestra, and dance band, and, belatedly entering sports in my senior year (1942-3), I won a letter in track.

World War II was then in progress, and I went off to college at Case School of Applied Science. I completed an accelerated freshman year in seven months, and, to my surprise, had the best record in the freshman class. But then, turning eighteen, I enlisted in the army. Thanks to a radio physics course taught by Howard Laub, my high school physics teacher, I had some knowledge of radio electronics, and I knew the Morse code, and so, after infantry basic training, I was transferred to a field artillery radio section, a much less-risky assignment. With a little more training, and still only eighteen, I became Radio Section Chief (Technician Fourth Grade) in the 220th Field Artillery Group Headquarters Battery. Before I completed my first year in the army, the 220th was shipped to England

and on to France. After the Battle of the Bulge, we were assigned to Patton's Third Army as it raced deep into Germany. Coming under enemy fire only sporadically, the 220th engaged in combat for six weeks. Members of the 220th were authorized to display two battle stars on their campaign ribbons.

When hostilities ended in Europe, Captain Beach from the 220th, a lawyer by profession, was assigned to Military Government at Third Army Headquarters in Bad Tolz in Bavaria. I went along as his assistant, and, on a couple of occasions, was treated to sightings of old "Blood and Guts" Patton himself. Then I was off to Shrivenham American University in Britain, a college established to provide education for GIs awaiting reassignment or discharge. It was there that I learned of the use of nuclear weapons to end the war with Japan. That solved the mystery of what had been going on in Oak Ridge, Tennessee. Early in the war, my father had sold his interest in the hardware store and had found employment as a purchasing agent there. Neither he nor I had any knowledge that nuclear weapons materials were being produced there, nor that nuclear weapons were even possible. With the end of the war with Japan, I knew that I would not be sent to the Far East and would soon be discharged.

After my brief stint at Shrivenham I returned to Germany, and was assigned to the 9th Division Artillery to mark time until discharge. A dance band, "The Divarty [for Division Artillery] Toot Sweeters" was being formed, and I joined it. My remaining time in the army was spent with the Toot Sweeters, happily playing in GI nightclubs and for United Service Organization (USO) shows.

Upon being discharged from the army I returned to Case (by then renamed Case Institute of Technology) and completed a Bachelor of Science Degree in physics. Then it was off to summer employment at Los Alamos Scientific Laboratory, which had seen the dawn of the nuclear age, for better or for worse. The science was exciting and the weekend mountain climbing with fellow summer employees in New Mexico and Colorado was exhilarating. And the local girls preferred dating summer employees, "because they had a carefree vacation attitude" that year-round employees couldn't muster in that remote mesa-top stronghold.

That fall, 1949, I entered graduate school at Yale University seeking a PhD in physics, and after a year of intense study put in another summer at Los Alamos. Returning to Yale in the fall of 1950 I learned of a Saturday-night dance to be held at 370 Temple Street, the women graduate students' residence. At that time there were no women undergraduates at Yale, but there were modest numbers of women in the graduate school and in the nursing school. And it occurred to me that I hadn't had a date in New Haven my entire first year at Yale. That wasn't normal. So why not attend the dance at 370 Temple? Well, for one thing there'd be ten times as many males as females there, and for another, those females would be, well, female graduate students. Who could imagine what to expect? Nevertheless, with little other entertainment in prospect that evening, I decided to chance it.

About Us

Well, would you look at that? There she was! What a beauty! Can you imagine? Intelligent enough to be one of the women graduate students, and looking like that? Just a little thing, couldn't weigh more than a hundred pounds. Sparkling gray eyes, a little reserved, but with an infectious smile, a dimple on one cheek only, dark wavy hair, a light complexion, and, I might add, very well proportioned. And hell, she's dancing with one of my fellow physics graduate students. And the room is packed with a huge excess of males. But it was no place for the faint of heart. Muscling my way through the throng, I requested, and was granted, a turn on the dance floor. Placing my arms around her, I found she was light as a feather and fit in a way I never experienced before. Fact is, I'm not much of a dancer. Always in the dance band, so never really got the hang of dancing. But with this little charmer it all came naturally. Turns out her name is Marjorie, she's Canadian, she's new here, going for a PhD in classics (Latin and Greek history and languages), and she's already accepted a date with my fellow physics graduate student.

Well, never mind, to make a long story short, Margie's been mine for the past fifty–three years. What good fortune to have such an enchanting, intelligent, and compatible mate in such an exquisite package! What's that? Nobody's *that* perfect? OK, I'll grant she's a bit obsessed with British murder mysteries, and, were she of lesser character, that could hint at a dangerous tendency.

Upon completing my physics PhD research at Yale, I found employment at the United States Naval Research Laboratory in Washington, DC, working in low temperature physics research. Six months later Margie and I were married, both innocent. Those were different times.

Diligent as ever, Margie completed her Yale PhD in absentia and found employment as a cataloger at the Folger Shakespeare Library. My research was going well at the Navy lab, which was (and is) an impressive institution, but, with the wanderlust of youth, I heard the siren call of the burgeoning aerospace activity in southern California. The Atomic Energy Research Department (later the Atomics International Division) of North American Aviation had an opening for a physicist to explore the basic electronic properties of nuclear reactor materials. To interview for that position I left Washington on a bitterly-cold, winter day. Snow blanketed the ground. At the Los Angeles airport, Dwain Bowen, my boss-to-be, met me in shirtsleeves and drove me to his home. We arrived after dark, and so I couldn't see much of the setting. The next morning I awoke in an upstairs bedroom to the sound of birds singing. Looking out the window, I was awestruck. The warm sun was shining brightly on acres of lemon trees, and in the distance were the majestic San Gabriel Mountains painted in soft hues of purple. With Margie's concurrence I accepted the position.

North American Aviation was of course noted for having produced some of the most noteworthy military aircraft of World War II and the Korean War, but when I arrived in 1955 the company was expanding rapidly into rockets and rocket engines, missiles, guidance systems, avionics, electronics, computers, and nuclear reactors. That was exciting! Again

I found fulfillment in my research and was soon appointed Group Leader of the Electronic Properties Group. That was a great privilege, for members of the group were very talented and productive, as well as most congenial. In addition, I was well rewarded financially by the company.

For Margie, employment opportunities were less attractive, but rather than sulk, she made things happen. A PhD classicist naturally looks for a university teaching position, but this was the McCarthy era, and state-supported institutions of higher learning in California required a loyalty oath. As a Canadian citizen, Margie couldn't pledge loyalty to the United States. She didn't have to work of course, but she liked to work, and having grown up under difficult circumstances, she found security in knowing that, in working, she was providing for a secure future. Off she went to a secretarial course and soon found employment as secretary to the Production Manager of Standard Brands, a food supply company. Then in 1956 she became a US citizen and found more appropriate employment at the Rocketdyne Division of North American Aviation, where she edited rocket engine operation, maintenance, and repair manuals. She did so well that she was soon appointed Supervisor of the Editorial Section and was classified as an "Engineer" by the personnel department. Never underestimate the value of a classical education.

We were happy. Our work was satisfying. We became homeowners in Woodland Hills. We learned to ski. We vacationed, and we discovered the Big Sur, Carmel, Monterey, and farther north, the Mendocino coast. The last, the Mendocino coast, was the least accessible, the least developed, and the most wild and rugged, and we fell in love with it. The S.S. Seafoam Lodge in Little River across the coast highway from Buckhorn Cove became a holiday habit.

Then, in the fall of 1958 Margie informed me that the production of a new family member was underway. That pleased me immensely, though it may have dealt a setback to the future advancement of women to supervisory positions at Rocketdyne. But Margie continued working until shortly before the arrival of Leslie Ellen Berlincourt on July 9, 1959. We could not have been happier, and over the years Leslie has proved to be a joy beyond description. Not wishing to trust Leslie's care to others for extended periods of time, Margie sought and found a part-time teaching position with the University of Southern California (USC), where she was able to limit her teaching duties to only two days a week.

At about the same time I began a research collaboration with Dr. Richard R. Hake, a highly talented physicist who had obtained his graduate degree from the University of Illinois. To our delight that collaboration yielded results of both scientific and practical significance. On the practical side, we discovered the superior high-magnetic-field, high-supercurrent-density superconducting properties of niobium-titanium alloys, which account for their use today in the windings of thousands and thousands of supermagnets in use for magnetic resonance imaging (MRI) medical diagnostics and for particle beam bending in enormous high-energy-particle accelerators literally miles in extent. Equally satisfying was the fact that we were able to account scientifically for these remarkable properties in terms of theories proposed earlier by the USSR scientists Ginzburg, Landau, Abrikosov, and Gorkov, but largely ignored in the United States. For their contributions to these theories, Ginzburg and Abrikosov received Nobel Prizes in Physics in 2003.

During all of this excitement in the early 1960s, Lee Atwood, CEO of North American Aviation, decided to establish a central research laboratory to serve all divisions of the company. The cadre for this new laboratory came primarily from Atomics International, and I was among those included. A new facility, the Science Center, was constructed for the laboratory at a magnificent site in Thousand Oaks, California, overlooking a deep canyon, and with picturesque mountain views.

About the same time the California Lutheran College (CLC) was being established in Thousand Oaks, and Margie left USC to become a part-time charter member of the CLC faculty. With both of our careers tied to Thousand Oaks, we purchased a very scenic half-acre parcel there high on a hillside overlooking the Conejo Valley with mountains of the Coast Range in the distance. There, in 1965 we constructed a contemporary house of our own design. (The process was without unhappy incident.) That same year I was appointed Associate Director of the Science Center. Our occasional visits to the Mendocino coast continued, and Buckhorn Cove became one of Leslie's favorite haunts.

Then, in 1967, Margie was offered and accepted a part-time teaching position in the History Department at what is now California State University at Northridge. With its much larger enrollment that institution offered greater scope for course offerings in Margie's field, but the downside was a long commute back into the San Fernando Valley. As Leslie grew older, Margie took on full time teaching duties at Cal State Northridge, but she still managed to see Leslie off to school each day and to greet her when she returned home. (I still marvel at how Margie managed all that.) In 1970 Margie was promoted to Associate Professor with tenure.

In the meantime the Science Center had been a success, attracting outstanding scientific staff and providing essential support to North American's operating divisions. The contacts with the company's ultra-high-tech challenges proved to be fascinating, and I found great satisfaction in Science Center solutions to those challenges. But North American Aviation had in a sense become a victim of its own success. The company had played the largest role of any company in the Apollo Program, the manned exploration of the moon. The first manned moon landing was accomplished with spectacular success in 1969, and so development and production for the Apollo Program and other large programs were being phased down. There had been a merger with Rockwell, and the new company was called North American Rockwell. As North American's fortunes declined, Rockwell's rose, and soon the company became Rockwell International, and Rockwell managers called the tune. Corporate support for the Science Center was drastically reduced, and I was one of the casualties of the subsequent staff reduction. Unfortunately, other aerospace companies were undergoing similar stress at the same time, and so, unlike in the past, one couldn't simply go across town and find employment with another high-tech company. University positions were also tight, but fortunately I received two university offers, and an offer to head the research department at the Leeds and Northrup Corporation. The decision was a difficult one. Margie, Leslie, and I retreated to Mendocino to ponder our future and consider the pros and cons of the various alternatives. How nice it would be simply to remain on the Mendocino coast and watch the waves roll in. But I was only 44 and not a dropout, and Margie wasn't either. In the end I accepted a position as full professor and Chairman of the Physics Department at Colorado State University (CSU) in Fort Collins with duties to commence in the fall of 1970.

What about our beautiful home in Thousand Oaks? Of course, with the aerospace malaise on the west coast, the bottom dropped out of the real estate market. Recall the famous Seattle billboard of that era, "Will the last person to leave town please turn out the lights!" Margie and I reached a painful decision. She and Leslie would remain behind pending sale of our home, and Margie would fulfill her teaching contract at Northridge, while I went off to Colorado. The only saving grace was that there was good airline service between Denver and LA.

I greatly missed Margie and Leslie, but fortunately CSU turned out to be a very congenial place, great dean, outstanding faculty members, fun students, and of course superb skiing nearby. And I even managed to have a second family of sorts. Seeking simple bachelor lodgings, I was about to despair, when someone suggested that I look into the College Inn, an off-campus student housing facility operated by the Prudential Insurance Company. It was a large, modern, substantial building with cheerful, inviting rooms with private baths. Delicious meals fit for adolescent appetites were included in a spacious and attractive dining hall. And the other residents, the students? They were fantastic, entertaining beyond belief. If I had to be temporarily parted from Margie and Leslie after the Rockwell disaster, I couldn't have chosen a better place to lick my wounds.

But time passed quickly. I worked hard, skied hard, flew home to California less often than I would have liked, and we bought a beautiful home under construction in Fort Collins, only a block away from a lake. And Margie found a buyer for our California home, although the transaction resulted in a significant financial loss. But never mind, in the summer of 1971 Margie, Leslie, and I were together again, and Leslie loved Colorado. And Margie had found a position as full professor in the history department at Metropolitan State University in Denver. She had also interviewed at CSU and at the University of Colorado in Boulder. In the latter instance, the Chairman of the History Department told her, "Oh, we never hire women!" What a juicy lawsuit that could have provoked in those early days of the feminist movement, but Margie believed her efforts would be better spent searching for opportunities elsewhere than in trying to reform the University of Colorado.

Whereas much was ideal at this juncture, Margie had a long commute to Denver. And I was troubled by the dearth of graduate students and of research funding in the Physics Department. I was of course aware of those realities from the outset, and I had accepted them because CSU was the best of the available alternatives. But those factors, combined with heavy teaching responsibilities made it difficult for the department to conduct vigorous research programs. Seeking expansion in the research arena, I campaigned actively for more research contract and grant funding for the department.

Then, early in 1972 I received an offer to serve as Director of the Physical Sciences Division at the Office of Naval Research in Arlington, Virginia, a suburb of Washington, DC. It was a supergrade civil service position with broad responsibilities for management of a contract research program directed toward Navy and Marine Corps needs, just the kind of high-tech activity I had so thoroughly enjoyed at North American. But it meant leaving CSU, which had been very good to me, and a physics faculty for which I had the highest regard. Margie and I talked it over and she agreed to the change, even though it meant that her career would be interrupted yet again. Such is life for contemporary two-career families. I'll forever bear guilt for being the cause of her career interruptions, though she's never chastised me for it. And we've never regretted our moves, because our subsequent careers have always been fulfilling.

Fortunately, our Colorado home sold quickly with a modest profit, and the transition to the Washington, DC, area went relatively smoothly. In short order Margie was teaching part time at Georgetown University and in addition working part time as a Program Officer for the National Endowment for the Humanities (NEH), a federal agency. Soon, as Endowment managers had opportunity to observe her performance, she was awarded a regular full time civil service appointment. With every career interruption she always bounced back.

We were to spend more than twenty-eight years in the Washington, DC, area. We lived comfortably but modestly in McLean, Virginia, most of that time, deep in the woods on a beautiful hillside, two-acre parcel, pretty much allowed to assume its natural vegetative state with towering old-growth hardwood trees. With both of us fully employed for a combined total of eighty-six years, we invested regularly and conservatively in mutual funds and in residential parcels and have achieved a comfortable retirement. But our careers in the Washington area were not without their pressures.

At the NEH Margie rose to serve as Deputy Director of the Division of Research, then Director of the Division of State Programs, and finally as Director of the Division of Fellowships and Seminars. In her NEH career Margie achieved Senior Executive Service (SES) rank and worked for five chairmen and three acting chairmen, all political appointees. Among them were Bill Bennett and Lynne Cheney (Dick's wife). (Incidentally, it was Lynne who established that female division directors were entitled to the same exalted SES rank as their male counterparts.) In recognition of Margie's career accomplishments, she's listed in *Who's Who in America*. She retired in December, 1994.

After several years at ONR I was assigned broader responsibilities as Associate Director of Research for Mathematical and Physical Sciences, which included mathematics, physics, chemistry, and computer science, all as they related to advanced military systems. In 1986 I was awarded the Department of the Navy Superior Civilian Service Medal and was appointed Director of Research and Laboratory Management in the

Pentagon in the Office of the Secretary of Defense. In this civil service position I held oversight responsibility for Defense-Department-wide Research Programs, developed policy for the management of Defense Laboratories and the Industrial Research and Development Program, and represented all of these areas in interactions with Congress. (Incidentally, during part of my tenure in this position Dick Cheney was Secretary of Defense, and his wife, Lynne was Chairman of the agency that employed Margie. Whereas Margie had frequent interactions with Lynne, I had no direct contact with Dick at the Pentagon.)

At various times during my career I served in an elective office of the American Physical Society, served on the Organizing Committee for the Applied Superconductivity Conferences, and served on, and contributed extensively to reports of, a number of National Academy of Sciences panels. I'm a Fellow of the American Physical Society, a Fellow of the American Association for the Advancement of Science, and am listed in *American Men and Women of Science, Who's Who in Engineering*, and *World Who's Who in Science*. More importantly, skiing in my late sixties (and, admittedly, aided and abetted by the generous age handicap) I finally captured a NASTAR silver medal. In October, 1992, I retired from the Pentagon, but continued to consult on technical matters for a few more years until becoming absorbed in efforts to build our home south of Elk.

With that extensive experience behind us, you might think our retirement would be a breeze, but, in truth, we weren't prepared at all for the game of Mendocino-style coastal roulette that lay ahead. Indeed, we were soon to find that lessons learned in Washington, DC don't necessarily apply in Mendocino County. The "rules" are different!

CHAPTER 2

From Land Purchase To House Plans

In 1980 Leslie graduated from Yale with a degree in geology, and in the fall she entered graduate school at Stanford to study geochemistry. Shortly thereafter, Margie and I traveled to California from our McLean, VA, home, bringing more of her belongings. We delivered them to the off-campus apartment she had rented with two other students, and then we headed off to the Mendocino coast for a romantic getaway. As always we enjoyed it immensely.

Driving back to San Francisco on a beautiful, sunny day, we decided to follow the coast part of the way, and, as we approached Elk from the north, we came upon those magnificent sea stacks. Transfixed, we stopped at the Cuffey's Cove turnout to savor them and then passed through Elk, hardly aware of the little village of some 250 souls. Then, half a mile south, there was a "For Sale" sign placed by Pacific Realty of Point Arena. Although we hadn't set out to shop for real estate, we were curious and stopped to investigate. Most of the parcel was impassably overgrown, but by following an old roadbed, which we later learned was part of the old abandoned Coast Highway, we came upon a small cleared patch with an unbelievably enchanting northern coastal view. Below us was Greenwood Cove where Greenwood Creek and its vast canyon meet the Pacific Ocean (Figure 2). A graceful crescent beach had been shaped by enormous foam-topped waves. And there again were the sea stacks, viewed now from the south. To the northeast the village of Elk lay nestled against a mountain backdrop.

Well, by the time we reached Point Arena some 17 miles farther south, I had to learn more about the property, even though I could sense that Margie wasn't too keen on my growing delusions of grandeur about the possibility of owning such a magnificent parcel. Besides, retirement for us was still a dozen or so years in the future. But, reluctantly, Margie humored me, and we stopped at the realty office in the old Point Arena Theater building. There, realtor Tom Wetterstrom informed us that the parcel consisted of a gently sloping eleven-acre point, lying about 160 feet above the sea. And it included a beach to the north and a beach to the south. To the west a small, lower-elevation land linkage connected the larger part of the parcel to a massive barrier stack, which contained a beautiful arch carved by wave action. The price was $250,000.

When we reached home we discussed it and discussed it and discussed it, I rashly, Margie cautiously, wary of indebtedness. We had never paid so much for anything before. Our home in McLean, VA, had cost $158,000. On the other hand, we were not inexperienced in purchasing and selling undeveloped residential parcels. That had been a part of our conservative investment activity. The approach had been to buy only high-quality parcels, parcels on which we ourselves would enjoy living. Of the twelve such parcels we turned over while engaging in that activity, we profited in all but one instance.

In any event, we kept flooding Wetterstrom with questions to avoid actually having to bite the bullet and make an offer. As we probed deeper, some aspects disturbed us. Most troubling, we were informed that Elk villagers and the local lumber mill had for a considerable period of time dumped trash over the northern bluff edge of our parcel into Greenwood Creek Canyon. We could see no evidence of this, nor have we since. We have, however, come across remnants of a railroad track that ran across our property in the days when a nearby lumber mill was in operation.

Well, on a fateful day, December 7, 1980, we did eventually bite the bullet. Against her better judgment, Margie consented to our offering $210,000, thinking that a safe $40,000 below the asking price would be declined and put an end to my goading. Surprisingly, the owners, the Sherwoods (he an airline pilot), accepted. The closing took place four months later. What had we done? We were city people, and Elk was really remote. And what would it be like to live in Elk next to the people we believed had defiled our property by using it as the village dump? Could the beauty of the surroundings compensate for such a past? (Fortunately, in 1994, when we applied for a building permit the Mendocino County Environmental Health Department reviewed the issue and concluded that the dump was on the parcel immediately to the north of ours, now Greenwood State Beach. That has lessened the stigma, but only slightly!)

Meanwhile, Leslie fell in love with David Yale, then also a graduate student at Stanford. They'd met earlier as Yale University undergraduates, but the fireworks didn't start until they encountered each other again at Stanford. A year later, 1981, they were married in McLean, Virginia. The newlyweds then spent their honeymoon at an oceanfront bed and breakfast just a half-mile north of our newly acquired property, further cementing our ties to the Mendocino coast.

A few years later, we sought to improve the appearance of our parcel by planting additional evergreen trees on it. On an informal basis, we submitted an extensive planting plan to the Mendocino County Department of Planning and Building Services. However, we were advised by a County Planner that a formal submission had little chance of approval, and so we didn't bother to pursue the matter any further. That proved to be a very costly mistake, for, had we persevered, we'd have had screening trees in place at the time we chose to build and might have averted the conflict that's the subject of this book.

FROM LAND PURCHASE TO HOUSE PLANS

As the years went by we paid off the mortgage. And we dutifully paid the real estate taxes, enriching the coffers of Mendocino County. Then In 1989 we learned that the five-acre parcel east of our eleven-acre parcel was for sale for $140,000. It fulfilled our usual investment criteria, and, although it lacked ocean frontage, it offered impressive ocean views, and it could serve as a buffer for our eleven-acre parcel. Again going into debt, we bought it. To the north of both parcels were 47 ocean-front acres purchased by the California Department of General Services in 1978 and transferred in 1983 to the California Department of Parks and Recreation. That land, our northern neighbor, was to become what is now Greenwood State Beach. At the time we thought it an advantage to be adjacent to state property, for it seemed unlikely it would ever be developed. We were of course unaware that the California Department of Parks and Recreation would prove to be a most undesirable neighbor!

Then in 1993, a year after retiring, I was eager to begin building our dream home in Elk. Margie was still working and was less than enthusiastic about the idea. But she agreed to a foray to get better acquainted with the Mendocino coast and to interview architects practicing there. We flew to California in October 1993, rented a car, and drove to Caspar, a small village between Mendocino and Fort Bragg. We'd reserved a vacation rental cottage there near the ocean.

We visited Fort Bragg, a lumbering, fishing, and tourist town of 6,000 souls some 25 miles north of Elk, and we found modern hospital facilities capable of handling all but the most severe cases. It appeared that the supermarkets, hardware stores, and drug stores in Fort Bragg would prove adequate for most of our needs. But shopping beyond that would require trips to Ukiah, 60 miles distant, or Santa Rosa, 100 miles distant.

To digress, Fort Bragg is an interesting (funky) town, a little rough around the edges, with modest homes. It boasts interesting art galleries, theaters featuring local actors, and occasional concerts by the Symphony of the Redwoods. Once primarily a lumbering and fishing town, Fort Bragg now depends heavily upon tourism, and to a lesser extent on an influx of retirees. Fort Bragg's harbor, Noyo Harbor, is the largest harbor between Bodega Bay and Eureka. It's a captivating place, a real working harbor, with fishing boats in profusion, seafood processing plants, a Coast Guard Station, seafood restaurants, and barking sea lions. Although, excursion boats take tourists fishing and whale watching, you'd never mistake Noyo Harbor for a slick Miami Beach marina.

Downtown in Fort Bragg, next to a small brewery, is the Skunk Train Station ("skunk" because of the odoriferous character of the diesel-powered rail cars). From there you can ride the rails through the redwoods and over the mountains to Willits and back. The railroad boasts a steam locomotive as well as the diesel-powered rail cars.

Fort Bragg is a little less liberal than Mendocino County in general, which is extremely liberal, and everyone is addressed by first name only, as if no one has a last name. The usual means of transportation is a pickup truck, and there's usually a dog (or two) in the back of it. Interestingly, I couldn't help but notice that when I made purchases in Fort Bragg stores I received dirty change, not dirty in the sense of the pristine currency that passes through the hands of Washington, DC, politicians, but literally dirty from having resided in the pockets of workers engaged in honest toil in Fort Bragg's lumber, fishing, construction, and agricultural activities. It was as if Fort Bragg was from an earlier era. There was no high-tech industry in Fort Bragg, no Macy's or Wal-Mart, and most certainly no Nordstrom's or Neiman-Marcus, and the residents prefer it that way. Having been raised in a small town myself I knew I could adjust, but I also knew that it wouldn't be easy for Margie, who grew up in Toronto. She loves to visit Nordstrom's and Neiman-Marcus, although she's too thrifty to pay their prices!

We were already well acquainted with Mendocino, about eight miles south of Fort Bragg and seventeen miles north of Elk. Its origins can also be traced back to lumbering. Mendocino is an exceptionally picturesque and charming seaside village of 1,000, magically situated atop the northern headlands of Big River. Flowers grow there in wild profusion amidst Victorian-style buildings (both old and new). Mendocino residents seek to maintain the appearance of bygone days with fanatic enforcement of development regulations. A Mecca for tourists, Mendocino abuts Mendocino Headlands State Park with its beautiful sand beach, and it boasts an abundance of delightful inns, restaurants, and art galleries. Except for a dearth of trees and the presence of tourists' fancy modern cars, it could be Carmel half a century ago. Every summer, a large tent is pitched on the headlands, and there the village holds a week-long music festival, featuring everything from jazz to opera.

Most Americans have visited Mendocino either on TV or in the movies. "Murder She Wrote," "The Russians are Coming," and "East of Eden" are but a few of the more than fifty productions filmed in Mendocino and environs. Outside the village proper, both north and south, are many beautiful coastal-zone homes. Perhaps the most exclusive area is Chapman Point to the south and across the bay from Mendocino, where a few-acre parcel can command more than a few million dollars.

But, overall, the County of Mendocino is poor, one of the poorest in the state. With poverty widespread, it's not surprising that County welfare and mental health expenditures command a considerable share of the County budget. In the mountains that isolate the coast from the inland valleys there's still a fair amount of lumbering, and further inland are large agricultural tracts and numerous noteworthy vineyards. However, the biggest cash crop in the County is said to be marijuana. Although there's no official record of that, it's estimated that income from marijuana is three times that of all legitimate agriculture. Interestingly, the Village of Mendocino's sister city in Japan is named Miasa. Translated into English that means "beautiful hemp" or "beautiful marijuana," but I suspect that that's more coincidence than indicative of drug use in Miasa. Then again, I could be wrong.

Against this backdrop, we found few architects to interview, but we were very favorably impressed by those we did find. It was fascinating to visit projects they had designed. Indeed, their creations, overlooking the rugged coastline, proved to be overwhelmingly seductive. Our rashness surprised us. We acted promptly, signing a contract with Leventhal, Schlosser, Architects (LSA) in Fort Bragg. In the initial planning phases, our primary contact was with Michael (Mike) Leventhal, who obtained his degree in architecture from the University of California at Berkeley. Robert (Bob) Schlosser, a tall, sturdily-built, pony-tailed Princeton University architecture graduate would become more involved in later phases as we encountered problems with the Mendocino County bureaucracy. Together they were an impressive team, and they assured us that we should be able to build a house of the type we wanted within our target budget.

We next engaged Doug Dennis to clear some brush at the western tip of the property, but only enough to allow us to gain our first glimpse of the southward panorama (Figure 4). That view was indeed very nice, but the northward view we'd first observed (Figures 2 and 3) was much more impressive. Not surprisingly, we expressed a strong preference for a siting to take maximum advantage of that northern view. However, Mike explained to us that we would have to deal with the California Coastal Act, the County Planning and Building Services Department, and the residents of Elk, and, according to Mike, all were more than a little hostile toward development in the coastal zone. His words were very sobering, and we began to realize that we might be in for a bit of trouble, maybe a whole lot of trouble. In the location we preferred, our house would be visible from most of Greenwood Cove beach and also visible to the residents of Elk. Mike suggested that our prospects would be much improved if we chose a building site farther to the south. That way our house wouldn't be visible from the beach (and it would also be a bit more distant from Elk). Ironically, the closest (350-foot-long) segment of Greenwood Cove beach is part of our parcel. Nevertheless, because the public had used that segment for considerably more than five years without having been denied access, they had long ago acquired prescriptive rights to continue using it. And, in any event, in the United States the public always has the right to use any beach below the mean-high-tide line. We could imagine a catch-22 scenario, in which we propose to locate our house where it is visible from our beach, and our permit application is denied because our house is visible to the public while they're using our beach. Reluctantly, we acceded to Mike's advice. Now, with the wisdom of hindsight and vast painful experience, we believe this to have been a major tactical error, not that we blame Mike, for who could have imagined what we were about to encounter? Had we instead applied for a permit to build on our preferred site the application would surely have been quickly denied, and, with our opponents' lust for a pound of flesh perhaps assuaged, they might have been more receptive to our second-choice siting. But then again probably not! In any event, we were beginning with a second choice. We'd made a major concession before even testing the County bureaucracy and local citizenry. And it dawned on us that when we purchased our dream parcel we had unwittingly entered into a high-stakes game of coastal-zone roulette governed by murky rules that are capriciously administered.

We prepared to return home, no longer naïve, now aware that Elk might be our retirement paradise, but it would be an imperfect one. And I itched! It seems that some of that brush we'd cleared was poison oak, and I was covered with blisters from head to toe, and in places you don't want me to mention! As we awaited our flight at San Francisco

Airport people gave me a wide berth as I scratched furiously at the blisters. A few days later, back home in Mclean, I shivered as sharp pains coursed up and down one leg, a nasty infection. But for the skill of Dr. Robert Lee Carter, our family dermatologist, and the efficacy of modern miracle drugs, Margie would have become a widow.

As the itching subsided we set about making detailed lists of features we desired in our house, and Mike and Bob quickly translated them into drawings, which we then critiqued. As an amateur architect I had designed our Thousand Oaks, CA, home and several more as examples to enhance the sales appeal of parcels we sought to sell, and so I couldn't resist giving our architects more "help" than they needed. But they were very patient, even though every change was a chore, for they hadn't yet fully completed their transition from T-square, triangle, and board to computer-aided design. After many, many iterations, in June 1994 we had a set of plans suitable for a Coastal Development Permit application to Mendocino County. I had even constructed a balsawood model.

The plans called for a main house, approximately 3,300 sq ft, consisting of a living room with a mezzanine (or internal balcony) with an external raised deck, a library/ study/bedroom, a dining room, a kitchen, a laundry, a powder room, and a master bedroom with his and hers bathrooms, all sited on a rise at the western tip of the parcel. A breezeway and ramp at the northern end of the main house connected it to a three-car garage three feet lower in elevation. (We didn't plan to have three cars. The third garage bay was intended to accommodate a workshop, a riding lawn mower, and the like.) On the northern end of the garage were another bedroom and a one-bedroom guesthouse. Total conditioned space was about 4,300 sq ft., the garage 900 sq ft.

The bedroom between garage and guesthouse was intended for a live-in caregiver in the event we might eventually need one. This was to be a retirement home after all. Also the house was designed to be wheelchair friendly, hence the ramp connecting the main house to the rest of the structure. In our discussions with Mike, Margie and I (both active and independent) found it uncomfortable to refer to the "caregiver's room." Anybody getting along in years prefers not to contemplate the need for a caregiver, and so we began referring to that room as the "maid's room," although we never had a maid (and at 77 and 80 we still don't). Henceforth the room was labeled "Maid" on the plans. This would prove to be a *BIG* tactical mistake!

CHAPTER 3

SCENIC-PRESERVATION MANDATES
AND PROPERTY RIGHTS

With an exciting set of house plans in hand in mid 1994, we were looking forward eagerly to building our dream home. However, we dreaded facing the bureaucracy that would judge and could deny our application for a Coastal Development Permit. Indeed, we anticipated that getting approval might require a long, hard slog. The reasons behind our dread are outlined in this chapter, as I interrupt the narrative to describe and analyze controversial issues surrounding land use, scenic preservation, and property rights in California (as well as a few other states). After noting the inequities and inconsistencies of those existing legal provisions, I propose reforms aimed at achieving a more equitable and congenial relationship between scenic preservation mandates and property rights. That sets the stage for resumption of the narrative in the following chapter.

A quick journey through Malibu, with its cheek-to-jowl oceanfront development, should be enough to convince even the harshest skeptics of the desirability of preserving as much as possible of the natural character of the remaining magnificent undeveloped coastal zone of California. But that admirable goal of preservation faces an enormous obstacle. Much of the coastal-zone property is privately owned. A simplistic approach to this dilemma would be for the government to

- o   Ban any additional development on already-developed parcels in the coastal zone, and

- o   Invoke the Constitutional right to eminent domain, condemn for the public good the remaining undeveloped parcels, pay the owners fair market value, and maintain the undeveloped parcels in their pristine state.

The first of these measures would likely be unconstitutional and doubtless lead to open rebellion. To finance the second would require an enormous increase in taxation of the public at large. That might also lead to open rebellion. So much for such simplistic approaches.

EUREKA! (That, incidentally, is the motto of the State of California.) Why pay for it if you can get it for nothing? Why not simply impose onerous regulations on what can be built and where it can be built in the coastal zone? That would impose relatively moderate burdens on owners of already-developed parcels, who just might accept this approach without insurrection. But, what of the owners of the as-yet-undeveloped parcels? Well, to conform to the regulations and make scenic preservation possible, many would simply have to abandon their plans to build at the most desirable building sites on their parcels. Obviously, owners of undeveloped parcels would object vehemently to this expropriation of value from *their* parcels alone in order to provide a public good, which should, by rights, be financed by the public at large. But then owners of undeveloped coastal-zone land comprise only a small fraction of the voting public, and so they have little political clout. Moreover, they can be picked off one at a time, i.e., to achieve scenic preservation for the benefit of the public at large, value can be extracted from the parcels of coastal-zone landowners one at a time as the owners seek to acquire Coastal Development Permits for their projects. This approach had great appeal to 54% of California voters, who in 1972 voted in favor of Proposition 20, a citizens' initiative that launched the "Coastal Conservation Initiative" on an interim basis. Then in 1976, the implementing act, the "California Coastal Act," was passed by the State Legislature, making the coastal protection program permanent. To oversee administration of the Coastal Act, the legislation created the California Coastal Commission.

Owners of coastal-zone property would soon come to view the California Coastal Act as an act of expropriation and a blatant exercise of tyranny by the majority. Interesting perspective on majority rule is to be found in a comment by Parker J. Palmer, who served for eleven years as Dean of Studies and Writer in Residence at Pendle Hill, a Quaker learning-living community near Philadelphia. Writing in the 7-8-07 issue of *APS News*, Palmer remarked,

> "When I asked why the community at Pendle Hill made decisions
> via a laborious, tedious, time-consuming and utterly maddening
> process called consensual decision-making, I was told, 'Because
> making decisions by majority rule is a form of violence.'"

The passage of the California Coastal Act was indeed one such violent act by majority rule. Under simple majority rule there's always that temptation for the majority to take from the minority. By such means the cat, the rat, the dog, and the duck can take and eat the bread that the little red hen acquired through dint of hard work, viz., by having planted the seed, cut the wheat, threshed the wheat, milled the grain, and baked the bread. Our founding fathers understood that danger. Accordingly, while some governing issues in the United States are settled by simple majority rule of citizens at large, others are settled by elected representatives, and still others are settled by appointed officials. And, because none of the foregoing decision-making processes are perfect, our forefathers wisely established certain overarching, fundamental, guiding principles that impose limitations and safeguards designed to protect citizens from their government and from each other. Those limitations and safeguards are contained in the United States Constitution. It provides a remarkably just, sensible, and fair framework for governance, but it's neither perfect nor complete. Indeed, it's a work in progress, and it can be amended by two-thirds majorities in both houses of Congress, plus ratification by three-quarters of the state legislatures. The Constitution has protected us from many rash and inappropriate citizens' and government actions, but, unfortunately, not all, the case in point here being the California Coastal Act. Unfortunately, when the Coastal Act and its originating referendum were approved, key guiding principles and limitations of the United States Constitution were simply ignored. Those key provisions, the Fifth and Fourteenth Amendments, require that "private property shall not be taken for public use without just compensation" and that, "No state shall make or enforce any law which shall…deny any person within its jurisdiction the equal protection of the laws."

Unfortunately, the takings clause in the United States Constitution is terse in the extreme and provides no listing of what government actions might reasonably be considered to be "takings." As a consequence, property owners' freedom to use their land as they wish has become a very contentious matter governed by complex legislation, zoning codes, land-use regulations, and judicial precedents, many of which take liberties with the Constitution. As a result land use is currently one of the most litigious of legal arenas.

Now what's a sensible, just, and fair meaning of the Constitution's takings clause, and how does that relate to the California Coastal Act? It's customary to classify a taking as either an eminent domain taking, or a regulatory taking. In the former instance the government acquires the deed to the property (i.e., acquires ownership) and pays "just compensation" to the person from whom the property was taken. Such an act clearly amounts to a taking in the Constitutional sense. Nevertheless, both the public need for the taking and the adequacy of the level of compensation are often disputed.

What constitutes a regulatory taking is more complex and hence more controversial. For purposes of public order and safety, government may place regulatory restrictions on the use of property. Such regulatory restrictions may be concerned with zoning, setbacks, fire safety, drainage, erosion control, geologic stability, pollution control, noise abatement, etc. In many such instances the regulatory restrictions benefit both the public at large and property owners, and they may protect or even enhance property values. Such regulatory restrictions are certainly not takings in the Constitutional sense.

On the other hand, some government regulatory restrictions sanctioned by the California Coastal Act provide a benefit to the public at large at the expense of targeted landowners. For example, a scenic preservation restriction may prohibit a landowner from placing his home at the most desirable site on his property, thereby benefiting the public at large by providing the public with scenic vistas free of development. In this instance the fair market value of the parcel and its value to its owner have both been greatly diminished. Although the government has not acquired the deed to the property, it has taken something highly coveted by the government and the public at large, viz., the owner's most cherished and valuable building site. Surely, in a rational world this must be considered a taking in the Constitutional sense, requiring that just compensation be paid to the landowner. Indeed, it would be totally inappropriate for the landowner alone to be forced to bear the cost of providing a public good, which, by all rights, should be financed by members of the public at large.

Accordingly, in what follows I'll use the term "regulatory taking" to designate government regulatory restrictions that devalue private property in order to fulfill the covetous desires of government and the public at large. Unfortunately, in the vast majority of such cases victims of regulatory takings are not paid just compensation. Many years of misguided judicial precedents have established the illogic that a regulatory restriction on the use of land does not constitute a taking in the Constitutional sense unless the restriction renders the land *completely* void of economic value. According to the judiciary, only then must just compensation be paid by the government. In other words, government can steal 99% of the value of a parcel without having to provide any compensation at all. By that same illogic, a burglar, who steals all of your household goods except the kitchen sink, could not be convicted of any crime. Only a total numbskull would fail to understand how government, and the cat, the rat, the dog, and the duck, will behave when given such license. Despite the multitude of ill-founded judicial precedents to the contrary, I maintain that a regulatory taking, as I've defined it above, requires just compensation regardless of whether the devaluation is 1% or 100%. Not only is that the definition I choose to use in this book, but it's the definition recently placed into effect in the state of Oregon by dint of a citizens' initiative (about which I'll have more to say later).

Could it have been the intent of the framers of the Constitution to sanction regulatory takings without provision of just compensation for the affected landowners? I think not. Imagine George Washington attempting to build his Mount Vernon home today. I doubt he'd consider it Constitutional if, without just compensation, he were required by the whim of a government bureaucrat to locate his home at a site on his estate with no view of the Potomac River. Likewise, imagine Thomas Jefferson attempting to build his Monticello home today. I doubt he'd consider it Constitutional if, without just compensation, he were required by the whim of a government bureaucrat to locate his home in a swale instead of at the summit of his 850-foot-tall "little mountain." Certainly, if, for public benefit, government denies a landowner a permit to build at the site that is blessed with the most desirable scenic vistas, then immense value has been taken, and it's a taking in the Constitutional sense. In short, a taking is a taking, whether by eminent domain or by regulatory restrictions, and it's only sensible, just, and fair that in both instances appropriate compensation be paid. However, government and the public at large have grown accustomed to acquiring such highly valuable, scenic exactions free of charge through regulatory takings. So long as such exactions are free to the government and to the public at large there will be no end to them. With governments loath to police themselves, this unjust disparity between eminent domain takings and regulatory takings has only recently begun to be addressed through citizens' initiatives. In the meantime, the unjust exactions continue.

Early on, the California Coastal Commission behaved as if its powers were unlimited. Not content with merely controlling visual impact, the Commission began demanding public access easements across private property as part of the price for granting Coastal Development Permits. Although this was without license of any law, the Coastal Commission justified such confiscations as compensation for the scenic damage that it was claimed the developments would inflict on coastal vistas. In *Nollan v. California Coastal Commission, 1987,* in Ventura County, the Supreme Court saw this differently, branding it as "outright extortion" and banned it. Indeed one can imagine the uproar if government sought to impose easements without just compensation across land already developed (whether coastal or inland). Yet, despite the Supreme Court ruling, many Coastal Permit Administrators still believe that would-be developers owe the state for the privilege of building on their land. In actual fact, owners have the right to build on their land.

The California Coastal Act is also inconsistent with the "equal-protection- of-the-laws" clause of the United States Constitution. By adopting the Coastal Act, a majority of voters established, for the benefit of the public at large, a process for expropriating value from coastal properties without justly compensating the owners. This singling out of a particular group of landowners, and subjecting them to more-restrictive land-use laws and regulations than are in effect in other areas clearly violates the "equal-protection-of-the-laws" clause of the Constitution. There can be no doubt that any attempt to subject all landowners to expropriation of their most desirable building sites at the whim of covetous government bureaucrats and without just compensation, would be soundly rejected by the majority of voters.

Not only does the California Coastal Act fail to provide equal protection of the laws for the coastal zone as compared with inland areas, it fails to provide equal protection of the laws within the coastal zone itself. For example, consider two oceanfront parcels, a quarter-acre parcel and a five-acre parcel. The space available on the quarter-acre parcel is so limited that the house can be placed in only one location, where it's in full view of the public, and where its owner enjoys magnificent ocean views. The Coastal Permit Administrator has no alternative but to approve that site, even though the house may obstruct public views to the ocean. On the other hand, the five–acre parcel possesses two possible building sites, one with the same desirable characteristics as the building site on the quarter-acre parcel, and one not visible to the public and offering the owner no ocean views. If in the latter case the Coastal Permit Administrator rules that the owner must build on the less desirable site, the government has "taken" the most desirable site from the owner and has also denied the owner equal protection of the law. Yet that's the usual ruling. Moreover, whereas the owner of the quarter-acre parcel provides no undeveloped open space for public enjoyment, the owner of the five-acre parcel would provide the public at large with four and three-quarters acres of undeveloped open space. Of course, with appropriate vegetative screening, both houses could be concealed from public view within ten to fifteen years.

The issue of vegetative screening to conceal development from public view is itself contentious. Many Coastal Permit Administrators demand that new development not be visible to the public, despite the fact that that's not an explicit requirement of the Coastal Act. That rationale is used to banish development to locations not visible to the public, often when that deprives owners of scenic views from their properties. Yet, vegetative screening at the owners' preferred sites could conceal their homes from public view within ten to fifteen years. Shouldn't owners have the right to their preferred sites and a reasonable period of time to achieve effective concealment?

A relatively minor aspect of Coastal Act regulations is further illustrative of the practice of imposing restrictions on coastal-zone construction that the majority of Californians would surely not accept. Specifically, Coastal Act regulations require that new development in the coastal zone be finished in dull, earthy colors, tones that blend in with the environment. In contrast, inland houses and houses built in the coastal zone prior to enactment of the Coastal Act may be painted any glaring colors the owners wish. Clearly, California politicians knew better than to attempt to regulate the colors of all houses (and they doubtless understood as well that the majority would not intercede when such restrictions were foisted upon a relatively small number of newcomers to the coastal-zone).

Prior to the California Coastal Act the laws and regulations governing development in the California coastal zone had been relatively permissive, and development had taken place with little regard for scenic preservation. That's no longer the case. Now the laws and regulations are highly restrictive and, as noted above, of questionable Constitutionality. While the machinery for implementing the Coastal Act was being activated, building moratoria were declared, lasting in some areas for several years. Then, regulations designed to preserve California's magnificent coastal scenic vistas took over with little regard for property rights. Nevertheless, like many owners of undeveloped coastal-zone property, Margie and I were willing to accept modest sacrifices in our use of our property to the benefit of scenic preservation for the public at large. Indeed, as noted in the previous chapter, we had at the very outset voluntarily relinquished the northern building site for our project, even though it would have provided us with the most desirable scenic vistas. We did so despite our belief that coastal-zone property owners should be entitled to just compensation if government mandates such a less-than-optimum siting. However, having voluntarily sacrificed our most desirable building site we believed we should, at the very least, be entitled to clear, objective, explicit, and quantitative laws and regulations so that the Coastal Development Permit approval process would be carried out without caprice, bias, or acrimony.

We were soon to learn if the process worked that way in practice. We found that the hoops through which a Mendocino County Coastal Development Permit (CDP) application must jump are specified by the California Coastal Act of 1976, as amended, and by the California Coastal Commission Regulations, the Mendocino County General Plan *Coastal Element,* and the Mendocino County Zoning Code *Coastal Zone.* After demonstrating that the latter two documents were not in conflict with the former two documents, Mendocino County gained authority to rule on CDP applications. All four of the above documents stacked altogether are two inches thick printed on both sides of the pages, and the provisions are obviously much too lengthy to discuss in any detail here. But they're not rocket science. With a little patience anyone of normal intelligence can understand them. Anyone contemplating buying land and building in the coastal zone would be well advised to obtain and carefully review the full set of laws and regulations applicable to the area of interest *before* purchasing land and *before* undertaking design of a structure. The better your understanding of the laws and regulations, the better your chances of choosing a parcel which will allow you to take optimum advantage of scenic vistas, and the better your chances of negotiating effectively with planners and regulators at the city, county, and state levels.

It's pertinent to our case that the Constitution of the State of California is even more-explicitly pro-private-property-rights than the Constitution of the United States. Section 19 of Article 1 of the California Constitution reads as follows:

> "Private property may be taken or damaged for public use only when just compensation, ascertained by a jury unless waived, has first been paid to, or into court for, the owner. The Legislature may provide for possession by the condemnor following commencement of eminent domain proceedings upon deposit in court and prompt release to the owner of the money determined by the court to be the probable amount of just compensation."

Addition of the words "or damaged" in the first line is highly significant. Certainly, if government-imposed use restrictions devalue a property in any way, then, by any reasonable interpretation, the property has been "damaged," and, under the California Constitution the owner is entitled to just compensation. There can be no doubt that that was the full intention of those who adopted those words in the California Constitution. But today there's apparently no place for such logic in California government, for it has strayed far from its Constitutional roots.

Since enactment of the California Coastal Act and the subsequent rezoning by coastal counties, pounds of flesh have been ruthlessly extracted from owners of undeveloped coastal property. Suddenly, owners were stripped of rights that had been enjoyed all along by their neighbors who had already developed their parcels. Many large parcels, which formerly could have been subdivided, were precipitously restricted to development of but one residence. *In that single stroke much of the no-development agenda has already been realized.* Low-population-density coastal-zone areas will no doubt remain so. Clearly, the public at large prefers it that way. Because owners of undeveloped coastal land are but a small fraction of the voters, it's not surprising whose ox is being gored.

Taken altogether, the many restrictions imposed by the California Coastal Act provide scenic vistas for the public at large at the expense of coastal-zone landowners, flagrantly violating not only the state and national Constitutions, but fundamental principles of fairness as well. When government extracts value from one segment of the public for the benefit of the public at large, then, by rights, the government should reimburse the abused segment for its loss. As so eloquently stated by Supreme Court Justice Hugo Black in *Armstrong v. United States, 1960*, the takings clause in the United States Constitution's Fifth Amendment was necessary to "bar Government from forcing some people alone to bear public burdens, which in all fairness and justice, should be borne by the public as a whole."

Obviously, the framers of the Constitution never anticipated the California Coastal Act, nor did they anticipate the most notorious measure of all for redistribution of wealth, the income tax. By no stretch of the imagination could either measure be judged as providing equal protection of the laws. In both instances, value is extracted disproportionately from some for the benefit of all. Nevertheless, the extent of departure from equal protection in income-tax law is less extreme, for a significant portion of United States citizens bear at least some of the income-tax burden (although the lion's share, 97%, is paid by the top 50% of earners). In contrast, the public at large pays nothing at all for the scenic preservation mandated by the California Coastal Act. Instead, the entire burden is borne by but a fraction of a percent of the populace, viz., owners of undeveloped coastal-zone properties.

Although atrociously cumbersome, income-tax laws are models of clarity and objectivity compared to the Coastal Act. Real power and authority reside in the *provisions* of income-tax laws, not in the administrators of income-tax laws. In contrast, the Coastal Act is so subjective that its *administrators* (county civil servants, county supervisors, and members of the Coastal Commission) are free to wield broad and arbitrary powers and exact harsh concessions from whatever hapless coastal-zone landowner they choose to select, while leaving owners of similar holdings elsewhere completely unscathed. Imagine an income-tax system with administrators who, at their whim, are at liberty to levy a tax against you while exempting your neighbor, all the while factoring in the opinions of the local citizenry as expressed in their protest letters, in their petitions, and at hearings. As taxpayers, we would never tolerate such a system.

Yet, through the Coastal Act, the voters of California imposed just such abuse on coastal-zone landowners by unjustly empowering government administrators to decide which owners of ocean-view properties will be allowed to enjoy ocean views from their homes and which will be denied such views, a clear violation of equal protection of the laws. Having little recourse, other than expensive and time-consuming litigation, most coastal-zone landowners simply concede, albeit grudgingly. But, there's danger in becoming so inured to such abuse that we accept more and more of it to the ultimate detriment of fundamental rights and freedoms.

Of course abusive land-use regulations are not confined solely to California. In 1986, ten years after passage of the California Coastal Act, the United States Congress passed the National Columbia River Gorge Scenic Act, imposing by law very similar expropriations on owners of property in an 85-mile-long corridor of the Columbia River Gorge encompassing parts of the states of Washington and Oregon. The Columbia Gorge Commission, established to execute the law, bears a striking similarity to the California Coastal Commission, and its functioning and regulations appear to have been modeled after those of its California predecessor (except that Commissioners are appointed by two states rather than one).

The National Columbia River Gorge Scenic Act simply compounded the regulatory abuse that citizens of Oregon had already long endured. Since 1973 they had been subjected to land-use regulations even more oppressive than those in the coastal zone of California. The despised Oregon land-use system extended throughout the state, and, in a clear violation of the Constitution's takings clause, it prohibited many unfortunate landowners from building anything at all on their parcels. In 2004, defiant citizens of Oregon took matters into their own hands and placed a countervailing citizens' initiative, on the ballot. That initiative, "Measure 37," was approved by a 61% majority vote. It requires that the state reimburse landowners for devaluations of their properties by regulatory takings. Specifically, Measure 37 includes the following language:

> "If a public entity enacts or enforces a new land use regulation or
> enforces land use regulation enacted prior to the effective date
> of this amendment that restricts the use of private real property
> or any interest therein and has the effect of reducing the fair
> market value of the property, or any interest therein, then the
> owner of the property shall be paid just compensation."

Measure 37 provides in addition that, in lieu of just compensation, the state may choose to waive the restriction. All of this is clearly a step in the right direction, but it remains to be seen how effective it will be in achieving justice and equal protection of the laws. Currently being disputed in Oregon is the extent to which land-use restrictions in the federally-designated National Columbia River Gorge Scenic Area are subject to Measure 37, which is a state measure. One thing is certain. Measure 37 will enrich the coffers of property-rights law firms in Oregon. (An excellent account of Oregon's land-use offenses appears in *Regulatory Overkill* by Bill Moshofsky, published in 2004 by Trafford.)

In 2006 a number of related citizen's initiatives followed in other states. They were spurred in large part by property owners' outrage over the Supreme Court's highly controversial *Kelo v. New London, 2005* decision, which upheld the right of the city of New London, Connecticut to take private property for *private* use despite the clearly stated Constitutional restriction of takings to instances for *public* use. Owners of private property naturally view that development with alarm. There can be no doubt that the Supreme Court erred grievously in that decision, and many states rushed to undo its damage by amending their own constitutions to counter it.

The new initiatives were intended both to counter Kelo and to duplicate Oregon's Measure 37. In the first instance these initiatives would ensure unequivocally that eminent domain could be invoked only for *public* use (as already mandated by the United States Constitution and seconded by state constitutions). In the second instance these initiatives would ensure that just compensation would be paid to owners whose properties sustained damage or devaluation as a result of regulatory actions. Unfortunately, California's Proposition 90 was defeated by a 52% majority; Idaho's Proposition 2 was defeated by a 76% majority; judicial action blocked Montana's Initiative 154 from the ballot; and Washington's Initiative 933 was defeated by a majority of 58%. Only Arizona's Proposition 207 was successful, winning by a 65% majority vote.

Thus, on the surface it would appear that the majority of voters in many states have little aversion to government condemnation and devaluation of private property. However, it's more likely that the losing initiatives were simply victims of very skillful political campaigns by left-wing opponents. With the help of sympathetic media, the latter very effectively exploited allegations that wealthy, right-wing, New York, real-estate developer, Howard Rich, had contributed heavily to the campaigns in support of the aforementioned initiatives. Most westerners would of course regard such meddling in their affairs by a New Yorker as repugnant, if not illegal. Secondly the opposition argued that if their governments were required to compensate owners for regulatory damages to, and devaluations of, private property, their governments would go bankrupt. In the states where the initiatives were defeated the majority of voters were evidently mesmerized by those two factors and simply failed to recognize that, if the private properties of others can be easily targeted for uncompensated regulatory takings, then their own private properties might also one day be easily targeted for uncompensated regulatory takings.

Had voters looked beyond the allegations of eastern meddling and the specter of government bankruptcy, they might have thought seriously about who should rightfully bear the burden of regulatory devaluations, the targeted property owners, or the public at large. They might also have interpreted the threat of government bankruptcy as simply an admission of the enormous magnitude of the regulatory rip-offs that their governments have all along been perpetrating against private property owners. Indeed, Measure 37 claims in Oregon are approaching $20 billion, making regulation waivers a far more likely outcome than compensated regulatory takings. One can only hope that, in the years ahead, property owners in all states will become more diligent in defense of their private property rights. In any event, the fact that government might not be able to afford to compensate property owners for damaging regulations does not comprise license for government nevertheless to impose those damaging regulations without just compensation, for that simply amounts to unacceptable expropriation.

One more especially flagrant act of unacceptable expropriation deserves mention. In 2004, the governing council of Washington State's King County (which includes Seattle and extensive adjacent rural land) enacted so-called "Critical Areas Ordinances." Those ordinances require (among other provisions) that rural landowners who haven't already cleared their land must leave up to 65% of it in a natural state. In this instance the urban-area members of the council simply outnumbered the rural-area members of the council and, at the expense of rural landowners, created vast areas of open space and natural habitat to the benefit of the public at large. You can imagine the reaction of rural landowners who planned on clearing some of their land for agricultural or other uses. Needless to say, the Critical Areas Ordinances are currently under legal attack by those whose land use has been harshly restricted. Had Washington's Initiative 933 been adopted by voters in 2006 this issue would already have been resolved in favor of the rural landowners.

As is abundantly clear by now, the scenic-preservation regulatory takings perpetrated in California, Oregon, Washington, and other states as well, all fit the same pattern. The government and urban majority covet scenic open spaces. Rather than purchase them at market value, the government and urban majority simply take them through imposition of regulations and zoning restrictions. The owners of the scenic open spaces, being in the minority, are powerless to retaliate. The judiciary, ostensibly created to assure compliance with the Constitution, simply sits by and watches it happen. The cat, the rat, the dog, and the duck dine greedily on the little red hen's bread. (And our founding fathers turn over in their graves).

Something akin to Oregon's Measure 37 is sorely needed in California (and elsewhere as well). Moreover, the development laws and regulations should be so iron-clad-explicit, quantitative, and objective that, initially, a Coastal Permit Administrator would have to focus exclusively on a checklist rigid enough to assure that all of those explicit, quantitative, and objective criteria are met. Then the Coastal Permit Administrator would be allowed but a single subjective judgment, viz., a recommendation on whether the proposed development should be located as proposed or should be moved to an alternate location for purposes of scenic preservation. In the latter instance an independent and impartial assessor would determine the amount that the proposed scenic preservation action would devalue the owner's property, and this would of course be subject to judicial review. In effect, a price tag would be placed on each scenic preservation action, so that, if it eventually took place, the owner would be reimbursed by the amount on that price tag. Whether or not that action would actually take place would be determined in a competition among all relocation recommendations made by all Coastal Permit Administrators in the area of concern. Reimbursements would be funded through taxation of the public at large. Obviously the amount of money available for such reimbursements would be determined by the extent to which the public at large would be willing to pay taxes for scenic preservation. With a price tag on each scenic preservation action, and a limit on the available funds, regulators would have to choose carefully and responsibly which preservation actions offered the most public benefit for the available funds. Such an arrangement would put an end to the current system of rampant and capricious, free-of-charge-to-the-public, scenic-preservation exactions and replace it with a system based on responsibility, accountability, and fairness. This is the approach I propose as means to achieve a more equitable and congenial relationship between scenic preservation and property rights.

Ideally, there should also be concern not only for scenic preservation but for scenic *restoration* as well, and *all* owners of property, developed or not, coastal or inland, should be under obligation to enhance the scenic character of their own properties. In effect, scenic preservation and restoration should begin at home. Instead of simply terrorizing coastal-zone property owners via the California Coastal Act, inland property owners should be doing something constructive to deal with their own scenic offenses. One could even imagine a "California Inland Commission" charged with effecting inland scenic preservation and restoration. Indeed, why not give inlanders a dose of the same medicine they crammed down the throats of coastal-zone property owners? Well, obviously, I don't propose that. Two wrongs don't make a right. Instead, what I do propose is reformation of the coastal laws and regulations along lines outlined in the preceding paragraph, and I propose application of those reformed laws and regulations to coastal and inland regions alike. If such equity were introduced into the equation, i.e., if all members of the public, coastal and inland alike, were treated in the same manner, I'm confident that, Californians (like their Oregonian neighbors) would demand that the laws and regulations be more fair, equitable, and reasonable. And, with both coastal and inland areas participating in scenic preservation and restoration, there'd be both equal protection of the laws and greater scenic enhancement.

A tough interpretation of the Coastal Act is deeply ingrained in the cultures of the Coastal Commission, the Commission Staff, County Supervisors, and County Staffs. Any applicant for employment in the coastal development planning bureaucracy would be well advised to display at least a hint of anti-development zeal. Surely, no one would like to be responsible for approving anything that can be criticized by the public as damaging to public views. It's much easier politically to be against, rather than in favor of, *any* development. California residents in general have an anti-development fervor. They have their homes, and would like the rest of the state to be simply one big park. Wouldn't we all, but raising taxes to pay to achieve it through just compensation is quite another matter. It's just a whole lot easier to abuse coastal-zone landowners alone than to force all California residents to pay enough additional taxes to enable purchase of land and scenic easements in order to achieve scenic preservation.

However, even with a highly-professional, unbiased, law-abiding coastal development bureaucracy, there would still be problems under the existing Coastal Act, for its language is so loose, subjective, and qualitative (as opposed to explicit, quantitative, and objective) that even two strict constructionist decision-makers are likely in good faith to reach different conclusions in any given case. In such a situation, decisions become capricious. If, as is usually the case, the bureaucracy is biased *against* development, the loose language of the Coastal Act makes it all too easy for the bureaucracy to achieve its agenda by ruling against those seeking development permits. Coastal landowners argue that this was the intent of the drafters of the Coastal Act. What are needed are laws and regulations so explicit, quantitative, and objective that Coastal Permit Administrators would be unable to inject their own biases into their determinations regarding whether or not a proposed development is in compliance.

Perhaps the most glaring example of the loose language of the California Coastal Act is the term, "subordinate to the character of the setting." Yes, "subordinate" is the dreaded "S" word I mentioned in the preface, the one I said was a lot like porn because you'd know it when you saw it. It appears in Section 30251 of the act, which states in part that,

> "New development in highly scenic areas such as those designated in the California Coastline Preservation and Recreation Plan prepared by the Department of Parks and Recreation and by local government shall be subordinate to the character of the setting."

(Incidentally, the Columbia Gorge Commission uses the term "visually subordinate" in the same context.) This language immediately raises the question, "In whose opinion?" As is so often stated, beauty is in the eye of the beholder. And by what criteria are "highly scenic areas" designated? Such ambiguous language generates conflicts that enrich California land-use law firms and provide justifications for expanding state and county coastal planning staffs.

Landowners should at the very least be entitled to clear, specific, objective, quantitative regulations, regulations that:

o   Assure that landowners can easily design projects to conform to the regulations with certainty.

o   Assure that the administration of those regulations will be straightforward and not subject to caprice, political corruption, or the whims of diverse administrators.

29

o   Assure that landowners will receive the equal protection of the law mandated by the United States Constitution.

An ideal set of regulations would place strict quantitative limits on square footage, height, setbacks, and color and require such extensive vegetative screening that strictures on siting and architectural style could be largely eliminated. After all, if, after ten or fifteen years, the public wouldn't be able to see the development, its style and appearance would be beside the point!

But in the real world we were to be subject to the California Coastal Act as it was then executed in Mendocino County. Given that reality, what was to be the fate of our Coastal Development Permit application?

CHAPTER 4

COASTAL PERMIT DEVELOPMENT APPLICATION

We soon learned that there's much more to a Coastal Development Permit (CDP) application in Mendocino County than merely a set of plans. The application must include in addition:

o   County Real Estate Tax Verification (certifying ownership)

o   Geological Report

o   Landscaping and Vegetative Screening Report

o   Soils and Septic Field Report

o   Botanical Report

o   Archeological Commission Release

o   California Department of Transportation Highway Encroachment Permit

o   Elk County Water District Approval of Application for Water Service

o   County Environmental Health Clearance

    o   California Department of Forestry and Fire Protection Preliminary
        Clearance.

Suffice it to say that most of these erect time-consuming barriers; some must be certified by licensed professional experts; most are costly; and altogether they comprise elements of a minefield, any one of which is capable of triggering denial of a project. Of course, many of these reports and clearances are in the best interest of owners. In earthquake-prone California owners are well advised to build only on sites that are geologically favorable. And owners in locations without sewers require soils suitable for septic fields. It's also in the owner's interest that combustible vegetation exist no closer than a safe distance from the house. But one finding of an archeological artifact or rare or endangered plant or animal can spell disaster. The landscaping and vegetative screening issue is equally treacherous as already noted. To what extent does the public have the right not to see the project? Must owners erect vegetative screens, which interfere with their own viewsheds, in order to render their projects invisible to the public?

I'll expand a bit here on but one of the above-mentioned reports simply to illustrate the level of scrutiny to which a parcel is subjected during evaluations of its suitability for development. The botanical survey of our parcel was conducted by Gordon E. McBride, PhD, who had previously conducted 350 such surveys for eight different agencies. In his report, McBride listed some 40 plant species that he had found on our parcel. Among them was a patch of Castilleja Mendocinensis (commonly known as Mendocino Paintbrush), which he referred to as "rare and endangered." Because of that designation, the location of that patch, and a hundred-foot buffer zone surrounding it, automatically became a protected no-development zone under Mendocino County regulations. Fortunately, this did not impact our plans, because the Castilleja Mendocinensis patch lay more than 400 feet northeast of our proposed building site. Interestingly, we've recently learned that Castilleja Mendocinensis was not included (nor is it today) in the official Federal and California listings of rare and endangered plants. Nevertheless, at the time, Dr. McBride's designation was good enough for the Mendocino County planners, who were all too eager to accept any excuse for prohibiting development in the coastal zone. Ironically, road crews regularly mow vegetation alongside highways in Mendocino County with no regard whatsoever for rare and endangered plants!

Now, once a CDP application has been submitted to the Mendocino County Department of Planning and Building Services (PBS), what procedures are followed? The CDP application is assigned to a Project Coordinator (PC) who's responsible for reviewing it meticulously and for providing opinions regarding its consistency with the Coastal Act and the County Regulations. As a part of this review, the PC sends project descriptions to other county and state offices and departments, as well as various entities outside government, providing them with opportunities to comment on aspects which might be of concern to them. In the meantime the CDP applicant is required to post on the property a "Notice of Pending Permit" with a brief description of the proposed development and a reference to PBS where additional information may be obtained. The CDP applicant must also provide a listing of all property owners within 300 feet and all occupants within 100 feet of the proposed development, together with the corresponding Assessor's Parcel Number for each owner/occupant. That enables the County to send notifications to those individuals. All of these measures assure that everyone gets a fair shot at the project. On the other hand, in Mendocino County adverse comments received by a PC on a proposed project are not automatically brought to the attention of the CDP applicant. To avoid being blindsided, applicants should consult the County file on their projects frequently and request copies of pertinent comments. Although inconvenient for applicants who live far from Mendocino County, that's a necessary task.

The PC considers comments from all quarters, calls to the attention of the applicant any inconsistencies with the regulations, and attempts to resolve controversies. (Incidentally, quite a heated debate took place between a member of the California Native Plant Society and Dr. McBride regarding the botanical survey the latter had conducted on our parcel. Fortunately, it had no adverse impact on our proposed project.) Upon completion of the PC's review, the PC prepares a "Staff Report," noting agreements and disagreements with regard to the CDP application's consistency with the regulations. The report contains a recommendation either for approval or denial. A recommendation for approval is usually contingent upon the satisfaction of a number of additional conditions that are usually quite troublesome.

The Staff Report is widely circulated, and a hearing announcement is published in the local newspaper soliciting public comment. Next a quasi-judicial public hearing is convened by the Coastal Permit Administrator (CPA), a county official who has authority to rule on the CDP application. If the CPA rules in favor of the applicant, objectors may appeal the ruling either to the County Board of Supervisors (BOS) or to the California Coastal Commission (CCC). Because the BOS charges a substantial fee, and the CCC does not, objectors invariably appeal to the CCC. Rulings of the CCC are final unless invalidated by a lawsuit waged either by the objectors or the CDP applicant.

If the CPA initially denies the application the applicant may reapply with a modified application after a specified period, or the applicant may, for a substantial fee, appeal to the BOS. If the BOS rules in favor of the applicant, objectors can then appeal to the CCC. Again, rulings by the CCC are final unless invalidated by a lawsuit. If the BOS rules against the applicant, the applicant may either reapply with a modified plan or initiate a lawsuit against the County. It should be noted that the playing field is steeply tilted in favor of anti-development forces. They can appeal at any stage free of fees. But the applicant can appeal only to the BOS and only then with a very stiff fee.

We were blissfully unaware of much of the above when, on 7-21-94, we submitted our CDP application to the Fort Bragg office of PBS. That we were cautiously optimistic about our CDP application is evident from the fact that we had placed our McLean, Virginia residence on the market a month earlier.

The Project Coordinator assignment for our case went to Linda Ruffing, about whom we knew very little. In contrast, we had been forewarned about the Coastal Permit Administrator who would rule on our project. That would be none other than the notorious Gary Berrigan, who supervised coastal planners in the Fort Bragg office of PBS. Infamous for his overly harsh interpretations of land-use regulations, he was beloved by antidevelopment zealots and reviled by CDP applicants.

On 8-15-94 Ruffing wrote to us seeking additional information on a number of topics. The tone of her letter was much less than accommodating, a fact we sensed with some unease. According to Mike Leventhal, we were getting much more than the usual scrutiny. All issues raised by Ruffing would be burdensome to deal with, but most, those having to do with archaeology, water supply, plot plan, septic system, geotechnical report, landscaping, highway encroachment, landfill, and botanical survey appeared to present no insurmountable obstacles and were significant only in showing that our application was being reviewed with a fine-tooth comb.

Other matters raised by Ruffing were destined to become continued sources of wrangling. The first of these issues had to do with the unusual room arrangement of our house. You'll recall that our proposed design consisted of a one-bedroom main house, a narrow roofed breezeway, a garage, and a maid's room and guesthouse all connected together under a common roof and in that order. Considered as one structure, our design would be allowed under County regulations. But if the garage/maid/guesthouse portion was determined to be a separate structure from the main house, we would be required by County regulation to reduce the size of the maid/guesthouse portion to 640 sq ft or less. Unfortunately the County regulation for distinguishing between "separate" and "connected" was (and is) ambiguous, and so this posed a difficulty. Just why the County regulations should favor one arrangement over the other is beyond my comprehension. In any event, Ruffing's letter chose a hard line on this issue, viewing our garage/maid/guesthouse as a separate structure and stating that, "Second residential units are prohibited in the coastal zone, and guest cottages are limited to 640 square feet." At the end of Ruffing's letter was the statement that a series of photomontages would have to be prepared for purposes of evaluating the visual impact of our project. This would also become a source of continued wrangling.

Mike Leventhal's 9-9-94 response to the issues raised by Ruffing was patient, polite, and meticulous. With regard to the 640 sq ft limitation, he commented that, "The residence as drawn is a three bedroom home with two of these bedrooms connected by a covered walkway to the main portion of the home. There is no intention of having a second residential unit, only semi-detached bedrooms for privacy." With regard to photomontages he sought more explicit information on what was required.

At this juncture, for reasons unknown to us, Ruffing resigned from her position with the Department of Planning and Building Services. Her replacement as Project Coordinator was to be Mary Stinson. When Bob Schlosser first stopped by to discuss our project with her, Stinson referred to us disparagingly as "Republicans" and chided him for assisting us in our attempt to move to Mendocino County. I have no idea what caused her to classify us as Republicans, but she'd evidently concluded that we were and should be treated as such in predominantly Democratic Mendocino County. Her comment was of course totally inappropriate for a civil servant, who's supposed to be strictly non-partisan in her official capacity, but it was prescient with regard to her subsequent relationship with us.

On 10-19-94 Stinson responded to Mike's letter of 9-9-94. She addressed some twenty items, most of which, though burdensome, could be handled without serious adverse impact. An all-inclusive recitation of the indignities of dealing with such minutiae would be out of place here, and so I'll focus on only a few that proved to be most troublesome. Stinson's letter reiterated the issues raised by Ruffing relative to the floor area of the maid/ guesthouse area, and she pointed out a County regulation prohibiting the kitchenette we had planned for the guesthouse. About that there could be no debate, and so this was not an issue we chose to contest, even though this regulation is without a logical basis and is widely flouted in Mendocino County.

Stinson's letter also identified five viewpoints from which photos were to be taken for use in preparation of photomontages. These included the Cuffey's-Cove Highway-One turnout two road miles north of our parcel, three sites in Elk approximately one-half mile north of our parcel (viz. the bluff-top burn circle of Greenwood State Beach, the beach level immediately below that burn circle, and the front of the Elk Garage), and the south end of the Highway-One turnout adjacent to our parcel.

Most of the issues raised by Ruffing and Stinson were appropriate for Mike to handle, and he did so, keeping us informed to assure that we concurred with his approaches. On the other hand, the task of preparing photomontages was one I was well equipped to handle, having been engaged in photography for some 60 years and having a physicist's technical capabilities. Accordingly, with a graduated house-height pole placed at the westernmost corner of the house, I took the required photos. The pole served as both a marker and a gauge. With knowledge of the house dimensions and the angle of view in each case, I was able to place a rectangle large enough to enclose and represent the house at the building site in each photo. I assumed that that would be sufficient for gauging visual impact. Also, I undertook the task with the firm conviction that a photomontage used for judging visual impact should show the scene as it's seen by unaided human eyes, not as seen with a telescope or binoculars. After all, the importance of an object in a scene is roughly proportional to its size relative to the remainder of the scene. Indeed, if you look at a house through a telescope or binoculars so that the house fills most of the scene viewed, the house dominates the scene, and it's not likely to be judged "subordinate to the character of the setting."

Unfortunately it's not possible with readily available photographic equipment to duplicate the remarkable field of view of a pair of human eyes, viz., roughly 180 degrees horizontally and 135 degrees vertically. The most practical scheme would be to use a 20 mm lens with a 35 mm film camera, both of which are fairly commonly available. But in this case the photo would depict only about one-sixth of the scene encompassed by human eyes, and so would place us at a six to one disadvantage. Nevertheless, we decided to accept that degree of disadvantage, but not without some misgivings.

However, in discussions with Mike, Stinson demanded, in addition, photomontages prepared using photos taken with telephoto lenses of focal length up to 400 mm. At the extreme magnification by a 400 mm lens, the fractional area of the scene occupied by the house would be 2,400 times that for the case of unaided human eyes! We took this to indicate that Stinson was either incapable of understanding the gross distortion her demands comprised or was fully aware of it and planned to use it as a weapon against us. Neither was acceptable. Nevertheless, under protest, we complied and produced montages for 50, 200, and 400 mm photos in addition to 20 mm photos. In each instance I represented the house by a rectangle large enough to contain the house. On several of the 20 and 50 mm montages this rectangle was about the size of a hyphen in this text, simply because the distances from camera to house site were so great, ranging from one-quarter mile to 1.6 miles. In any event, my montages, submitted on 12-20-94, were rejected, in part because Stinson insisted that the house be depicted in detail and in part because she would accept evidence only if prepared by an independent professional. Accordingly, most of that exercise was wasted. However, during the process we at least established unequivocally that our house would not be visible at all from the beach level of Greenwood State Beach.

So it was back to square one as we contacted a professional recommended by Stinson. After struggling with the task for a couple of months, he was unable to produce the photomontages, and so he recommended that we approach his mentor, George Omura, located in Albany, CA. Omura succeeded, and in April 1995 provided the required montages. They verified the sizes of my house-enclosing rectangles and, in the high-magnification telephoto montages, depicted details of the house.

While all of this was in progress, Bob Schlosser added his voice to Mike's, protesting in principle the use of magnified views for the photomontages. Bob made the point that, when the legislature created the California Coastal Act, the portions concerned with visual impact had obviously been concerned only with the visual impact on unaided human eyes, rather than on views accessible only with telescopes, binoculars, and telephoto camera lenses. Bob's FAX of 3-14-95 elicited the following response from Stinson:

> "This letter is in response to your March 14, 1995 FAX regarding the applicability of magnified views for the required photomontages. This office cites the following sections of the coastal element and the Zoning code to substantiate our requirement for those photomontages:
>
> 1. Chapter 3.5 of the Coastal Element requires that new development comply with policies of that chapter.

2. Sections 20.532.025 (A) and (G) of the Zoning Code have to do with information required for Coastal Permit applications.
3. Sections 20.504.015 (A) (3), and (C), 20.504.020 (C) and (D) regarding visual resources in Highly Scenic Areas.

You do have the option to appeal this determination to the Planning commission pursuant to Section 20.532.035 (G) and Section 20.544 within 10 days. The filing fee is $970.

Should you have any additional questions concerning this matter, please contact this office."

Of course, none of those regulatory citations mention photomontages, let alone magnified views. Stinson either missed the whole point or deliberately chose to ignore it in order to force preparation of misleading evidence. From the hostile tone of her letter it appeared most unlikely that she would recommend approval of our permit application. In any event, her letter appeared to us like a declaration of war. Whether she was our main antagonist, or whether she was merely a proxy for Berrigan, we had no way of knowing. But the reality of it was that we had just paid $1,670 for magnified-view photomontages that comprised misleading adverse evidence against our own CDP application. We subsequently learned that photomontages had been required by the County in only one previous instance. In all other cases, so-called "story poles" had been erected on site to enable Project Coordinators to gauge visual impact. We had of course provided story poles in addition to the photomontages. What was so special about our modest project that elicited so much special attention? Instinctively, we sensed that something was going on behind the scenes, and we weren't privy to it.

In the mean time, shortly after we received Stinson's rebuke, Ray Hall, Director of the Mendocino County Department of Planning and Building Services sent us a form letter telling us of a review of the CDP application process aimed at streamlining it. He sought our "thoughts and comments as a property owner on ways to improve the permit process." Our response expressed appreciation for his efforts to streamline the process, and it continued, "However, we would like to delay responding until our permit application (submitted in 1994) has been favorably acted upon, and our retirement residence has been completed. In that way we will be able to view the entire process in retrospect, and we will also avoid the possibility that any in-process criticism could adversely impact our interactions with staff currently handling our application." I doubt that he could have interpreted our response as a ringing endorsement.

CHAPTER 5
COUNTY AND STATE PARKS ATTACK

Throughout the fall of 1994 and the spring of 1995 we and our architects attempted as best we could to deal with the myriad issues raised by the Department of Planning and Building Services. Mike, always the optimist, had commented on his winter holiday greeting card to us "Expect Christmas 1995 in Elk!" But relations with the County had deteriorated badly. The issues of photomontages and maid/guesthouse square footage outlined in earlier chapters, were only illustrative of other unsettled issues too numerous to address here in detail. In attempts to respond constructively to comments (unwritten) by Stinson that the house was too large, we had in December, 1994 submitted a new plan showing a significant reduction in size, with conditioned space reduced from 4,288 sq ft to 3,843 sq ft, even though a house ten times larger than our proposed house would not exceed the coverage limit set by the County regulations for our eleven-acre parcel. Also, belatedly recognizing that labeling a room as a maid's room might be judged offensive in a County as poor as Mendocino, we had Mike relabel the room between the garage and guesthouse as Bedroom 3. To deal with the attached/detached issue the connection between the main house and garage was redesigned so that it was no longer a breezeway. The new version included both a common wall (with a door and a window) and a common roof.

At one point, impatient with the pace of progress on our application, I had telephoned Stinson to address a number of issues, pretty much to no avail. I had then telephoned Ray Hall, Director of Planning and Building Services to voice my concern on a number of issues and request that he look over the shoulders of his staff. He promised to review our case, but expressed no opinion on the issues.

Badly in need of diversion from our all-consuming battle with Planning and Building Services, Margie and I had earlier arranged for a two-week tour of Japan beginning in the middle of April 1995. On our way, we spent a day in southern California and returned to our motel in the evening to find a telephone message that had been left by Mike. It stated simply, "Submitted letter to County. All is well. Have a safe trip." Buoyed by that note we thoroughly enjoyed our travel in Japan.

Returning home, we were informed by Mike that, finally, all issues had been resolved and pretty much agreed upon, and that all that remained was for Stinson to write her

Staff Report. Mike was upbeat. We were only cautiously hopeful. Six weeks went by, and on 6-7-95 Stinson signed off on her Staff Report. It was a disaster! It imposed 13 "Special Conditions." Some were tantamount to denial of our project. Others were constraints to which we had already agreed and, although burdensome, were not of major concern. Just as we feared, the first two of the photomontages displayed in the Staff Report were 200 mm and 400 mm lens views from Cuffey's Cove, which greatly exaggerated the visual impact of our proposed project. In fact in a 20 mm lens view from that site our house height would be less than the thickness of a raster line on Omura's computer screen and hence would not show up at all. But the Staff Report included only one 20 mm lens photomontage, specifically for a view of our house from the highway turnout to the south. Thus, it was evident that the cards were stacked against us for our permit hearing before Coastal Permit Administrator Berrigan, which was fast approaching on 6-22-95.

Among the Staff Report special conditions was one which required that our residence be set back an additional 60 feet from the western bluff edge. Because of the unusual topography this would seriously degrade our ocean views, while yielding no benefit to public views to the ocean. We couldn't accept that.

Another special condition required that our structure "must be redesigned and limited to one story.... and substantially reduced in size." This was unacceptable for several reasons. County regulations are silent on whether or not a mezzanine is counted as a story, but the Uniform Building Code does not count a mezzanine as a story. Moreover, the County regulations contain no prohibition of a second story for a marine terrace site, such as ours, as opposed to a ridge site, where there is a clear prohibition of two stories. As our interactions with County planners wore on, the two-story issue arose again and again. They seemed completely incapable of accepting their own regulations. Height considerations were less controversial, the planners sometimes expressing willingness to allow a foot or so above the usual 18-foot limit. I say usual, because the regulations allow additional height when, "an increase in height would not affect public views to the ocean or be out of character with surrounding structures." Nevertheless, to conform to the overall 18-foot limit the ceiling height in our mezzanine today is nearly a foot less than the usual eight feet, and incidentally, that mezzanine is the crown jewel of our house with magnificent views in all directions, most of which are denied to the lower level by the relatively uncooperative nature of the topography of the site where we were ultimately allowed to build.

The further size reduction ordained by the Staff Report was also unacceptable. As already stated, the County limit for our parcel is a full ten times larger than the structure we proposed, and the phrase "substantially reduced in size" provides no guidance regarding what size *would* be acceptable. In addition we had already reduced the size by 445 sq ft.

The final unacceptable special condition stated that, "Prior to connection to the Elk County Water District the boundaries of their service area shall be expanded to serve this site or the appropriate County Land-Use Maps amended to reflect the existing situation whichever is appropriate." This was unacceptable for several reasons. The ECWD water supply line runs across our property and was already servicing a multitude of residences beyond our parcel (i.e., farther from the source). We had already paid for and been granted an ECWD tap. Even if denied access we could always drill a well. Waiting for the ECWD to expand their service area and for the County Land-Use Maps to be amended could very well delay our project for several years. (In fact, today, eleven years later, the County Land-Use Maps have yet to be amended!) This ridiculous issue, which would be discussed *ad infinitum* in subsequent hearings, brought to mind scenes from old western movies, which often featured murderous conflicts over water rights.

Apart from unacceptable special conditions, the Staff Report contained numerous factual errors, factual errors that were destined to work against us. I'll mention but a few. The project description at the beginning of the report described our proposed project as "an approximately 5,000 square foot two story single family dwelling including an attached three car garage, guest and maid's quarters..." Actually, the square footage of the conditioned space was 3,869 with a 960 square foot garage. Moreover, according to the uniform building codes the structure was not two story, and the average height of the proposed house was only 12.9 feet. Perhaps most likely to inflame opposition were the words "maid's quarters." And elsewhere in her Staff Report, Stinson continued to refer to the third bedroom as the "maid's room," despite our having relabeled it.

In an attempt to understand what had occurred, we belatedly telephoned Planning and Building Services requesting all information in their possession bearing on our case. We followed it with a formal request in writing. Of course we should have been requesting such information all along. As ex-civil servants with full knowledge of freedom-of-information statutes as they relate to public activities we should have been more inquisitive.

So what had been going on behind the scenes? Recall that County coastal planners had received our CDP application on 7-21-94. The very next day they dispatched a description of our project to, and requested comments from: the Native Plant Society, the California Department of Transportation, the County Health Department, Norman de Vall (County Supervisor from the Fifth District and resident of Elk), Sonoma State University, the Archeological Commission, the County Farm Advisor, the County Agricultural Commissioner, the California Coastal Commission, and the California Department of Parks & Recreation in *both* Mendocino and in Sacramento. Recipients were notified that, "If we do not receive a response within fifteen (15) days we will assume no response is forthcoming." We had no idea that our CDP application was about to be subjected to such massive scrutiny.

Moreover, we were not pleased with the description of our project in that solicitation for comments, for it included the words, "...detached garage with attached maid quarters and apartment unit...," words which were certain to ignite opposition. There were still other very troublesome aspects to the solicitation. It was odd indeed that Norman de Vall, County Supervisor for the Fifth District and resident of Elk, was included, because the County Supervisors could sit in judgment of our case in the event of an appeal, and California's Brown Act required that if one Supervisor receives information on a case, all other Supervisors must as well. Most shocking was de Vall's hand-written response passed to Ruffing on a small, undated 4" x 6" slip of paper. It read,

"I did phone in my concerns re this proposal AnD have serious questions re the design – which to me is a minature shopping MAll. If invisAble to Town, Highway AnD Beach – I cAn livE w/it - Otherwise – it's back to the DrAwing board - pls -

Norman "

In our view this was totally improper and illegal. In effect a potential judge was telling the civil servant what position to adopt on the case. Equally troubling was a critical letter from former Elk resident and Chief County Planner Alan Falleri, of the Ukiah office of the Department of Planning and Building Services, superior to both Stinson and Berrigan in that department. His name had not appeared on the solicitation list, but he nevertheless proffered his opinion, stating flatly that the proposed project, "is not subordinate to the character of its setting," and further that it should be moved eastward and down-sized. With such comments from her superiors (de Vall and Falleri), how could Stinson render an independent and objective judgment? And who could guess what pressure her immediate supervisor, Berrigan, might be applying?

A more-professional response was received by the County from the California Coastal Commission's Jo Ginsberg. Not having visited the site herself, she was careful not to take firm positions on the critical issues.

The California Department of Parks and Recreation showed no such restraint, aggressively attacking our project in a letter to the County. It was written over the signature block of Bill Berry, State Parks Superintendent for the Russian River/Mendocino District, but, significantly, it was signed "for" him by Gary Shannon. The Berry/Shannon letter harshly attacked the visual impact of our project as seen from Greenwood State Beach viewpoints, claimed incorrectly that mitigation of the visual impact with vegetative screening would not be feasible for the proposed location, and argued that the structure should be relocated "further toward the east" (where our views of the ocean would be severely diminished). This attack was most surprising, for our proposed house would be a full one-half mile from the nearest public view point in the state park. Moreover, the tone of the letter was clearly hostile. Yet, we knew that in very restrained and accommodating communications with the County two years earlier, Berry had offered only minor criticisms regarding plans for an enormous (17,200 sq ft, 216 ft long, 42 ft high) ocean-front, "single-family residence" that Kenneth and Linda Rawlings proposed to construct a mere 87 feet from van Damme State Park near the village of Mendocino. That project subsequently failed to gain County approval, but Berry had appeared willing to accept it, even though it would have obstructed public views from the State Park to the ocean. Why then had Berry adopted such a highly negative attitude toward our project, which would be miniscule in comparison, would be vastly farther from State Park view points, and would not block public views from the park to the ocean? There had to be an ulterior motive, but what could it be?

Interestingly the Berry/Shannon letter stated erroneously that, "The proposed plan also shows a portion of the structure to be encroaching into the minimum 40-foot setback." Now that was odd. Those words looked familiar. Indeed, in her Staff Report Stinson erroneously wrote, "The plans also indicate a second story deck encroaching into the 40' setback area." Further examination revealed additional coincidences. In fact, it appeared as if, prior to release of her Staff Report, Stinson had provided State Parks with some of its ammunition for use in the Berry/Shannon letter. Moreover, on the coversheet faxing the Berry/Shannon letter to Stinson, Shannon had written, "Sorry this took so long. I will call you later today." It thus appeared that the Berry/Shannon letter had been prompted by Stinson. (And it had almost certainly been written by State Parks employee Gary Shannon rather than Berry. I wonder if Berry even knew what was in the letter.) Significantly, the letter had not met the 15-day response limitation specified in Ruffing's original solicitation letter. In fact, it was dated almost a year later, 6-6-95, *only the day before Stinson signed off on her completed Staff Report!* It thus appeared that Stinson was not merely gathering comments, but had taken sides and, instead of being the impartial public servant, was actively recruiting opposition. Or am I being too harsh? Could Stinson's superiors in PBS have been pulling her strings? I don't know. In any event, it would have been most improper for Stinson to have taken sides in what had become a controversy, and it would likewise have been improper for her to have prompted Shannon. Also, the information we received from the County failed to include any disclosure of the nature of the discussions between Stinson and Shannon, which had to have taken place. That should have been included in the County response to our freedom-of-information request. Adding further confirmation of the cozy relationship between the County and State Parks, Stinson had brazenly incorporated extensive quotes from the Berry/Shannon letter word for word into her Staff Report. She had allowed one party in the dispute prime coverage in her Staff Report without offering equal space for a rebuttal, clearly improper etiquette for such a report.

Disturbed by these events, we hired a lawyer, Richard Henderson, from Ukiah, to represent us at our upcoming hearing before Coastal Permit Administrator Berrigan. There wasn't time for Henderson to get up to speed on the details of the case, but his presence at our hearing would demonstrate to Berrigan that we would not accept an abridgement of our property rights without a fight. In the meantime Mike and Bob wrote a hard-hitting letter to Berrigan refuting the claims of the Staff Report. In addition to points recounted above they reported an independent ruling from Jim Spence, Chief Coastal Building Inspector for Mendocino County, who stated that our proposed project was a single structure, and hence there was no problem with our guesthouse/third-bedroom arrangement. Also, according to Mike, Stinson had verbally approved the guesthouse/third bedroom arrangement before later issuing her Staff Report with its negative determination on that matter. Thus the stage was set for the CPA hearing before Berrigan.

CHAPTER 6

COASTAL PERMIT ADMINISTRATOR HEARING I

The two-week interval between the release of the Staff Report and our hearing before Coastal Permit Administrator Gary Berrigan was a period of intense activity for us as we developed rebuttals to the assertions in the Staff Report. As fate would have it, on the eve of the hearing, we found buyers for our Virginia house, which had been on the market for almost a year. To deal with that Margie remained behind, while I flew to California for the hearing (my fourth transcontinental round trip in our quest for a permit). To make certain I covered all of the disputed issues in the Staff Report, and to be certain my comments became part of the official record of the hearing, I prepared written comments, some 27 pages of double-spaced narrative plus numerous illustrations. I arrived on the Mendocino coast early enough on the day before the hearing to take, and have developed, additional photographs pertinent to our case.

The next morning the hearing began in the nondescript conference room of the Fort Bragg office of the Department of Planning and Building Services. Gary Berrigan, a fortyish man, above average in height and of medium build with thin graying hair and a pony tail entered, turned on a cheap music-box-type tape recorder, and called the meeting to order. By then I was looking forward to finally being able to confront Stinson, to face our accuser, to point out her errors, and to demolish her arguments. But that was not to be, for she didn't appear. That was very odd. In such hearings it's customary for the Project Coordinator first to summarize the Staff Report as well as any written comments received from interested parties including other government offices and the public at large. Applicants and their representatives testify next followed by any other attendees who wish to comment. But here was Gary Berrigan fulfilling his role as Coastal Permit Administrator and in addition playing the role of the Project Coordinator summarizing the Staff Report in this quasi-judicial hearing. It was as if in a trial the judge acts not only as judge, but also as prosecuting attorney as well, thus leaving little doubt about the probable outcome of the proceedings. In any event Berrigan ran through the assertions of the Staff Report with dispatch, almost as if he'd written them himself. But Stinson's absence was a mystery. Is it possible she didn't fully subscribe to the positions in her report and couldn't bring herself to participate in the public lynching? Or did she believe in her report and simply have stage fright? I don't know.

As might well be expected, given the nature of the special conditions contained in the Staff Report, I was combative in my comments. It was evident to me that the visual impact issue was central, and that the photomontages had played a prominent role in the County deliberations on the matter of visual impact. Accordingly, I devoted a lot of time showing how various focal length lenses depict various scenes, and I presented peel-back masks on photos to show how the importance of a particular feature in a scene changes in going from wide-angle to telephoto lens. To demonstrate that a 400 mm lens was not the kind of thing your typical tourist carries around I showed Berrigan my own camera with a 400 mm lens attached. From back of camera to tip of lens hood it extended nearly a foot-and-a-half. I also made the point that, as seen from Cuffey's Cove, 1.6 miles distant, our house would occupy only one one-millionth of the field of view of a pair of human eyes, and hence could only be judged subordinate to the character of the setting. I presented photos showing that our house would not block public views to the ocean. And I showed diagrams indicating how moving our house eastward would not benefit public views to the ocean, i.e., would provide no benefit to the public, while devastating our views. I expressed our willingness to plant trees to screen our house from public view and disagreed with the assertion of the Berry/Shannon letter that vegetative screening was not feasible. The day before, I had taken photos from Greenwood State Beach, and I showed Berrigan how the recently-created park had been established deep within the existing village of Elk with houses packed around it in all directions except oceanward. I also showed him pictures of oceanfront houses recently approved by the County that are much more prominent visually than ours would be.

Next to speak was Gary Shannon from State Parks. Not only did he share his first name and Irish ethnicity with Berrigan, but his age and stature as well. As to be expected, he simply reiterated what was already contained in the Berry/Shannon letter. Mike and Bob then disputed Shannon's position on the feasibility of vegetative screening, and they seconded many of the points I had made. Henderson, our lawyer, had little to say on the contentious issues and sought only to steer discussions along lines where some agreement might possibly be achieved. I doubt that anyone could have succeeded at that task.

As the hearing dragged on, it became apparent that Shannon was the only person (apart from Berrigan) to come to the hearing to oppose our project. That was actually quite encouraging, for, as subscribers to a couple of Mendocino coast newspapers, we were well aware that land-use matters in the area often resulted in very contentious battles with lots of public participation. Yet, despite the fact that our hearing was widely publicized via mailed hearing announcements and local newspapers, our hearing was very sparsely attended. Just maybe, without a lot of public support for his position, Berrigan would not be comfortable denying our project. But as Berrigan began his deliberative comments I soon realized that that was just wishful thinking.

Berrigan commenced by emphasizing that visual considerations are subjective. In effect he dismissed as beside the point all of the information I had presented regarding use of various lenses for photos depicting visual impact. He mentioned for the record that he had never been on our property, although he had seen it from the highway. He claimed,

> "It is much more highly visible than what's depicted in these [20 mm] photos. That's why I say that the visual aspects of this are very subjective, and I do have the authority and discretion to deal with this matter."

More remarks followed on his authority and responsibilities. He then expressed his concern regarding what effect any approval of our pending permit application would have on the development of our adjacent 5-acre parcel. Next he addressed the attached-detached issue relative to the allowed square footage for our third bedroom and guesthouse, and he dismissed the ruling from the Building Department inspector, claiming a different criterion for the Planning Department. With regard to size, Berrigan argued that, "The maximum lot coverage is a maximum. You don't automatically get it." And he again stated that, "…the Coastal Permit Administrator has the authority and ability to approve, conditionally approve, or deny a project." After a few words lost in a tape change, Berrigan continued:

> "Look at it more simply. I don't think it's quite subordinate. I agree with your comments relative to conditions and their wording saying that recommending that it be redesigned subject to the Coastal Permit Administrator's approval. I agree with you, and, in large part, it's not that it provides me with too much discretion, because I do have that discretion, but I don't think that it's proper or legal for that discretion to be exercised outside of a public hearing."

A bit later he commented:

> "It's not subordinate to the setting at all…as proposed, no, I could not approve this as proposed, quite frankly, and solely based on the highly scenic policies. As proposed, no, I could not approve that. I simply would not and will not."

After some further comments to the effect that size remained a problem, Berrigan allowed that he was willing to continue the hearing to another date if we wished to submit a landscaping plan for consideration at that time. However he included a caveat:

> "I'm not sure that the landscape plan is going to resolve my concerns, because quite frankly, my, I do not want to be

responsible for approving something that's going to be there for a very long time, that's going to be my negative memorial as an action that I have taken. As I, you know, looking at the policies and everything, I want to be careful if a project is approved here. At least in my role that I'm satisfied that, that I can live with that particular decision. If I can't, then I'll deny it and then you can appeal to the board and let the Board of Supervisors make that particular decision, and let it rest on their shoulders… but the guidelines are, make it subordinate by making this structure as invisible, I mean if it can be made invisible from Elk, the state park and the scenic turnout by the cemetery, then that's all the better."

That attempt by Berrigan to impose invisibility, even though the law does not require it, echos de Vall's admonition in his highly-improper 4" x 6" note to Ruffing. Actually, the above quote is but a fraction of Berrigan's long harangue, but it's enough for you to get the drift. On the spot I decided to go for the landscaping plan, even though the odds were stacked pretty conclusively against us. There was just the slightest possibility that before the next hearing, Berrigan might study and understand the copy of my hearing remarks that I left with him. But then, given his stated position, it appeared most unlikely that anything would change his mind. Still, nurturing a glimmer of hope, before the hearing closed we invited Shannon to meet onsite with our architects and our to-be-selected landscape architect so that he could represent State Parks interests in the development of our landscaping plan. And, with vegetative screening having become a critical issue, I couldn't help but note the irony in the fact that twelve years earlier we had abandoned plans to plant additional evergreen trees on our parcel when we were advised by a County Planner that a formal application for that purpose would likely be denied.

Back in my motel, I telephoned Margie to report the outcome of the hearing, which was not at all unexpected. We agreed that the odds against us were so unfavorable that we would have to decline the offer on our Virginia house and take it off the market. Ironically, the couple who had made the offer to purchase our Virginia house were Richard Latter, a physicist, and his wife, Natalie, a linguist. With their offer on our house rejected, they too met disappointment as a consequence of the actions of a Coastal Permit Administrator in far away California.

I spent the night in Fort Bragg, and the next morning I tuned my rental car radio to Joe Regelski's KOZT, Fort Bragg, news broadcast. Much to my chagrin, I was assaulted with a greatly condensed version of the previous day's awful experience all over again. So that's who the unidentified hearing attendee was. I stopped at the radio station's office in downtown Fort Bragg to retrieve a transcript of Regelski's report for the record.

CHAPTER 7

ATTACK BY THE ELK ANTI FACTION

After the hearing our activities branched out in several directions. Mike arranged for landscape architect Sara Geddes of Satre Associates in Eugene, Oregon to develop our landscaping plan. With bachelor's degrees in both fine arts and landscape architecture from the University of Oregon and with extensive experience in west-coast projects, Sara was a most welcome (and very attractive) addition to our team. She'd been actively involved with the large, award-winning Sea Ranch development some forty miles to the south of Elk, where she was responsible for administering the Sea Ranch Architectural Design Review Committee, directing community planning programs, and overseeing environmental management efforts.

The onsite meeting was soon arranged with our architects, our landscape architect, and Gary Shannon of State Parks. The meeting was in fact quite encouraging in that Sara found conditions highly suitable for successful vegetative screening. She noted a number of evergreen trees already thriving on the parcel. Also, the meeting assured that Shannon had an opportunity to see the extensive existing brush and ceanothus trees, which at the outset would pretty much obscure the bottom half of our proposed structure from public view. Within short order Sara produced a landscaping plan that more than fulfilled the specifications outlined in the County's Special Condition 10.

In two FAXs regarding the attached/detached controversy, Mike challenged Berrigan to point out what County regulation wording led him to his ruling that differed from the ruling of the Chief Building Inspector. Berrigan ignored him. Seeing that this was leading nowhere, Margie and I wrote on 7-12-95 to Hall seeking his ruling. After all, both planners and building inspectors reported to Hall, and so his determination would be binding, not that we expected him to be able to cite any legal definition. The point was that we had to get this settled one way or the other so that we could prepare suitable plans for the upcoming continuation hearing. As expected, we received the answer we didn't want, and it made no reference to any definitive regulation. Hall ended his letter with the caveat,

"…this is one person's interpretation which may or may not be shared (and is certainly not binding) upon whomever hears the Coastal Development Permit."

In short, Mendocino County is governed, not by law, but by the caprice of Coastal Permit Administrators! So much for equal protection of the law. We could only concede defeat on the attached/detached issue.

Because of our general displeasure with both Berrigan and Shannon we decided to take remaining issues to their superiors. This is always a risky thing to do, but at this stage we had little to lose, because our relations with Berrigan and Shannon could hardly get worse. Besides, in an earlier telephone conversation Hall had agreed to review our project. Accordingly, a few days after our hearing we dispatched copies of my hearing comments along with displays, figures, and photos to both Hall and Berry. I planned to meet with each of them separately late in July or early August.

In the meantime, what I'll designate as an "anti faction" of Elk residents was awakening, and they had no intention of welcoming us to their "friendly little community." A little historical background is appropriate to place them in context. For nearly a century, from the 1860s to the 1960s redwood lumbering was the primary activity in the environs of Elk, then known as Greenwood. Lumber milling operations took place in the vicinity of Greenwood Creek, and indeed the present site of Greenwood State Beach was host to one such large mill. At considerable peril, ships were tethered to a large offshore sea stack (rock outcrop), and a treacherous cable arrangement was used to load milled lumber (and passengers) for transport to San Francisco. In those days Greenwood was a boomtown of sorts with a population many times its present 250 or so residents. Saloons and bordellos flourished on the proceeds of lumbermen's wages. Lumber-mill refuse, garbage, and raw sewage were all unceremoniously dispatched over the bluff into the ocean. Only within the past decade have the thought-to-be-last remaining offending sewage lines been redirected, their effluent now being pumped up to a septic field established on land acquired uphill and to the east of the village.

Some descendants from the lumbering days are still to be found in Elk, but they're not part of the anti faction. Rather, engaged in agriculture, construction, and business, old Elk families tend to have high regard for property rights. Likewise for most recently arrived retirees. The latter have found the Mendocino coast to be as beautiful, if not more so, than other California coastal regions. And they've found it to be more affordable, because of its remote location.

In contrast, most members of the anti faction were swept into Elk by the vacuum created when the lumbering activity ended, the population plummeted, and real estate bargains became irresistible to those seeking low-cost housing. Many were sixties-generation hippies, many were environmentalists, many were anti-Vietnam-War activists, and many were hoping to practice their drug culture without interference from authorities.

Attack By The Elk Anti Faction

Where better than this remote Eden? As reported in an Associated Press article by John Howard in the 11-27-98 issue of *The Washington Post*,

> "The rule of law seems to have a weak hold in this county of spectacular forests, canyons, rocky cliffs and some of the finest marijuana in the world. In Mendocino County, pot is the biggest cash crop, and the new district attorney is an ex-con.....
> [Norman] Vroman, a lawyer, served nine months behind bars during the early 1990s for failing to pay several thousand dollars in income taxes....On Nov. 3 Vroman, running on a platform that included decriminalization of marijuana, defeated a three-term incumbent who was president–elect of the California District Attorney Association." [Used with permission of The Associated Press Copyright© 2008. All rights reserved.]

Many Elk residents relish the prospect of decriminalization. Beside Highway One, at the southern entrance to the village, a sign proclaims that the highway has been adopted by the "MEDICAL MARIJUANA PATIENTS UNION." And each August the union's members march proudly with their banners held high in the annual "Great-Day-in-Elk" parade.

Today's quiet village of Elk is a far cry from its rowdy, boomtown, lumbering days as Greenwood. Many of the buildings date back to those days and are modest, and plain. But some are noteworthy. A few miles north is a nineteenth century shingle house perched high on a bluff above the Pacific. It was lovingly restored by its retiree owners, Dean and Ramonda Wisdom, who have surrounded it with enchanting flower gardens. Their handiwork is also evident in the riot of flowers that decorate the compact grounds of the small, century-old nondenominational Greenwood Community Church, a pure white sentinel with clean simple lines, that stands at the center of the village. Across from it, very extensive flower gardens enhance the quaint lodgings, shops, and restaurant of the Greenwood Pier Inn. And in the summer the entire front yard of the nearby Joel and Jania Waldman residence is densely packed with yellow daisies, giving the appearance of a bright-yellow elevated carpet. Across the road, within Greenwood State Beach, is the old lumber mill office building, now a small museum with exhibits that depict the early lumbering days of the village. Nearby is the recently-built and attractive Elk Post Office. Adjacent to it, in a converted home of recent vintage, is the Elk Studio Gallery, a cooperative endeavor of local artists. In addition to their works, the gallery features beautiful South American weavings and other works of art.

But, were it not for the adjacent spectacular ocean scenery, passing motorists would take little note of Elk. Although the County's General Plan *Coastal Element* states that, "It is hard to imagine any change that would improve Elk," the village is in dire need of more trees to soften its stark appearance. Ironically, while many in the Elk anti faction are tree huggers when it comes to attacking what remains of the lumbering industry, it seems that, within the village, they've adopted a "not-in-my-back-yard" (or front or side yard) attitude toward trees! Ignoring the impacts of their own homes on the scenery, they've focused instead on scenic issues having to do with properties outside the village. The possibility that it might be a good idea for scenic enhancement to begin at home with their own properties evidently hasn't occurred to them.

Situated in the poorest county in California, Elk offers scant opportunity for employment, a garage, a small grocery, several bed-and-breakfast inns (some without official County sanction), and a few small restaurants, none of which pay lucrative wages. Many residents live below the poverty level, and many are struggling artists. Some live in the wilds of Greenwood Ridge in makeshift homes that lack modern sanitary facilities and other amenities. They enjoy virtual immunity from County building codes courtesy of lenient enforcement measures adopted during de Vall's tenure as Fifth District County Supervisor. Powerless in many ways, members of the anti faction achieve satisfaction and the illusion of power by demonstrating against the "establishment." They were delighted when, by vote of County citizens, Mendocino County became the first in the nation to ban the cultivation of genetically-modified crops. No matter that their own breeding activities comprise a form of experimentation in genetic modification, often, I might add, absent the formality of wedlock. Indeed, according to United States Census Bureau data, Mendocino County has the distinction of being the county with the highest proportion of unmarried opposite-sex-partner households in the nation, 11% compared to a national average of 5%.

The anti faction regularly protests what they perceive as scourges of the modern industrialized world, including what remains of the lumber industry in northern California. Those fortunate enough to have participated in noteworthy protests in San Francisco, or having taken part in the celebrated anti-globalization protest in Seattle regale their cronies with reminiscences of their "triumphs." The anti faction is well organized. Some of its members, the waste matter of the higher education establishment, are quite articulate in espousing liberal causes. They are the ringleaders, and they have efficient online communication networks. And they can get their ultra-left, hate-America fixes on weekday mornings by tuning to Amy Goodman's "Democracy Now" on KZYX/KZYZ, the local NPR radio stations, which unapologetically espouse liberal causes while enjoying financial support by US tax payers of both liberal and conservative persuasions. "Fair and balanced" they're not!

The anti faction also makes certain that their Fifth District member of the Board of Supervisors is suitably liberal. In 2002 there were 278 registered voters in the greater Elk area. Democrats numbered 155, Republicans 42, American Independent Party members 8, Libertarians 5, Greens 27, and those with no party affiliation 41. In 1996, at one of a series of annual Mendocino County "Living Communities Conferences," anti-development activist Joan Curry, from the nearby village of Mendocino, summarized conclusions reached. In the 10-31-96 issue of *The Mendocino Beacon* she was quoted as saying, "In general, we like it rural, with a focus on education, we're pro-environment and object to wealthy colonization..." Although the term "wealthy" wasn't defined, it would seem that retirees who've each worked diligently for more than forty years, have lived moderately, and have saved for a secure retirement, just might not be welcome.

What acts would awaken this anti faction to the threat we posed to their way of life? Well, Berrigan certainly gave it the old college try. Asked by Ray Hall in late August 1995 to reveal what public notice measures he had taken with regard to our case that were beyond the minimum legal requirements found in the coastal zoning code, Berrigan reported in a 9-1-95 letter marked CONFIDENTIAL (which we obtained later only by virtue of our lawsuit) that,

> "1. When the public notices were mailed for the June 22, 1995 CPA hearing (when the item was first scheduled), I had Mary Stinson prepare a separate public notice (attached) to be posted in Elk."

> "2. A copy of the hearing notice, staff report and exhibits were sent to Norman de Vall for availability at the Elk Community Center. (Prior to the public hearing I viewed the Berlincourt site from various locations along Highway One. At that time I checked the Elk Post Office, Elk community Center and a couple of other bulletin boards in Elk to see if the notices and/or reports were at these locations. I found none.)"

After all that effort (above and beyond minimum legal requirements) to recruit opposition to our application it must have been a keen disappointment to Berrigan that only Shannon showed up to voice his opposition at our hearing. But Berrigan didn't have to wait long for satisfaction. On 6-23-95, the day after our hearing, he received a telephone call from Elk resident, Ron Bloomquist, who at that time wrote the weekly columns on Elk for *The Mendocino Beacon* and *The Fort Bragg Advocate News*. Those two newspapers, published weekly, were near copies of each other from the same publisher.

Here it's worth digressing a bit to acquaint you with Bloomquist, for he was to figure prominently in the campaign against our project. His perspectives are shared by many in the anti faction, and a glimpse into his background and his worldview provides some understanding of the anti faction in general. Like many of them, he's interesting and colorful, though complex. He's highly articulate in presenting his viewpoints, and he's quite talented artistically, having produced meticulous pen-and-ink drawings of the local scene. And he obviously possesses more than a little mechanical skill, having replaced the original engine in his old VW microbus with one from a Toyota. He painted that van with the large black and white spots of a cow and referred to it as the "Road Cow." The Road Cow was further altered so it emitted a moo, instead of a honk, to announce its presence. While all of this might be suggestive of a lighthearted outlook on life, Bloomquist is deeply troubled by mainstream society. His alienation would best be described in his own words from a portion of his 9-24-94 column in *The Mendocino Beacon*. But, alas, he denied me permission to quote the column here. His words can, nevertheless, be savored at his web site (www.blabberon.com, click "where I live," click "Greenwood/Elk columns"). In the meantime, here's my less-articulate summary.

For a period of nine years Bloomquist had lived on Saint Anthony's Point in a trailer serving as caretaker. To his regret, the point had been sold, and he announced that he would be moving. He hoped to remain in or near Elk and to continue writing his column. By then he'd written more than 230,000 words in the column, and he estimated that it would take a quarter of a million to do justice to the little village.

Bloomquist told how he had owned two houses while married, but after his divorce he'd chosen not to own real estate and had sought a simpler existence. For a while he'd lived with relatives, later moving to apartments in Seattle and still later moving to a rural cabin. He eventually found employment in Los Angeles with the Northrup Corporation and began living in his 1967 VW microbus in the company parking lot, which offered convenient access to the company cafeteria and company showers. On weekends he sought solitude and camped at remote wilderness sites like Mojave, Joshua Tree, and Los Padres National Forest. It took the Northrup security detail six months to notice Bloomquist's living arrangements. Upon being evicted from the Northrup parking lot, he bought a small trailer and took up residence in an El Segundo trailer park. But after two years he was fed up with Los Angeles and big city life in general, and he moved to Elk, renting a space at the (now abandoned) trailer court a few miles south of Elk. Offered the caretaking job at Saint Anthony's Point, he moved there, where he took pride in how well his 1959 Airstream trailer fulfilled his wish to keep life simple.

Next Bloomquist recalled that the Community Center Board had at one time mentioned the possibility of his serving as a caretaker at the Community Center, but nothing came of that, because trailers had become unacceptable in the coastal viewshed. (Evidently Bloomquist hoped that, by telling his story in his column, he would be offered another location for his trailer.)

In the final paragraph of his lament, Bloomquist told of usually feeling like an ordinary person, but that he sometimes felt like a sub-species. He recalled having been content when he spent weekends camping in the desert, but when he drove back into Los Angeles the sight of the luxury cars, ostentatious homes, and hustle and bustle made him feel uncomfortable and shoddy. Yet he recognized that he could choose to be a part of all that. He could join the rat race, take on a mortgage, and max his credit cards. But he'd chosen to keep it simple. Nevertheless, it had become complicated, because he now had to find another place for his trailer.

As it turned out, friends soon provided Bloomquist with a spot for his trailer up on Greenwood Ridge a few miles outside Elk. That enabled him to continue writing his column for the local newspapers.

ATTACK BY THE ELK ANTI FACTION

Now, as firm believers in live and let live, we had no quarrel with Bloomquist's life style. But, unfortunately, he and the anti faction would have objections to ours. They were not inclined to live and let live, and, indeed, they would view *us* as an undesirable sub-species.

From his 6-23-95 telephone call to Berrigan, Bloomquist learned the outcome of our hearing and, while he had chosen to "keep it simple" in *his* life, he set out to make it complicated in *ours*. As the Paul Revere of the Mendocino coast, he would sound the warning, not that the British were coming, nor that the Russians were coming, but, rather, that the Berlincourts were coming! In his next *Mendocino Beacon* column (6-29-95), Bloomquist quoted the County's erroneous project description and chided Elk citizens for not having protested the Berlincourt project, "...when normally we raise hell over just about anything." His column also mentioned that the public notice was posted on the bulletin board in the Elk Store, and that additional information could be obtained from Mary Stinson at the Planning Department in Fort Bragg. There was no mention that de Vall had a complete set of information locally as well. A notorious anti-development activist, de Vall, was no longer a County Supervisor, having been replaced by Charles Peterson, who was of the same persuasion. In any event, Berrigan could rest assured that de Vall would also fan the flames of opposition.

Our copy of *The Mendocino Beacon* with Bloomquist's incendiary column in it reached us about a week later. I immediately (7-9-95) dispatched a letter to him along with a copy of my hearing statement. My letter was cordial. I provided a little information on our personal backgrounds and invited Elk residents to visit our parcel. My letter noted that, "Perhaps the most realistic perspective on what can be expected can be gained by visiting our building site, looking toward Elk, and observing how little impact the buildings of Elk have on *our* view." I also mentioned that I would be visiting Elk in a few weeks and would bring 20" x 30" photomontages that I had recently prepared with 20 mm lens photos. With montages this size I was able to show details of the house. Most importantly, a viewer standing at the burner circle viewpoint of Greenwood State Beach, while holding one of these montages at arm's length, would see the depicted scene in exact size registration with the actual scene. Accordingly, these montages represented about the most realistic means possible for judging visual impact.

Of course, my letter to Bloomquist was a complete waste of time. The damage had been done. Some 18 letters protesting our project were received by the Planning Department in the next two months. They attacked every conceivable aspect of our project mentioned in Stinson's error-riddled project description, and they were personally vicious in their indictments of us. Readers wouldn't tolerate a tiresome repetition of their contents here, but I can't resist inserting one to illustrate the problem. The letter was from Mary C. Comerio, Professor of Architecture (and onetime Department Chairman) at the ever-so-prestigious University of California, Berkeley, owner of a vacation home on Greenwood Ridge. Comerio, obviously too impressed with her professorial status, used university stationery. Her letter should be a source of extreme embarrassment to the architectural profession and to her colleagues at Berkeley. She wrote in part:

"I have three major concerns about the house as proposed."

"1. The property is zoned for a single-family residence and the house is really designed as three units. Although the owners say they intend to use it for themselves, their children's families, and a caretaker, their intended use is not the criteria for zoning permission. In fact the house will have three separate kitchens in three separate living quarters. Any architect or Realtor would acknowledge that this constitutes three units."

"2. The proposed dwelling is nearly 5000 square feet if one includes the caretaker quarters over the garage and all other inhabited space. This is simply out of scale with any dwellings in the Elk community. The size has more in common with Bed and Breakfasts in town. The opportunity to convert from residential to tourist use is obvious and wholly inappropriate to the site."

"3. Because the owners propose a caretaker unit over the garage, and because the scale of the proposed dwelling is so large, it will be extremely difficult to conform to any masking of the structure, even through landscape and siting. The simple fact that living space over a two car garage space must be nearly 20 feet tall without a roof prevents architectural attempts to minimize the bulk of such structure."

Actually, our plans showed only one kitchen; the total conditioned living space was 3,843 sq ft; there were no caretaker quarters over the garage, which is less than 14 feet tall; and, after our combined 86 years at the grindstone, the last thing we wanted to do was spend our "retirement" years running a bed and breakfast catering to the whims of tourists. Is it possible that Comerio, an architect, can't read plans? If so, I suppose I should be willing to forgive ignorance. But, if she never saw the plans and simply accepted someone else's fallacious description, that's another matter. On the internet Comerio's biography claims, "…she is the nation's leading authority on post-disaster reconstruction," but it's fair to wonder if her so-called scholarly publications are as flawed and unprofessional as her letter quoted above. Nonetheless, that letter was one of the nicer ones the Elk anti faction sent to the Planning Department.

Interestingly, sometime around the middle of July, 1995, protestors began addressing their letters to Berrigan rather than Stinson, and we learned that Stinson had resigned from the Planning Department. I'm still curious about her motivation. Did she simply have other career goals, or might it have been guilt over her attack on us? In any event, we sought information on who would succeed her as Project Coordinator. It was to be none other than Berrigan. In our view it was improper and illegal for him to serve, in effect, both as prosecuting attorney and judge, but then this was Mendocino County. We certainly hadn't anticipated that we'd be spending our retirement years dealing with such blatant lawlessness.

In the meantime still another Mary, Mary Pjerrou, an Elk resident, ex-college professor, and President of the Redwood Coast Watersheds Alliance, had also set her sights on us. Like Bloomquist, she's complex and bitter regarding mainstream society. Only many years after our first encounter with her, and only after we had gained access to the internet, did we learn of the extent and intensity of her activities. For many years she has mounted aggressive, sixties-style protests against clear-cut lumbering, herbicde use, loss of wildlife habitat, clothing industry child and slave labor, free-trade agreements, corporate greed, election fraud, and war. In addition, Pjerrou found time to author a science- fiction novel entitled "Coz." In 2002 she received the $1,000 Anthony prize from the Rose Foundation for "her work to restore Greenwood Creek." The Rose Foundation report of her award also credits her with having "…won a series of citizen suits forcing lumber companies to develop long-term Sustained Yield Plans to guide timber harvesting."

Pjerrou's early sit-in campaigns against lumbering were directed against Louisiana Pacific Corporation, which owned large forest tracts in Mendocino County. But her most vigorous campaigns have since been directed against the Fisher family, which holds a controlling interest in the Mendocino Redwood Company, which acquired the 235,000 acres of Louisiana Pacific forest properties in 1998. The Fishers also own controlling interests in the Gap, Banana Republic, and Old Navy. The facts that the Fishers have contributed liberally to the Natural Resources Defense Council and are represented on the board of that organization have not spared them from Pjerrou's wrath, as she has shrewdly mounted protests against the Fisher's apparel companies as means to apply leverage against their lumbering activities. I'll briefly mention one of her campaigns here, just to provide a flavor of her tactics. (For additional entertainment you can google her.)

Together with Mary Bull, Pjerrou co-founded the nationwide "Save the Redwoods - Boycott the Gap Campaign." They organized and led demonstrations against Gap stores in major cities across the nation and in a few other countries as well. Disorderly protestors were arrested at some of these demonstrations. Little wonder! The following are quotes from an 11-17-03 Miami Beach, Florida, press release authored by Pjerrou.

> "Gap protestors will strip off their clothes to the chant, 'We'd rather wear nothing than wear Gap!' amidst radical cheers, songs and leafleting, at the Miami Beach Gap store, today, Monday, November 17, at 2:00 p.m., to protest Gap sweatshops, forest

destruction, and the Free Trade Area of the Americas (FTAA) agreement."

"The Miami Beach protest is the culmination of the Gapatistas' 3,000 mile journey across the southern United States, with protest stops at Gap stores in five cities along the way –- Los Angeles, El Paso, New Orleans, Tallahassee and Miami Beach –- heading for mass protests against the FTAA in Miami Nov. 17-21."

Obviously this press release was crafted with the aim of prompting wide media coverage (no pun intended). However, my admittedly inexhaustive search of the internet yielded little evidence that the above press release (and a multitude of earlier ones promising similar entertainment elsewhere) received much attention from the press. But when the promise of a strip show came to the Westwood community of Los Angeles, home of UCLA, you could expect that a "curious" budding undergraduate journalist might be in attendance to witness the event and cover it for the university newspaper. Sure enough, the 2-7-00 issue of UCLA's *Daily Bruin* carried an article by Timothy Kudo entitled "Group strips in protest of Gap's alleged practices." According to him, on the previous Sunday some 25 protesters, led by Mary Bull, had "exposed their half-naked bodies" at an intersection a block south of the UCLA campus, while chanting, "We'd rather wear nothing, than wear Gap!" He added that the group had originally planned to strip completely, but when informed by police that that would lead to arrest for indecent exposure, they had determined that the media coverage was insufficient to justify enduring arrest. According to Kudo, Bull had claimed that her group had stripped completely in other cities, including San Francisco, Amsterdam, and New York, and had added that, "We didn't know that L.A. was so straight-laced." Accompanying the article was a photo by Jared Dever, which featured a shapely young female in the process of half-stripping.

It's noteworthy that by 1998, when the "Boycott the Gap" campaign was launched, Pjerrou apparently had no scruples about directing inflammatory charges against those she attacked, even if those charges might be construed as defamatory. In an article by Ted Williams in the May/June 2000 issue of *Fly Rod & Reel Magazine*, Pjerrou is said to have claimed that all the forest's owners past and present and all regulatory personnel past and present are liars. And in a continuation of the 2003 Miami Beach press release quoted in part above, Pjerrou wrote,

"The Gap is one of the worst of these big corporations that prowl the globe for the cheapest labor and natural resources. They're destroying redwoods forests, polluting rivers and seas, busting unions, and using worker-slaves in fifty-five countries to sew

Gap clothes. The FTAA will expand this kind of global piracy throughout our hemisphere."

By the time Pjerrou issued these charges it's evident that she had no fear whatsoever of being sued for defamation by the Fishers. Yet in her earlier attacks against us she had openly expressed her fear that we would sue her. Perhaps in the more recent instance she'd been assured by legal counsel that she was immune to suit by "public figures," such as the Fishers, who command an empire of approximately 150,000 employees and annual revenue in the vicinity of 15 billion dollars. A critical assessment of Pjerrou's accusations of the Fishers is of course outside the scope of this book. Suffice it to say that the Fishers have had to deal with Pjerrou's charges in their own way, just as we, in our own way, had to deal with her charges against us. I suppose the Fishers simply ignored her, which must have infuriated her. But, unfortunately, we couldn't ignore her.

So, with much bigger "Fishers" to fry, why in the world would Pjerrou bother with our modest project? Well, because of its location one-half mile across Greenwood cove from her home. She evidently regarded our distant property as part of *her* front yard. And so, in July 1995, aided and abetted by Benton MacMillan, who owned and operated the Elk Store, and amidst all of her other activities, Pjerrou gathered signatures on a petition designed to thwart us. The petition featured a picture of the magnificent view from the Cuffey's Cove turnout with an arrow pointing to our building site. Next to the arrow were the words, "Berlincourt, 2-story, 5,000 sq ft, bldg. project." Needless to say there was no mention that the building site was 1.6 miles distant as the crow flies. Under the picture was the caption, "Help preserve the most magnificent view on the California Coast," followed by the County's erroneous project description. At the scale of the photo, our house would amount to little more than a hyphen in her petition, but there was of course no indication of that. Over a six-week period 163 signatures were obtained, 70 from Elk residents and the remainder from whatever tourists from Fairbanks, Alaska, London, England, and Yazoo, Mississippi happened to stop in at the Elk Store for bubble gum. Some Elk residents took exception to the petition and stopped shopping at the Elk Store. It hadn't been our intention to ignite a conflict between different factions of Elk, but the little village was, after all, just a powder keg waiting for a spark.

Margie and I reasoned that if the anti faction could have a petition, then so could we. And so we composed a letter, which we sent to all Elk residents, pointing out the errors and distortions in the County representation of our project. We attached copies of a portion of the 20" x 30" photomontage I had recently prepared. We encouraged villagers who might be sympathetic to our cause to write to the Planning Department in support of our project, and we enclosed a petition page on which they could register their support for our proposed project. We were much encouraged by the many kind responses to our appeal. Nine of our supporters sent letters to the Planning Department, and 49 signed our petition. Many also sent letters of encouragement to us. We sent letters of appreciation to all who supported our cause. They've since become steadfast friends.

One of our supporters, Don Daniels, a mechanic at the Elk Garage and son of one of the lumber mill owners during the mid 1900s, pointed out that from his house across the cove he would have the village's closest view of our house, and he had no objection.

It still remained for me to meet with Hall and Berry regarding the problems we were encountering with their subordinates, Berrigan and Shannon. Recall that I had sent copies of my hearing statement and other information to each of them. I telephoned Berry on 7-17-95, and I reviewed what had been in the letter that Shannon signed on Berry's behalf and pointed out that the error in Shannon's contention that vegetative screening would not be successful. Berry seemed very unconcerned, but he did agree that he and Shannon would meet with me at the State Park view point on 8-1-95. Then he added that it was, "State Parks policy to oppose any development next to State Parks." Whereas I couldn't imagine that State Parks could possibly make that official policy, I had begun to suspect that it was nonetheless common practice. To check on this, without being identified, I asked my son-in-law to write to Donald Murphy, Director, California Department of Parks and Recreation concerning the department policy regarding development adjacent to State Parks properties. The response, dated 8-8-95, made it clear that there were no statutes, regulations, policies, or guidelines which dictate State Parks positions relative to development of properties adjacent to parks and that the issue is a matter for the Coastal Commission and County authorities. Parks were in effect like any other neighbor, and so Berry had no State Parks policy license on which to base his opposition to our project. Later, at a deposition and under oath, Berry would deny he ever made the offensive statement.

I flew to California on 7-31-95, my fifth cross-continent round trip devoted to seeking a permit for our retirement home. Unfortunately, Shannon failed to appear at my meeting with Berry. I had wanted to be certain that, if Berry and I reached an understanding, that Shannon would also be bound. At the State Park burn-circle view point I demonstrated to Berry how, holding the 20" x 30" montage at arms length beside the actual scene, he could approximate the visual impact of our proposed home. I also showed him sketches which made it clear that, because our parcel was basically a terrace, moving our house eastward would provide no benefit to public views. I pointed out that if our quest for a building permit were to go smoothly henceforth, Margie and I were willing to place a no-development deed restriction on our five-acre parcel, and in addition would be willing to donate the northern beach portion of our eleven-acre parcel to the State of California. (Whereas neither the County nor State Parks could legally demand such concessions from us as conditions for granting a building permit, there was no restriction against our taking those actions on our own volition.) I also explained that if things did not go smoothly, ultimately there would be two houses, one on each parcel. I showed him maps I had prepared depicting the two different visions for the future. As a final inducement, I offered to underground the telephone line, which runs across our property, and whose unsightly poles mar the view from the State Park. My vision for the future was for one house and no telephone poles, and I asked him what he thought of it. He expressed his agreement with my vision and assured me that he would put a leash on Shannon. He even said, "You know, you're a really good guy!"

My meeting with Hall was much less agreeable. I won't bother you with the details other than to say that he was totally dismissive of my large photomontage and was totally supportive of Berrigan's position. He even muttered about not being able to afford to live on the coast himself. Clearly, there would be no reasoning with him.

Back in Elk I met with Ben MacMillan at the Elk store and Mary Pjerrou at her home in attempts to explain the true character of our project as opposed to the way it was portrayed by the County and by their petition. That accomplished nothing. Both were openly hostile. Both claimed not to know the source of the petition, claiming it just appeared one day on the Elk Store Bulletin board. Nonetheless, MacMillan and Pjerrou were openly "managing" the petition. Pjerrou was even inappropriately using a public agency's (the Elk County Water District's) fax machine to transmit petition pages and letters to the County Planning Department. It was during my brief meeting with Pjerrou that I discovered, to my horror, that, like me, her brother is a physicist. I also learned that her eyesight was not particularly good. When I showed her the 20" x 30" photomontage, she was unable to find the house until I provided her with a magnifying glass! Ironic wasn't it? But I suspect she's just far sighted and wouldn't have the same problem seeing our finished house.

Another incident on this trip illustrates the state of my relationship with the Planning Department at this point in time. By now you're doubtless well aware of my addiction to photography. The morning of 8-2-95 I took a picture of the Spruce Street offices of the Planning Department in Fort Bragg to add to my Mendocino County memorabilia collection, which by then had grown quite extensive. Later that day, while I was visiting Mike and Bob, Officer Doug Silva, of the Fort Bragg Police Department sought me out and told me that there had been a hit-and-run accident near the Planning Department. A BMW had been damaged, and someone in the Planning Department had seen me taking pictures at about that time and suggested that I might be involved and that I might be found at the offices of Leventhal, Schlosser, Architects. Officer Silva wanted to inspect my rental car to see if it showed any evidence of that encounter. Of course it didn't, and, as Silva's official report of the incident stated, he took photographs of my rental car to confirm my innocence. Thereafter I began to notice that Berrigan was always a little nervous about my photography.

I was meeting with Mike and Bob on this trip in order to confirm further accommodations we were willing to make to meet the Stinson/Berrigan special conditions. We abandoned the third bedroom by converting it into a workshop (i.e., so that it would no longer be conditioned space); we had already abandoned the kitchenette in the guesthouse; we reduced the garage to a two-car garage; we increased the setback from the northern bluff edge by ten feet (to 141 ft); and we further reduced the conditioned living space to 3589 sq ft, a reduction of 700 sq ft relative to our original submission. This information was provided to Berrigan on 8-8-95 along with the landscape-screening plan in ample time for it to be included in the announcement for the upcoming CPA hearing on 8-24-95. We had in effect agreed to 12 of the 13 special conditions, still holding firm only with regard to the western setback. However, when the hearing announcement appeared it was *de'ja vu* all over again! The Planning Department had *again* issued the original fallacious project description, *again* misrepresenting our project as a "5,000 square foot two story single family dwelling, 3 car garage with guest quarters and maid's quarters..." To add insult to injury, the announcement still listed Stinson as Project Coordinator even though she had long since departed, and Berrigan was acting (in our view illegally) as both "prosecuting attorney and judge."

Things continued to unravel. An 8-21-95 letter to the Planning Department from State Parks and signed by Shannon "for Berry," in effect repudiated the agreement I had reached with Berry. The letter was even more critical than the earlier Berry/Shannon letter, saying,

> "We question how successful plants will grow, when observing little
> plant growth (except grasses) out on the point. Our confidence
> for successful screening would improve with greater protection
> that could be achieved by moving east."

Thus the outlook was bleak indeed as we prepared for the continuation hearing.

CHAPTER 8

COASTAL PERMIT ADMINISTRATOR HEARING II

On 8-22-95 Margie and I began another transcontinental round trip (my sixth) devoted to realizing our retirement home. The occasion this time was our crucial continuation hearing before Coastal Permit Administrator Gary Berrtigan. In the stressful times preceding this hearing Margie and I worked very intensely together trying our best to develop approaches to cope with our adversaries, and, yes, we counted Berrigan among them, despite his supposed role as impartial judge. For the first time in our 42-year marriage Margie and I argued fiercely with each other. But, it was never personal. We knew that with good intentions we were both striving for the same goal, and it was never easy to agree on what approaches might be most effective in helping us achieve it. True to form as a scientist, I tended to be analytical, quantitative, and technical, even mathematical in my approach. After all, that was my nature. On the other hand, Margie, a humanist, saw our adversaries' approach as purely emotional and subjective and believed that we had to approach the problem on that plane. She reasoned that the opposition didn't understand my technical arguments and wouldn't trust the conclusions I reached in any event. But we could agree that the real challenge lay in trying to convince Berrigan to conform to the County's own regulations. Unfortunately, neither of us could conceive of a way to achieve that. In any event, it was good to have Margie by my side for this hearing.

Early on 8-24-95 we arrived at the Planning Department's Fort Bragg hearing room only to find a notice posted on the door announcing that the hearing would be held at the Veteran's Memorial Building. We managed to find our way there and entered its vast auditorium. Present were only five or six attendees in addition to our architects and us. We were delighted that two individuals, who'd written letters of support for us, were in attendance. They were "Mac" McKnight, a retired building contractor (and in retirement a highly accomplished, award-winning wood carver), who lived a few parcels south of ours, and John Raffety, a retired military medical doctor, who lived in the village. Opposition attendees included Shannon, Pjerrou, and Eleanor Lewallen. Lewallen lived in Philo, which is about 15 miles inland from Elk. With her husband, John, Eleanor often harvested seaweed on our beach for their Mendocino Sea Vegetable Company.

At the appointed hour Berrigan announced that he would be starting a little late because of the change of venue. We waited, and we waited, and we waited. Because of the large number of letters and petition signatures bearing on our case Berrigan had assumed that the attendance would be much greater and for that reason had moved the meeting to the larger facility. When it finally became evident that there would be no more attendees, Berrigan led off ever so briefly noting that since the first hearing we had submitted a landscape plan and modified house plan. He mentioned only our elimination of a garage bay, failing to note a number of other changes from our original submission, viz., our abandonment of the guesthouse kitchenette, our conversion of the third bedroom to a workshop, our 10-foot increase in setback from the northern bluff edge, and our 700 square foot reduction in conditioned living space. In other words he simply ignored the accommodations we had made in attempts to meet the special conditions proposed in the Staff Report.

When Berrigan called for comments. Margie spoke first, expressing our appreciation to the many residents of Elk who supported our application through letters and through our petition. She mentioned the encouraging telephone calls and personal notes from several of them, and she noted that we had received calls from a few people who had signed the Pjerrou/MacMillan petition and later withdrew their signatures when they learned the truth about our project. Then Margie expressed her great concern that the County had continued to circulate the original fallacious project description in the hearing announcement and through the local newspapers. She remarked that,

> "The house for which we're seeking a permit is not two story. It's one story with a loft in one room. It's not 5,000 square feet. It's not a three-car garage. There are no maid's quarters. We've been married 42 years. I've never had a maid. The so-called guest quarters, the bedroom and a family room, are so that [our family members and friends, not tourists,] can come to visit us."

I spoke next and pointed out that we had accommodated to virtually all of the special conditions of the Staff Report and that the only remaining matters at issue had to do with visual impact and the western setback, issues which I planned to address in detail. With regard to the former I called Berrigan's attention to the 20" x 30" photomontage. I had earlier provided him with a report explaining in detail how the montage was generated, and so I asked if he was willing to grant that the approach was legitimate. He replied, "I have read the information that you submitted, and that's all I'll say." Thereupon I reviewed the process to establish its validity for the record. I then remarked that,

> "...it's possible to visit the site with that photo, that is, the site where the photo was taken, hold it out at approximately arm's length, that's about 18 inches, and you'll see the very same size in that

that you see in the real panorama. So you can use that type
of picture to get the most, most realistic idea of what it's really
going to look like."

As to whether our house would be "subordinate" I quoted the definitions from the
Random House Unabridged Dictionary and *Ballantine's Law Dictionary*, both of which
amounted to "of lower order or rank, of less importance, secondary..." I remarked that,

"By both of those definitions ninety-nine cents is subordinate
to a dollar, just as fifty cents, ten cents, and one cent are
all subordinate to a dollar. Clearly, a line has to be drawn
somewhere, and legally it's generally drawn in accord with again
'the reasonable mind' criterion."

I continued,

"Now, in fact, our residence will cover less than one one-
hundredth of the area of the parcel... and the bulk or volume
of our structure will comprise less than one one-thousandth of
our portion of the headland that rises above the sea. Moreover,
our house will occupy only one one-hundred-thousandth of the
human field of vision when viewed from the upper-level picnic
area of the State Park, and will occupy only about one one-
millionth of the human field of vision when viewed from Cuffey's
Cove."

Continuing further, I commented that,

"To be other than subordinate, our house would have to be
'superior' or 'dominant' relative to the setting, which clearly it is
not, as you can see right there. There's too much else that's
going on there that's wonderful to focus all your attention on..."

In hindsight it would have been best to leave it at that, but, in an attempt to place
this issue in better perspective, I showed a photo of a famous face, that of supermodel
Cindy Crawford. Pointing out her famous beauty mark, I remarked that it comprised a
much larger one-twelve-thousandth of the scene, yet millions of us still find pleasure in
gazing at her face.

I then showed pictures of the six-to-twelve-feet-tall brush, which already existed on
our building site, which, at the outset, would provide significant screening of our house
from public view. Our rental car in the photos allowed some gauge of height.

Addressing the matter of western setback, I showed simplified sketches of the headland with our house situated at different locations, demonstrating that, viewed from the State Park, it made no difference in visual impact where the house was sited. Thus, increasing the western setback would not advance any legitimate state interest. In fact, increasing the western setback would make the house more visible from Highway One and would place it in a location where there's less favorable brush for initial screening. I mentioned that when I met at the State Park with Berry he agreed on these points and said he would email Shannon to that effect. In light of that I found it hard to understand how Shannon had adopted the counter arguments regarding this issue in the Shannon/Berry letter of 8-21-95. We learned later on in the hearing that Berry had been on a one-month vacation.

Next, I showed numerous photos of ocean-front projects recently approved by the County. All were far more prominent visually than ours would be (and many were near state parks). I referred to them as precedents, even though I knew full well that Berrigan refused to accept precedents as having any relevance to our case. One, the Corwin-Wolsky house a few miles south of our parcel, was particularly apropos from my perspective. It was a half-mile from public view, the same distance as from our house to the park viewpoint, but it was clearly two story, appeared to be significantly taller than eighteen feet, and it blocked views to the ocean. Since Berrigan had approved it as being subordinate to the setting, then surely our house had to be judged as subordinate as well.

Finally, I discussed the possible no-development deed restriction on our five acre parcel and the possible beach property donation I had earlier discussed with Berry, noting that of course it would be inappropriate for the County to condition our permit on those actions, but that, given equal protection of the law on our permit application, we were always at liberty to take those actions on our own volition.

Others who spoke in support of our project included both of our architects, Bud Kamb (a local real estate consultant we had engaged), Mac McKnight, and John Raffety. All added further support to my comments. The first to speak in opposition was Shannon. He followed the script of his most recent 8-21-95 letter, expressing his skepticism, "...about the success of the vegetative screening," and adding that, "...our preference would be, be to see the house moved further back..."

Pjerrou spoke next. Immediately she pounced on the Cindy Crawford analogy. What I had referred to as a "beauty mark," she referred to as a "mole or mar," and she argued that, if it were on the end of Crawford's nose, it would be "ridiculous." That was a shrewd attack, but it was not an apt analogy. Our house would not be located at the western tip of our parcel. Seen from the park, it would be set back from the western tip by over ninety feet. Nevertheless, there could be no doubt that Pjerrou's comment would be implanted in Berrigan's brain. Pjerrou continued at considerable length. Her comments are summarized in the snippets which follow:

"...it is an outrageous violation of all of the values stated in the Local Coastal Plan for protection of the coastal environment, particularly the coastal views...my heart reaction is this is an outrage to build a visible structure out on one of the last remaining open views from the town of Elk to the ocean...I wish that the solution to this problem could be that the State Parks Department purchase these parcels...I have my concerns about those mitigations, whether they're going to be enough, whether they're not going to wreck my view, whether or not you'll see this huge stretched-out house out there with lights all over at night ...All I'm saying is that, in terms of looking at the mitigations required by the, by the [County] staff, if that's what, if that's what they recommended, I don't think it's enough. I think the further the building is pushed to the southeast the more it will disappear from the view from the town of Elk."

Whether the last of these comments planted another seed in Berrigan's mind, or whether such a seed had long ago taken root there, I don't know, but from that moment, I knew what the outcome of the day's hearing would be. Pjerrou's demand for even more western setback than proposed in the Staff report would surely appeal to Berrigan, so much so that he would ignore the fact that moving the house still further southeast would make no significant difference to views from Elk, would increase its visibility from the highway, and would even partially obscure public views to the ocean from Highway One, which is also considered as a precious view corridor by the Coastal Act. (A small digression here: Pjerrou's complaint that she would "...see this huge stretched-out house out there with lights all over at night" was surprising, in view of the fact that the humongous, unshielded mercury-vapor barnyard security light on the front of her own house turns night into day in the middle of Elk.)

We were so highly incensed by Pjerrou's call for greater southeastern setback that we took little notice of her expressed wish for State Parks to purchase our parcels, nor did we pay any attention to a similar sentiment expressed by de Vall in a FAX he had sent (inappropriately on the Elk County Water District fax machine) to Berrigan two days prior to our hearing. In hindsight, those were clues we should not have missed.

Next we were to hear from Lewallen. She described the beach as a "very holy place." She spoke of weddings there and how people "buried their dead at the beach." She worried that our septic field would pollute the beach where she harvested sea vegetables [seaweed] for human consumption. (Apparently she was less worried about contamination from the dead who'd been buried there.) She didn't "...think humans should be living on the bluff." She feared the bluff was not geologically stable. And, to make certain that Berrigan hadn't missed Pjerrou's call for greater western setback, she seconded it.

By then Margie and I were seething over the still-greater-setback suggestion, and Margie couldn't resist taking a shot at Pjerrou. When Margie referred to the opposition petition that "...Ms. Pjerrou started," Pjerrou snapped, "No, that's incorrect. I didn't start it." In any event, Margie went on to make her point, which was that the framer(s) of the petition had continued circulating false information about our project even after our letter, which went to all Elk postal patrons, had informed them of the true facts. Margie then noted that,

> "...publication of false information which results in injury is
> defamation...this petition incites adverse, derogatory, unpleasant
> opinions about us...it injures our reputations."

Well, despite Pjerrou's attempt to distance herself from the petition, she had transmitted to the Planning Department batches of signature pages with numerous long cover letters that were abusive to us. Subsequent events would show that she was fearful of being sued. People who defame usually know very well that they're defaming, and they can't help but fear being called to task on it. But we had no plans to sue her, because that wouldn't get us a building permit. About all we might obtain from a suit against her would be a humongous mercury-vapor light fixture and the satisfaction of her public humiliation. Tempting though the latter was, we chose instead to keep our eyes on the prize, specifically, the permit to build our dream home.

At this point Berrigan said he had a few comments to make before adjourning for lunch. Without apologizing, he admitted that some of the noticing errors were "probably the county's error, and not intentional, certainly." He wasn't man enough to say that they were, only that they "probably" were. Then he remarked that he, "didn't review the revised plan." In retrospect I now question why in the world he would then be qualified after lunch to pass judgment on our case. Had we caught the significance of that statement at the time we could have demanded a rehearing, but I doubt the outcome would have been any different. Berrigan's parting words before departing for lunch were,

> "I'm going to consider this over lunch, and we can come back at
> one thirty, and I will make some kind of decision at that point. At
> this point I don't have a clue, so I'm adjourned."

Can you imagine comments like that from a judge? After lunch Berrigan recited a list of the correspondence he had received on our case since the previous hearing and claimed to have "read every single piece." Apparently that correspondence was more entertaining to him than reviewing our plans so as to become informed on the facts! Responding to my having cited as precedents other oceanfront houses (many next to state parks), Berrigan defended some as less prominent than ours would be. With regard to others, he said in effect that if the County made mistakes that was no excuse for compounding them. Interestingly, we had earlier shown pictures of the Corwin-Wolsky house among the precedents. Berrigan now commented,

> "Uh, Corwin-Wolsky that's real interesting, because coming back from vacation last week I drove down Highway One. Came back all the way from Highway One and was very surprised to see that uh our required landscaping had not been installed at the Corwin-Wolsky house, and uh sort of made a mental note to review the file, and uh getting ready for this particular hearing. I had forgotten about it. I thank you."

It would thus appear that Berrigan reveled in his authority to score on the Corwin-Wolskys (and by inference, on us.) In hindsight I regret having reminded Berrigan of the Corwin-Wolsky house, inasmuch as Beth Corwin and her husband Tom Wolsky have since become very good friends. They had had their own unpleasant battle with Berrigan in order to get their building permit. (And, I wouldn't be surprised if at that time their landscape screening was still so young as to be scarcely discernible from the highway one-half mile distant. In any event, their vegetative screening is now coming along very nicely.)

With the Corwin-Wolsky matter off his chest, Berrigan turned next to the dictionary definitions of "subordinate" that I had quoted, and he took issue with them. Like Humpty-Dumpty in Lewis Carroll's "Through the Looking Glass," Berrigan began to invoke his own definitions, not the dictionary's definitions. It was as if he'd become Humpty-Dumpty, and I was facing the same predicament Alice faced. That's perhaps best illustrated by the following quotes from Carroll's description of Alice's encounter with Humpty-Dumpty.

> "'When I use a word,' Humpty Dumpty said, in a rather scornful tone, 'it means just what I choose it to mean, neither more nor less.'"

> "'The question is,' said Alice, 'whether you can make words mean so many different things.'"

> "'The question is,' said Humpty Dumpty, 'which is to be master – that's all.'"

Asserting his Coastal Permit Administrator status as "master," Berrigan disputed my claim that 99 cents is subordinate to a dollar. Thereupon I responded, "Good. I'll give you 99 cents. You give me a dollar." Berrigan replied, "What? Thank you. It's less than a dollar, but it's not subordinate to a dollar. It's less than." To which I responded, "That's the dictionary definition [of subordinate]. 'It's less than.'" Obviously, this didn't help our cause at all, but his arrogant disregard for dictionary definitions had pulled my chain, and anyway, there was little doubt where this was going. All I could think of was Eubie Blake's song, "I'll Give a Dollar for a Dime!" combined with Abbot and Costello's "Who's on First?" Berrigan then chastised me with, "Mr. Berlincourt, did I interrupt you except for a clarifying question?" I responded, "You're very welcome to." To which he replied, "Thank you very much." I added, "I was clarifying…" At this point he cut me off with the following monologue, which I quote at length so that readers can make up their own minds regarding Berrigan's arguments:

> "You weren't. You were arguing, and, pardon me, it's over. Uh, so, I don't believe that 99 cents is subordinate to a dollar. It's less than. Our policies indicate that, uh, and it's noted in the Staff Report, that it needs to be subordinate. A question was raised, will moving this make a, quote, significant change uh as recommended in the Staff Report? Uh, I'm not sure whether it will make a significant change, but certainly the further distance that the house is from Elk, the more subordinate it will be. Uh, the more secondary it will be. Uh, as noted on the, uh, and from, on the photo submitted, uh it's right now located on the promontory in a very predominant location, and, uh, you know, everyone has indicated that it will be visible regardless of where it is. The question is how dominant will it be? Uh will it, and, uh, the reverse of dominant is subordinate, and what I have to do is look at uh the policies and determine in my own judgment whether or not what's being proposed is subordinate to the character of the setting. Uh, unfortunately, Mr. Berlincourt revised his notes. I would have brought with me the uh legal opinion from the uh discussions regarding subjective and objective studies uh as a result of some court cases in California that apparently he missed. Uh but we do use uh, you know, consider what are objective studies and what are subjective studies, and uh visual analysis is considered a subjective study. Uh I'm not going to argue any points regarding uh mathematical calculations of scales based on whether one used 20 mm, 200 mm, or what have you. Uh I think that the purposes of this, or the purpose that this has served is to indicate what the area looks like, uh its setting, and what residential development would look like uh on the property, and I think that, you know, whether one considers that yours are more to scale, which you know, is fine, I mean your drawings were much more precise and concise than the others, uh but it's still significant, so I'm not real comfortable with the design. Uh, I

believe that the design is client generated, as uh Mr. Leventhal sometimes refers. I think that they've done a, they've made an attempt to design the structure uh into the environment, but I do not believe that, if they were on their own uh to design something they felt was subordinate to that location, it would have been different, but I think that they have to recognize their clients' uh desires, and so I think that this is more client generated, because I personally believe that uh better design could be uh could be located there. Uh it would be more subordinate, so anyway uh, as proposed, I can't approve what was proposed. Uh the next question is whether to simply to deny it, and uh go from there, or whether to condition it. Uh the part of the problem with that is that my inclination is that it should be located to the south and to the east of where it's uh proposed right now. Uh we have an entry road designated, and I believe that it should be located to the south of that entry road uh, as far, I mean, yes, to the south of that entry road and to the east. Uh I agree that the, the landscaping, I have concerns about uh landscaping out on that area where you're proposing it, because of the uh salt spray, the harsh environment. Uh also it's indicated that there's a 30 foot uh fire clearance area uh, so that the question in my mind is, should it be relocated, approved and relocated as uh designed, or should it simply be denied, and uh say try again, uh and *after an hour-and-a-half I still don't know what to do*, but I get paid for things like this is, so, I'm going to make a decision, and I'm going to deny the project without prejudice, which means that uh, a substantially revised project uh could be re, would be accepted by me with uh within a year. Uh, but I will deny it without prejudice, and uh any substantial revision to the project that reduces its impact uh I would accept a reapplication in less than a year. I also notice that the uh government post date uh is October 9th, and so what that's going to require is that uh the, the decision is denial, and at the next uh coastal permit hearing in September uh this will be on the agenda to adopt the findings uh to support the decision uh that I just made, and uh after the findings are adopted, then that is when the time for any appeal periods will, will begin, uh because the decision won't be effective until the findings are adopted, and so uh with that the application is denied."

There followed raucous exchanges involving our architects, Berrigan, and us, as we sought clarification of the steps in the appeal process and why Berrigan had to prepare additional "findings" and have them adopted at another hearing. It was then that Berrigan revealed that, "I don't believe that the findings in the Staff Report go far enough to support a denial, so additional findings have to be developed to support that particular denial." Whereupon I said, "You don't have a case, and now you've got to develop a case?" Berrigan then again launched into his visual-impact-and-subjective-studies speech and got back to the two-story controversy. Of course whether or not our plan was judged to be two stories was completely beside the point, because the regulations allow two stories on a terrace site such as ours. He seemed never able to grasp that fact, although he should have been an expert on that matter. Mike challenged him to show us any regulation to the contrary. Berrigan turned red in the face and blurted, "OK I'm not going to go into this wor…" He never finished that word or that sentence as he literally ran out of that vast auditorium!

The next morning, KZOT's Joe Regelski broadcast the news the Elk antis were hoping to hear. Margie and I had already met with Mike and Bob at their office and had composed and mailed an appeal letter to the Board of Supervisors. Included was the mandatory check for $635 and a request for additional information on the Board's appeal process.

Then, back home in Virginia, on 9-4-95 we received a letter from Mark Goldowitz of the California Anti-SLAPP Project. Margie's comments to the effect that the anti faction's circulation of fallacious information in their petition amounted to defamation had obviously struck a nerve in Pjerrou, and she had contacted Goldowitz! Along with a lot of legal gobbledygook, Goldowitz's letter stated, "Please be advised that any effort on your part to sue citizens for such petition activity could land you in serious hot water." But this attempt at intimidation caused us no concern, for we had never intended to sue any of the anti faction. After all, as already noted, they couldn't grant us a Coastal Development Permit. At the time we simply dismissed the Goldowitz letter as a sign that, having based her petition on false premises, Pjerrou felt vulnerable to a lawsuit and was very nervous about it. We now wonder if, having declined to sue her, we might have emboldened her to make her subsequent even-more-likely-to-be-construed-as-defamatory charges against the Fishers. In any event, in retrospect we can be grateful she hadn't employed her ultimate weapon by disrobing at our hearing.

CHAPTER 9

Our Appeal To The Board Of Supervisors

Meanwhile, it became evident that Bloomquist was not content with simply reporting the news in his *Mendocino Beacon* column but intended instead to use it to wage war against our project. He was in rare form as he rallied the anti troops in a column published on 8-24-95, coincidentally the same day that Berrigan denied our project. Because Bloomquist refused permission for me to quote that column here, you'll miss a lot of its passion and nuances as you read my admittedly-less-articulate summary of a portion of it. (Alternatively, you can access Bloomquist's own words at www.blabberon.com.)

Bloomquist reported that he'd been away for more than two weeks, during which time he visited the Seattle area. He'd camped along the way and exalted in the wilderness, but he found the cities and traffic congestion very disturbing.

He noted the contrast between the wilderness (with its scenic beauty, mountains, and rivers) and the cities (with their freeways and hoards of people rushing about meaninglessly). He deplored the spread of bedroom communities consuming forests and farmland.

As Bloomquist passed through urban and wilderness areas on his journey he kept thinking about the house we planned to build on our parcel south of Elk. What would it mean to the little village?

He commented that he'd talked with the Elk "old timers," who've spent their entire lives in Elk, and he characterized them as having the viewpoint that people who wish to come to Elk and spend money to construct a house should be welcomed, and, moreover, the new residents would benefit the economy. It appeared to Bloomquist that the old timers would also welcome high-rises, condos, K-Mart, McDonalds, etc., anything that provided convenience and stimulus to the economy.

In contrast, Bloomquist identified with those he referred to as the Elk "newcomers." By that term he was referring to the wave of hippies that had settled in Elk, not the still-more-recently-arrived retirees. Bloomquist's "newcomers" were opposed to any new construction and want Elk to remain as it is. They'd all experienced the big cities, the smoke, the clogged freeways, and now, living in Elk, they value the surrounding pristine beauty.

Bloomquist then expressed the view that the old timers hadn't cared much for the hippies when they arrived two decades earlier. At that time the local economy was depressed, and property values had dropped precipitously, so much so, that Elk became an affordable destination for the hippies. He claimed that, although the hippies had been despised, they'd been at the forefront of community service in building the community center and the health center, but he argued that community spirit had diminished greatly in recent times. He then noted that property values had now skyrocketed and that "retirement fortresses" were coming to Elk.

Bloomquist saw money as the root of the problem and argued that only the very wealthy had the resources to buy the land and engage the architects and lawyers needed to build on the coast. He estimated the need at a million or two. He scoffed at the belief by some that people with money must be great people, allowing that they might be in some instances, but he didn't think they were likely to show up for work details and other community activities. Instead he claimed they'd simply build their fortresses, donate a token amount to the volunteer fire department, and, after a year or so of sunsets, conclude that life in Elk is boring. He predicted that they'd then put their fortresses up for sale or rent and move to Aspen or Telluride, leaving their "artistic statements" behind to defile Elk's scenic vistas thereafter, and he added, "Big whoopie!"

Bloomquist then sounded the alarm that the retirement boom was fast approaching and that there would be a proliferation of retirement fortresses, with the winner being the biggest one nearest to the ocean. He saw it as the end of community spirit.

Finally, he called for vigilance and expressed his belief that the best things in life are free.

That some residents of Elk might actually be offended by his column had evidently never occurred to Bloomquist. Imagine that! Well, there followed a number of responses, one of which nicely sums up Elk retirees' sentiments regarding Bloomquist's foot-in-mouth comments. It appeared a week later, 8-31-95, as a Community Forum article in *The Mendocino Beacon*. It was entitled "Check Your Facts" and was authored by Lee ("Mac") McKnight and his wife, Barbara. (You'll recall that Mac spoke in support of our project at our hearing the week before.) I quote the entire text below.

> "In response to the column written by Ron Bloomquist in the Greenwood/Elk column of Aug. 24.
>
> As ... retirees who moved to Elk permanently 11 years ago, we are greatly outraged by the statements made regarding the retirees who are living here. He claimed only the hippies who moved here 20 years ago are the only ones who "do community work, volunteer for work parties, build a community center and health center."

If you'll remember Ron, the Elk fire Department is made up of many retirees. It was retirees who helped secure the land and build the new firehouse on Greenwood Ridge. We are the ones who are always there for a medical call and drive the ambulance, even at 3 a.m. in the morning. It was Rusty Gates, a retiree, who supervised building the addition to the community Center and Del Wilcox, a retiree, who did the planning. They did hours and hours of work and then had to hire boys to do the actual work because not enough volunteers were available. Del Wilcox also spent innumerable hours getting a grant for the basketball court and a grant for the new stage.

We've been the treasurer of the fire department for 10 years and know every penny that has been contributed. Your statement that "rich folks… may donate a few bucks to the fire department" is so erroneous it's laughable! For years the fire department existed on donations and it was only through the "rich folks" could it have functioned.

The same 20 or 25 people donated every year but we never saw a check from you or your hippy friends. One anonymous donor (a retiree) paid for the entire new roof on the firehouse. Because the fire department needed more funds for equipment the fire district was formed through the efforts of the "rich folks and retirees." They taxed themselves for the benefit of ALL Elk.

Are you paying any taxes, Ron, for the benefit of the fire department? Whether you are of not, if your travel trailer/house burned you know the retirees would be out there fighting as hard to save it as if it were their own. As for the health center - who was the driving force? Dr. John Frankel, another retiree. If it wasn't for him and his building, it never would have existed.

The ladies of the Greenwood Civic Club, another group of retirees and old timers, have worked hard and long to have rummage sales to contribute to the community. They purchased the defibrillator for the ambulance, provided scholarships to deserving [high school] seniors, purchased and trimmed the community Christmas tree, sponsored a community Christmas party for the children of Elk, and who gave a considerable sum to keep your precious computer center going this summer for the children of Elk.

Where would the Visitor Center be if it wasn't for the hard work and devotion of Ann Daniels, another "old timer?" Where would the Greenwood community Church be today if it wasn't for all the hard work of Dean and Rae wisdom, Dorothy Nielson, Lea Almanrode and Dave Brotherton, all retirees? We wouldn't even have the church! And wonderful May Berry, Sharon Mitchell and other "old timers" have kept the Catholic church alive and beautiful for 47 years putting on wonderful St. Patrick's Day dinner and Dance.

Where would this town be if it wasn't for the Matson family who for years and years have contributed time, money and hard work to provide a garage that's always willing to pull you out of a ditch or fix an old clunker. In fact, Ron, you wouldn't have a job for several winters if it wasn't for "old timer" Bob Matson who's the hardest worker in all of Elk.

As for the new house on the bluff which you and your buddies have stopped (temporarily, we hope), we don't see how you had the gall to start up the petition you did and then conveniently leave town. Did you bother to find out that a lot of statements you made about it were incorrect? It was only one story, not two, it didn't have a maid's quarters, it only had a two car garage, not a three car, etc., etc. You got a lot of people riled up who had no business getting involved. It's great to say everyone is entitled to a beautiful view at the beach, but this man has owned this property for 14 years and has paid over $80,000 in taxes alone.

Do you own any property? Do you pay taxes? What's the matter Ron? Are you just mad because we all worked hard for 40 or 50 years and "made it" but you didn't? Would all the land owners on the ridge who came 20 years ago want us coming and saying we want to walk in their woods and experience the forest so they can't build but they still have to pay taxes? This couple have had the dream of living on the ocean for years just as we did.

We bought our property in 1969 and every other weekend for 15 years drove up from the Bay Area to build our house. And during the week we worked hard jobs to pay for it and to make our dream of living by the ocean come true. You didn't even have the guts to appear at the hearing and see Mrs. Berlincourt, with tears streaming down her face, tell how hurt she was by the insults and condemnations they received from people they didn't even know and how it had been their dream to live by the ocean and become a part of the Elk community. What's your dream, Ron? To make everyone go away and leave you to the "starry nights?

We're so disappointed in you, Ron. We've always known you're on the opposite political side than we are but we've always respected your right to believe as you do. We always felt we had such a great community because "hippies, retirees and old timers" could work side by side and what a great example for the whole world. It's diversity that makes such a great country if everyone will contribute what they can and not divide communities into the "haves" and "have nots."

We just wanted it known that you and your views are not accepted by every one in Elk."

The writers of the above letter are among our dearest friends, and we can never thank them enough for their kindness and support. Their letter very aptly describes aspects of Elk sociology. Note that the McKnights' letter interprets Bloomquist's attack on the old timers as an attack on more-recently-arrived retirees as well. Also, interestingly, their letter points to Bloomquist as initiator of the petition against our project. I have no evidence of that. But I'm certain that Pjerrou and MacMillan were the major participants in the "management" of the petition. One other aspect of the McKnights' letter is forgivable poetic license. There were no tears streaming down Margie's face. She may look delicate and vulnerable, and it's true that she was deeply disappointed by the outcome of that hearing, but there's a tiger in there, and believe me, at that hearing the tiger had been angered!

As uncivil war raged in Elk, Margie and I contemplated how best to deal with the anti faction, the County Planners, the State Parks Department, and now the Board of Supervisors. With regard to the anti faction it was pertinent that one of their recurring criticisms was that from the outset we had not engaged in a dialogue with Elk residents regarding our plans and that we had not fully informed them of our intentions. That despite the fact that the plans we submitted to the County Planners had been fully accessible to the public. Nevertheless, in an attempt at engagement, I wrote to Bloomquist, MacMillan, and Pjerrou on 8-31-95 telling of my plans to visit Elk from 9-28-95 through 10-3-95 and of my willingness to meet with them. I further stated that if they would choose an evening and a location, and publicize the meeting to Elk residents of all points of view, "I will be pleased to be there and do the best I can to respond to questions and concerns." The arrogant and gloating rejections I received from MacMillan and Pjerrou displayed their unconcealed delight with Berrigan's denial of our Coastal Development Permit application. Bloomquist's response was less explicit, though not at all cryptic. It consisted of a copyrighted card showing one of his very skillfully executed artistic creations, entitled "Greater Elk, Home of Fog, Rain, Slugs, Sharks, and Malcontents." At the center of the scene was Pjerrou's house flanked by the Elk Garage, and MacMIllan's Elk Store. Rising behind those buildings were the mountains that lie immediately east of the village. Then beyond the mountains, and towering above them, were enormous Los Angeles-style high-rise buildings dominating all else. Inside the card was the following message.

"Here's another item for your Elk collection. I drew this in 1984.
Most folks seem to enjoy my sense of humor. Hope you do too."
"Ron"

We had no trouble deciphering this as a rejection. So much for seeking detente with the anti faction.

As for our relations with the County Planners and the State Parks Department, and our appeal to the Board of Supervisors, we felt a very compelling need for legal assistance. And we had little confidence that we could find the kind of help we needed simply by picking an attorney out of the Mendocino County telephone directory. Obviously, the arrogant and blatant exercise of power by the Planning Department that we were experiencing was well entrenched in Mendocino County. Presumably, that would not be the case if the area possessed effective legal representation for defense of property rights, and so we decided to look elsewhere. Fortunately, about a year earlier I had noticed an article about the Pacific Legal Foundation in *The Wall Street Journal*. PLF, located in Sacramento, is a non-profit organization devoted to upholding private property rights and other conservative causes. On 7-6-95 we wrote to PLF describing our case. We didn't expect them to mount a lawsuit on our behalf, because, at considerable sacrifice, we could manage to pay for legal representation ourselves and, also, because our case was not yet "ripe," i.e., we hadn't yet exhausted our appeals. Rather, we wanted to add our case to their catalog of government abuse of power and alert them to the kinds of issues that cry out for remedy. The first issue was of course the very subjective matter of "subordinate to the character of the setting." The second, and related, issue was the use of magnified-view photomontages in judging visual impact. It was our hope that PLF might in the future have enough influence to convince lawmakers to amend the Coastal Act by inserting objective visual impact criteria in place of the capricious subjective criteria.

In our letter to PLF we included much of the same background material we had used at our first hearing before Berrigan and that we had sent also to Hall and Berry. Later, in September, after Berrigan's denial of our project, we received a telephone call from Mark Gallagher of PLF, who requested additional information on our case. He cautioned, however that he could not make a commitment that PLF would write to the Mendocino Board of Supervisors on our behalf. We responded on 9-9-95 with a transcript of our June hearing (which we had laboriously transcribed from the very-poor-quality tapes we had obtained from the County), copies of Margie's and my hearing statements, copies of a number of the County regulations, a concise listing of what we believed to be abuses of power by the County, and finally a quote regarding the *Goldblatt v Hempstead (1962)* case from a Supreme Court ruling on *Penn. Cent. Transp. Co. v New York City (1978)*, specifically,

> "….a use restriction on real property may constitute a taking if not reasonably necessary to the effectuation of a substantial public purpose, or perhaps if it has an unduly harsh impact on the owner's use of the property."

To us, that appeared particularly apropos to Berrigan's insistence on a setback which would destroy our ocean views and at the same time yield no net benefit to the public view.

When Berrigan's "findings" on our case were issued later in September 1995, we sent a copy to PLF along with our planned rebuttals to each assertion of the findings. PLF found our arguments compelling and prepared a very-well-crafted letter in our support. Over the signature of James S. Burling it was sent to the Mendocino County Board of Supervisors in October.

After Berrigan's denial, our appeal was in the hands of the Supervisors, but we still had unfinished business with the Department of Planning and Building Services. On 9-4-95 Margie wrote to Hall pointing out erroneous and misleading statements by Berrigan in descriptions of our project in public notices and demanding that they be corrected. She quoted the Administrative Regulations of the Coastal Commission (Article 6, Application Summaries, 13057, Contents), which state, "The summary [of a permit application] shall be brief and understandable, and shall fairly present a description of the significant features of the proposed development, *using the applicant's own words wherever appropriate."* And Margie again tabulated the errors, viz., maid's quarters, 3-car garage, two-story, exaggerated living area, and the listing of the long-since-departed Mary Stinson as Project Coordinator, when in fact Berrigan was acting in both that and the Coastal Permit Administrator's role.

Only after our lawsuit was in progress and we had access to additional County internal records did we learn that Hall had requested Berrigan to explain why the notice for his second hearing did not note the changes we'd made. In a 9-20-95 memorandum responding to Hall, Berrigan wrote, "There was no clear indication from the agent [Mike Leventhal] that the project had been reduced in size." In fact Mike's submittal letter of 8-8-95, mentioned among its seven enclosures, "Two sets 24 x 36 revised drawings of the project, consisting of pages A-1 (Site Plan), A-2 (Floor Plan), A-3 (Exterior Elevations), and L-1 (Landscape Planting Plan from Satre Associates)." In addition to the enclosures mentioned in Mike's letter, a copy of my planned comments for the upcoming hearing was included, and that of course described our new plans and accommodations to the thirteen special conditions. Berrigan had three days to go over all of this material prior to the mailing of the hearing notice. Why did he think another set of plans, a "revised" set, had been sent if it wasn't pertinent to the 8-28-95 hearing?

Margie's letter to Hall produced some improvement in the project description listed in the notice for the 9-28-95 public hearing on Berrrigan's report of his finding's on our project. But this was too little and too late. The erroneous description had already done its damage. And, besides, Berrigan proceeded to resurrect several of those false issues in his findings. He attacked size, "second story," height, and visual impact. And, although he had never set foot on the site, he mandated a location on our plot plan where he said our house must be placed. That location was devastatingly harsh, as could have been anticipated from his comments at our August hearing. Not content with Stinson's Staff Report recommendation, Berrigan mandated that we place our house 300 feet farther back from the western bluff edge. That would harshly degrade our ocean views, while providing no benefit to public views from the State Park. Moreover, Berrigan's site would place the house close to Highway One, from which it would be highly visible and where it would obstruct public views to the ocean.

Berrigan also claimed that we had chosen the most-prominent location on the parcel for our house. But, at the outset we had foregone the most-prominent location near the northern bluff edge in order to reduce visibility of the house from the State Park and Elk and to hide the house completely from the beach level of the park. So, if, as Berrigan claimed, our proposed plan was for the most-prominent site, then the northern bluff edge site had to be less prominent and hence subordinate, in which case, shouldn't Berrigan approve locating our house at the northern bluff edge, which was our most favored location? Obviously, Berrigan's reasoning was faulty.

While complaining that our house would be highly visible from Elk and the State Park, Berrigan failed to point out that literally scores of existing structures are already much more visible from Elk and the State Park. They are in fact immediately adjacent (not one-half mile distant) and hence are much, much more prominent! Berrigan also dismissed our landscaping plan out of hand. He stated flatly, "The applicants' proposed landscaping plan would not result in the proposed structure being subordinate to its setting." Thus, he ignored completely the very favorable evaluation of prospects for successful screening by an expert witness, our highly-experienced professional landscape architect, and, equally significantly, he ignored the vigorous tall stands of evergreens that exist on the points north and south of ours.

OUR APPEAL TO THE BOARD OF SUPERVISORS

And Berrigan just couldn't resist having the last say on the dictionary definitions of "subordinate." His findings quoted my comments from the August hearing regarding the dictionary definitions of "subordinate" and then made a final ruling on that definition as follows:

> "The Coastal Permit Administrator has considered the definitions
> and statement, and believes that 99 cents is <u>less</u> than a dollar,
> not <u>subordinate</u> to a dollar. Fifty cents may be subordinate, and
> ten or less are clearly subordinate."

After all, the Coastal Permit Administrator had been allowed to invent his own set of County coastal planning regulations. Why shouldn't the Coastal Permit Administrator (like Humpty Dumpty) be allowed to invent his own dictionary?

In his final nasty jab Berrigan quoted my comments about Cindy Crawford's beauty mark and wrote,

> "In later testimony at the hearing while expressing concern about
> the siting of the structure, a member of the public continued this
> analogy. It was noted that this mark would not have the same
> effect if it were located on the end of Ms. Crawford's nose."

Naturally, he didn't mention that, viewed from the State Park, our house would be seen as ninety feet from the western tip of our property rather than at the tip itself.

I decided to make another trans-continental round trip (my seventh on this quest) at the time of the 9-28-95 public hearing on Berrigan's findings. I had telephoned Berrigan on 9-1-95 to determine if there would be an opportunity to debate his findings at the 9-28-95 hearing, and, if so, whether the findings might be subsequently altered based on the debate. As I fully expected, his answer to both questions was "no." Because the hearing would thus be pro forma, there was no reason to attend it other than to glare at Berrigan (which I did). But I had other more important reasons to make the cross-continent trip. I needed to meet with Mike and Bob to sharpen arguments and exhibits for the upcoming appeal to the Supervisors. I also wanted to meet with Berry to see if it might still be possible to turn around the State Parks' position relative to our project. And, finally I wanted to stop in Sacramento, get acquainted with Pacific Legal Foundation, and leave a copy of the 20" x 30" photomontage to help convince them of the validity of our claims. The first and last of these three tasks went smoothly, but my meeting with Berry was wasted effort.

Recall that Berry had been on vacation when Shannon wrote his second letter to County planners arguing against the possible success of vegetative screening for our project. This was counter to the agreement I had reached with Berry, his supervisor. On 9-12-95 I wrote to Berry expressing my concern, reminding him of the two visions we discussed, one house on two parcels, or two houses on two parcels. I reminded him also of his promise to email Shannon to inform him of his change of position regarding our project. Nonetheless, over Berry's signature block, Shannon had written his negative 8-21-95 letter to the County planners. I explained to Berry that, "I want to believe that this was not your intent and that it is a case either of a communications failure, or of Mr. Shannon's having slipped the leash." I then turned to Shannon's letter noting for example that it wrongly implied that our chosen site did not take advantage of existing vegetation, whereas during his onsite meeting with our architects he had had every opportunity to observe the brush barrier eight to twelve feet high that lay between our chosen site and the bluff edge in the direction of the State Park. During the survey clearing we had deliberately preserved that brush for screening purposes. Shannon's letter also questioned the chances for success of vegetative screening, completely ignoring the tall and vigorous stands of evergreens on nearby points. I urged Berry to write a letter to the Board of Supervisors disavowing Shannon's unfounded claims (but of course very-much doubted he would).

When I telephoned Berry on 9-18-95 on his return from vacation, he agreed to meet with me on the afternoon of 9-28-95. That was to be the same day of Berrigan's findings adoption hearing. Berry said that he hadn't had a chance to review the letter Shannon had written over his signature block. And he apologized, saying the letter didn't come out the way he intended, and he expressed his continued commitment to the one-house vision of the future. Then our conversation took a strange turn in which he discussed how hectic things had become because of a fracas that had occurred in Mendocino involving beach visitors and State Parks personnel. Our house issue just didn't compete with that problem at the time. He then added that, "Besides the County planner told Shannon they would deny your project anyway." Aghast, I listened without comment! That was a most surprising disclosure of impropriety on the part of the planner (presumably Berrigan), much like a judge divulging ahead of time and in confidence what his decision was going to be to one party to a lawsuit! Then Berry talked at some length and in general terms of the difficulties of working within the State Park bureaucracy. He seemed to need a shoulder to cry on, and I listened attentively. Then trying again to excuse Shannon's behavior, Berry commented that, "Shannon was under a lot of pressure from the County!" Again, I restrained myself from commenting, but that too was highly improper. So the judge was telling a witness what to say, and since when did the County make State Parks policy? I was speechless. Finally Berry said he would be discussing our project with his boss before taking any action. And that concluded our 9-18-95 telephone conversation.

The subsequent 9-28-95 face-to-face meeting with Berry was not a pleasant one. Berry said that he and his staff had looked over the Berrigan findings and the whole situation. They concluded that the beach property that we were considering donating to the state was of no value to State Parks, because the public had access anyway.

Furthermore, it was their position that, while the Stinson-mandated setback had offered no advantage to State Parks, the Berrigan-mandated setback would, and so they now supported the latter. Why was State Parks so intent upon defeating our plans? Why had Berry renounced his interest in the one-house-on-two-parcels vision? Could there be a hidden agenda of some sort? We were still very much in the dark.

So much for trying to negotiate with State Parks. We now had to focus on the Board of Supervisors. It was essential that the Shannon letters regarding vegetative screening be countered. At my request, Mitchell Custom Farming, who had done the clearing for the survey of our building site, sent a letter on 9-9-95 to the Supervisors telling them about the tall brush he had cleared and about the brush barrier which he'd been instructed to leave in place to provide screening of our house from the State Park. Contrary to the Shannon assertion, a lot more than grasses would grow there. And, indeed, a 9-24-95 letter to the Supervisors from our highly-experienced professional landscape architect, Sara Geddes included the comment, "I can state without reservation that the prospects for establishing trees and shrubs on the Berlincourt site are excellent."

Although Mike and Bob informed us that it was most unlikely that the supervisors would overrule Berrigan, we were nevertheless determined to make every effort to secure a favorable ruling. The odds were that Seji Sugawara (First District), Liz Henry (Fourth District), and Charles Peterson (Fifth District) would all vote against us. Likely voting in our favor would be Frank McMichael (Second District) and John Plnches (Third District). To make our case, Margie and I put together a 54-page notebook, and we sent copies to the supervisors. The notebooks telegraphed the arguments we planned to make at their hearing of our appeal. They were mailed on 10-20-95. A section on proposed findings was followed by a section replete with charts, photos, and diagrams showing how our proposed project was in full compliance with the County regulations. There followed a brief section on pertinent laws and regulations, and a listing of 49 Elk residents who had expressed support for our project. The next section detailed the improprieties of the Department of Planning and Building Services, the California Department of Parks and Recreation, and the anti faction of Elk. This included a listing of false statements and unsubstantiated claims in the County Staff Report, three public notices, the Coastal Permit Administrator's findings, letters and statements from the Parks Department, and in the anti faction's petition. At the end, because so much erroneous and malicious information had been circulated about us, we provided very brief personal information along with a listing of our expenditures in Mendocino County, viz. $80,000 in real estate taxes (1980-95), $140,000 for our five-acre parcel, and $54,000 for architectural fees. (The $210,000 price for our eleven-acre parcel had been paid to out-of-Mendocino-County sellers.)

Our notebooks were very aggressive and hard-hitting. Our adversaries were seeking to abridge our rights, and we wanted the County and State Parks to know that there had been enough improprieties within their establishments that they would be vulnerable if our case ended up in the courts for adjudication.

Public notices of the upcoming 11-13-95 Supervisors' hearing of our appeal in Ukiah were mailed by the County around the first of November. They were sent to 169 addresses from Elk to Fairbanks, Alaska. Evidently petition signers from outside the United States had been dropped from the list. On 11-2-95 Bob Schlosser received our architects' copy of the notice. Incredibly, the project description had reverted to the old original erroneous version! Bob Schlosser immediately telephoned the office of the Board of Supervisors to inform them of the error. After some consultation with County Counsel it was determined that if a corrected version were to be mailed by 5 PM that same day it would meet the statutory noticing requirement. It was a busy day for the County's clerical staff as they sent out the revised version to all 169 addresses. Much to our surprise the revised version was much improved, but still not as we would have written it. It failed to distinguish conditioned living space from garage space.

In the meantime both our supporters and the anti faction sent letters to the supervisors. Almost all of the anti faction's fifteen letters struck emotional chords and emphasized the effects our home would have on scenic views. But among the anti faction's submittals were two copies of Berkeley architecture professor Mary Comerio's highly-flawed letter, the one sent earlier to Berrigan which so erroneously and unprofessionally claimed our non-compliance with the County regulations. The anti faction had solicited far and wide for letters opposing our project. One, dated 11-9-95, from Nadya Williams of San Francisco, might not have reached the supervisors prior to our hearing, but it's worth quoting here as representative of the anti faction's emotional appeals. It read:

> "As a long-time admirer and 21-year resident of Elk, I stand with my friends and neighbors in opposition to the proposed monument to wealth, namely the Berlincourt project.
>
> What kind of "single family" needs 5,000 square feet? Wealth has its place, but not as so often occurs, at the expense of working families and the natural environment. This ostentatious and out-of-place structure, complete with "maid quarters," not only does not belong in Elk, but would be opening the death knell for higher rents and land prices and Sea Ranch-style developments for rich, absentee residents.
>
> I am a native Californian of 51 years and no one can tell me this state has not suffered from the onslaught of tract homes burying strawberry fields, strip malls covering orchards. As a former reporter for the weekly newspaper The North Coast News, I was proud to be a member of a committed group of professionals who dared to stand up to those who would exploit the beauty

of the coast for profit. We were financially punished for our stand, but we gained much more.

Ted and Marjorie Berlincourt are welcome to join the community of Elk if they respect its history, beauty and unique character - things that none of us can own or buy."

As is apparent in this letter (and in many others from the anti faction), our opponents' aversion to us appeared to be, to a considerable extent, sociological, with scenic preservation serving merely as a convenient vehicle for expressing it. Given the modest level of our affluence, their scorn would have been more profitably directed at Bill Gates and Warren Buffett.

In contrast, most letters from our supporters emphasized that we had met all County regulations. However, one from Erna Smith, Elk Postmaster (she preferred that as opposed to Postmistress), mentioned what we believe to have been improper behavior by County planners. She wrote:

"...a man and woman came into my office with area maps and prints of the Berlincourt's proposed house plan. They said they were from the Planning Dept. and that they were seeking feedback from the residents of Elk, on the proposed building. After looking over the plans, I said that I had no objection to their building on that large a site, and that I didn't think that anyone else would either. By the expression on the man's face, I felt that was not an acceptable answer."

Smith made another interesting observation:

"It is my understanding that the State Parks had some interested observers at the [8-28-95] hearing. It may be that they just want to know about anything going on, on adjoining properties; but I do know that they tried to take Anne Daniels property a few years ago, and that it was only through the intervention of [state] Senator Keen, that she was able to keep her home. I also know that, not only her home but other properties adjoining Park land in Elk is still on the list of properties targeted for acquisition by the State Parks, despite the insistence of property owners that their properties be removed from the list."

That should have set off alarm bells, especially in view of the covetous wishes expressed earlier by Pjerrou and de Vall at the time of our second hearing before Berrigan.

But, curiously, it didn't. Why, in hindsight, didn't we follow up on Erna Smith's information on State Parks' expansionist aspirations? Somehow, at the time, it just didn't stand out among all of the other distractions assaulting us. And besides, we possessed no hard evidence whatsoever of any overt moves against our property by State Parks. Had there been any such moves, then, by government rules, State Parks would have had to notify us. Also, they would have had to disclose their conflict of interest when passing judgment on our project to the County. They had done neither.

As our encounter with the supervisors drew near, the anti faction weighed in again in the media, and the media itself weighed-in in the media. Pjerrou was in rare form. On 11-2-95 she rallied the opposition in a 25- square-inch column in *The Mendocino Beacon*. It contained the usual false claims, chastised us for not accepting Berrigan's mandates, and urged the anti faction to protest our project by writing to the Supervisor's and attending our hearing. The following week our case was addressed three times in the 11-9-95 edition of the same newspaper. On page one a modest (16-square-inch) reportorial article included an accurate project description and mentioned that Berrigan had denied our application and required greater setback from the bluff edge. The article also mentioned our offer to install vegetative screening and our claim that the house would occupy only a tiny fraction of the headland vista. On page 2, Bloomquist's Elk column contained a 29-square-inch announcement from Pjerrou, which Bloomquist claimed to be "…accurate on all counts as far as I can determine." Nevertheless, Pjerrou repeated Berrigan's fallacious findings. Her announcement then took on a sinister tone as she noted that we had contacted the Pacific Legal Foundation! Moreover, according to her, we had sent a 10-pound package to the Supervisors mentioning the Constitution of the United States, property rights, and rebuttals to Berrigan's findings. (I'll grant that those are pretty serious offenses, but at twelve ounces of written material per supervisor our information package actually came in at a little under four pounds.) Her trump card was reserved for her last paragraph. We were guilty of owning additional properties in Albion and Mendocino!

The final shot in the 11-9-95 issue of *The Mendocino Beacon* was fired by the paper itself in an editorial on page 4. It was a two-barrel shot. The first one was aimed at Fetzer Vineyards, who had a retail outlet on Main Street overlooking the bay in the village of Mendocino. Fetzer had sought to enlarge their only window facing the street with a view of the bay. It was a puny three feet wide by four feet tall. Adjacent buildings had much, much larger windows, but, nevertheless, the Mendocino Historical Review Board (known locally as the "Hysterical Review Board") had turned down Fetzer's request. Fetzer appealed to the Supervisors just as we had. The Newspaper editorial's second shot was aimed at our appeal. The editorial urged the supervisors to deny both appeals.

Incidentally, Margie and I visited Mendocino recently and found that the pitiful little three-foot-by-four-foot window still adorns the front of the structure that used to be Fetzer's retail outlet. That space is now occupied by "The Mendocino Wine Company." It's still a little dark in there, but the wine is well worth the visit!

CHAPTER 10

BOARD OF SUPERVISORS HEARING I

With our hearing before the Mendocino County Board of Supervisors fast approaching, we prepared intensively. We created numerous viewgraph transparencies, charts, diagrams, and exhibits. And of course we planned to show the 20" x 30" photomontage, which, when held at arm's length presented the scene in exact size registration with the actual scene. Margie and I had researched every issue meticulously, and we had argued each issue ad infinitum until we both agreed on how best to address it. Would this be an opportunity to trump Berrigan's disregard for the facts and regulations? Would the Supervisors listen attentively to the facts, weigh them critically against the regulations and reach the only right decision, or, as we anticipated, would they simply vote their politics?

On Friday, 11-10-95, we began another trans-continental round trip journey (my eighth on this quest). Our destination was Ukiah, the Mendocino County seat. We had called ahead to the Supervisors' office to make certain that a viewgraph projector would be available. We were assured that it would be. (Neither we nor Mendocino County administrators had yet mastered powerpoint.) Despite the County reassurance on the viewgraph projector, we decided to rent one in Santa Rosa on our way to Ukiah. We had experienced great difficulty transcribing audio tapes from the County's inadequate audio recorder used at Berrigan's hearings, and we didn't want to take any chances with our visual exhibits. Besides, with the rental we could rehearse our presentation in our motel room. We arrived in Ukiah early enough on Friday 11-10-95 to be able to preview the Supervisors' hearing room, and we found that they shared a modest commercial building with "Char's Hair Now" beauty parlor on State Street, Ukiah's main street. It was fortunate indeed that we had rented a projector, because the County's projector proved to be a dysfunctional antique. But, unfortunately, the screen was undersize, and we wouldn't be allowed to turn off the bright lights directly above the screen. We could make do, but our visuals were not going to have their full impact.

After spending the weekend refining our presentation in the motel we arrived at the Supervisors' chamber on Monday morning 11-13-95 ready for combat. By the time the meeting commenced at 9 AM there was standing room only in the small hearing room. Perhaps thirty members of the public were in attendance in addition to the principals. The anti faction probably had a slight edge in numbers. Pjerrou and Bloomquist had been effective in their efforts to stir up the opposition. Pjerrou was, of course present herself, and so was Bloomquist, perhaps shamed into attending by the McKnights' "Community Forum" newspaper article.

With no introductory comments, Chairman Sugawara called on Berrigan for his testimony. Berrigan quickly summarized his findings, claiming that our house would not be subordinate to the character of the setting, that our building location should be restricted to a different site far to the east and south, that our chosen site was the most prominent on the parcel, that vegetative screening would not be adequate at our site, and that our house was two-story and hence not allowable. In justifying his denial, he added that there are two other vacant oceanfront parcels in the immediate vicinity, and that our proposed house would set the tone for their future development. Yet, at our hearings before him, he had always disregarded as irrelevant the precedents that we had cited! In other words, it was quite all right for him to invoke precedent arguments, but not for us to do so.

Next Chairman Sugawara called on us. I spoke, and Margie handled the viewgraphs. Having rehearsed repeatedly, we worked smoothly together. I pointed out that our house would amount to only one one-hundred-thousandth of the view as seen from Elk and the State Park, and so it would be subordinate. I disputed Berrigan's claim that our chosen site was the most prominent on the parcel, noting that nearer to the northern bluff edge would be much more prominent. Also disputing Berrigan's claims, I promised to show how our proposed loft and height were both in full compliance with the Coastal Element and the Zoning Code. I attacked Berrigan's claim that the landscaping would not make our house subordinate by arguing that it would already be subordinate even without the landscaping we planned to add.

I noted Berrigan's reference to other vacant parcels, that were near our parcels, and I stated that only one of our parcels would ever be developed if Berrigan's denial were to be reversed. I then described our proposed house, noting that it would cover less than one percent of the parcel on which we wished to build, would not block public views to the ocean, would not be visible from the east nor from the beach of the State Park, and would be partially screened initially by brush up to twelve feet tall.

Then I turned to a discussion of the Corwin-Wolsky residence, approved by Berrigan, and constructed the previous year a few miles south of our parcel. Just maybe the Supervisors would grant that precedents had some relevance to our case, even if Berrigan would not. I pointed out that the Corwin-Wolsky house is situated the same distance from public view points as our house would be and that the Corwin-Wolsky house presents a larger face to public view than our house would. Then I showed viewgraph photographs of the Corwin-Wolsky house taken with a 20 mm lens and a 400 mm lens to demonstrate how the latter magnifies the visual prominence of the house. And I told how we had been required to part with $1,670 for 400 mm lens photomontages, which were then used in the Staff Report to incite opposition to our project.

Next I produced the 20" x 30" photomontage for our proposed house produced from a 20 mm lens photo taken from the State Park viewpoint and asked each Supervisor to view it at arm's length. In that way they would approximate most closely the actual scene. I passed a magnifying glass to them so they could study the details of the house up close if they wished. Again I mentioned that, viewed from the State Park, our house would occupy only one one-hundred-thousandth of the scene.

Returning to precedents I showed a chart listing the numbers of houses visible from each of six coastal State Parks in Mendocino County. All told there are approximately 320, or, on average, about 53 per park. The actual number for Greenwood State Beach is 59. The point I was making was that Greenwood State Beach was created within the village of Elk. From almost any location in the park visitors looking toward our house would at the same time have other much-closer, and more-prominent houses in their fields of view. Why were we getting so much special attention? After all, the County had no problem with those other houses, all of which were much more prominent than ours would be.

Next I presented a chart showing how we complied with all pertinent County regulations. The chart also showed the "unlawful and more-restrictive regulations" invented by Berrigan in his attempts to thwart us. It's worth mentioning one of them at length here. Berrigan consistently insisted on calling our proposed house a two-story house. Yet the County regulations are silent regarding mezzanines. On the other hand the Uniform Building Code, the Standard Building Code, and the BOCA National Building Code all agree that a mezzanine having less than one-third the floor area of the room in which it is contained does not count as a story. Having erroneously declared our house to be two story, Berrigan then argued that the regulations do not permit a two-story house. Yet the pertinent County regulation states that, "...new development west of Highway One in designated "highly scenic areas" is limited to one-story (above natural grade) unless an increase in height would not affect public views to the ocean or be out of character with surrounding structures." So, even if we were to grant that our proposed house was two story, which it is not (according to the building codes), it would still be allowed, because it would not affect public views to the ocean, nor would it be out of character with surrounding structures. Indeed, at the time of the hearing, the nearest surrounding structures, though approximately one half-mile distant, were all two-story-or more structures!

I next listed accommodations we had made far beyond what the regulations require. So that Elk citizens and park visitors would not see our house from the park beach, we had voluntarily chosen a site with much-less-than-optimum ocean views for us. And we did that even though 21 other houses *are* visible from the park beach. To illustrate what we had relinquished, I showed a viewgraph photograph of that magnificent view from our northern bluff site. For comparison, I showed viewgraph photographs of the much-poorer northern views we would have from our proposed site. I also pointed out that our setbacks far exceeded the geological dictates and that we reduced the size twice (our original plan was 18 percent larger). Also, I noted, we relinquished the third bedroom, which had been intended to accommodate a caregiver at such time as failing health might dictate that need

Then I told of our intent to donate our northern beach property to the public and to place a no-development deed restriction on our adjacent five-acre parcel. I illustrated our vision of one house on our two parcels with photos and maps. But I also stated a caveat, viz., that our vision would be fulfilled only if our project were approved as proposed and not appealed. County Counsel Peter Klein confirmed that that was not something that the County could require, only something we could grant of our own volition.

Next I returned again to the "subordinate" issue stating that our house would amount to only one one-millionth of the view from Cuffey's Cove and one one-hundred-thousandth of the view from Elk and the State Park. The volume of our house would be only one one-thousandth the volume of the above-the-sea portion of our parcel. How could it possibly be anything but subordinate?

And I mentioned our full commitment to implementing our extensive landscape-screening plan, which called for more trees than mandated in the Staff Report special conditions. I showed pictures of the existing brush barrier on our parcel as well as pictures of tall and vigorous growths of evergreens on points north and south of ours. It was clear that, contrary to Berrigan's and Shannon's misleading distortions, prospects for effective vegetative screening of our house were excellent.

Then I attacked Berrigan's arbitrary and capricious 300-foot western setback requirement with a diagram showing how it would have no beneficial effect on public views from Elk and the State Park. And I quoted excerpts from precedents cited in the Supreme Court ruling in the *Nollan v. California Coastal Commission (1987)* case, specifically,

> "...one of the principal purposes of the takings clause is to bar Government from forcing some people alone to bear public burdens which in all fairness and justice should be borne by the public as a whole.
>
> In short, unless the permit condition serves the same governmental purpose as the development ban, building restriction is not a valid regulation of land use but an out-and-out plan of extortion."

We viewed Berrigan's position as expecting us alone to bear the burden of paying for our parcel, paying taxes on it, and sacrificing our ocean views all on the presumption of public benefit, when in fact there would be no public benefit. Worse still, a house at the

Berrigan-mandated site would not only block public views to the ocean from Highway One's highly-valued view corridor, but, being so close to Highway One, the house would completely dominate the scene. I showed all of that with the help of diagrams and a photomontage.

Returning to the issue of precedents I mentioned our June request in the County Planning Office in Fort Bragg for the plans to the Corwin-Wolsky house. A file was delivered to us, but it contained no plans, so we asked again specifically for plans and were told there were none. All we could learn from the scanty information in the file was that the living area was 2796 square feet and the height was 18 feet. Then, just a week prior to the Supervisors' hearing, Bob Schlosser managed by chance to obtain a copy of the Corwin-Wolsky plans in the planning office. The plans revealed a height of 23.5 feet and a living area of 3475 square feet, almost identical to our planned living area. *And the plans showed three split level stories and a loft!* So at the Supervisors' hearing I was able to show a viewgraph depicting in cross-section our house and the Corwin-Wolsky house side by side. I then asked whatever happened to the Constitution's guarantee of equal protection of the law? Further, were the Corwin-Wolsky plans deliberately withheld from us? I then declared that, since the County had ruled that the Corwin-Wolsky house was subordinate, then surely our proposed house must also be subordinate.

I followed that attack by charging that County planners applied constraints on our project that were more restrictive than County regulations; issued false statements and unsubstantiated claims in their reports, public notices, and findings; and incited opposition to us through the press and State Parks. I presented viewgraphs listing those offenses, and I reminded the Supervisors that we had sent them a list of what we believed to be egregious violations of due process.

Next, I took on the anti faction with their erroneous petition and malicious letters. Their petition claimed only to raise questions. In an attempt to evade legal liability the petition didn't condemn explicitly, but it did so implicitly (and maliciously). Not surprisingly, Berrigan's and the Staff Report's false statements were repeated by the anti faction in their letters, but there was also a lot of embroidery designed to characterize us as unworthy and insensitive plutocrats with three kitchens, servants, and caretaker's quarters over our garage.

I summed up with the following words:

> "We believe that you, the Supervisors, will see through the
> deliberate falsehoods, the biased and unethical attacks, the
> violations of due process, and that you will focus on what this
> hearing is all about, not about attacks on us, not about the
> numbers of signatures on our competing petitions, not about
> taking our side or taking the Coastal Permit Administrator's side,
> but rather about our compliance with all legal requirements.

> We're confident we're in full compliance. We've played by all the rules. Please accept our thanks for your attention in hearing our case."

Obviously, I'd made no effort to conceal my anger. Would the Supervisors see through Berrigan, or would they believe him and not us? I knew for certain they wouldn't take the time and make the effort to investigate and find the truth for themselves. They are eternally condemned to deal with mountains of superficiality, too many issues, no opportunity to get to the bottom of anything (the way scientists do). Easier just to be political. As Winston Churchill once remarked, "No one pretends that democracy is perfect or all-wise. Indeed, it has been said that democracy is the worst form of government except all those others that have been tried from time to time."

Well, Mike Leventhal followed, skillfully addressing matters of compliance with the regulations. But he couldn't resist taking a number of shots at Berrigan, even though it could very well place other projects of his in jeopardy when he had to deal with Berrigan in the future. It was courageous of him to support us in this manner.

Bob Schlosser spoke next. He focused first on the flawed public notices, detailing all the times the planners had issued erroneous notices and detailing his and Mike's calls to the planners to try to correct them. The botched notice for the hearing before the Supervisors was but one of a long trail of such unprofessional and inexcusable instances. Bob made a comparison between the public notices for the Corwin-Wolsky project and ours, pointing out the more faithful project portrayal in the former case, and the abuse in our case. Bob asked if it was now County Policy to use the project description as a means to favor one applicant over another. He next turned to a discussion of the special conditions, then to matters of compliance, and then to the findings. Without using notes he touched all of the bases with remarkable verbal skills. It occurred to me that if we were ever again cursed with another (expletive) hearing we would be well advised to use Bob as the featured speaker. Interestingly, Bob diplomatically excused the anti-faction Elk residents for their actions, saying that they had simply been misled by the "false and erroneous" notices issued by the planners. (The fact of the matter is that very soon after the anti faction's petition was initiated, Margie and I had sent letters to all Elk postal patrons informing them of the facts of the case, and so the anti faction was unworthy of the olive branch that Bob was offering.)

During the fifteen-minute break, which followed Bob's presentation, a tall, sixtyish woman approached me and introduced herself as "Doctor" Hillary Adams. Later I would learn that, as the daughter of Charles and Imogene Snyder, she was known in her youth as Judith Ann Snyder, became Judith Ann Snyder Schaeffer upon her marriage to the Rev. H. Paul Schaeffer, but assumed the name Hillary de Mandeville Adams, Adams having been her mother's maiden name. Doctor Adams had been a university professor, and her specialty was ancient Greek art and archaeology. That might have been a basis for some comity with Margie, but that was not to be, for she said that she had come to the hearing to protest our project, and that I should not take it personally. She went on to explain that no matter what the outcome of our attempts to build on the coast, if we ever did move to the area, we would be welcomed as if none of the controversy we had caused had ever happened. I instinctively sensed that she was really big trouble with a "capital T" in River City, and there was only one response that came to mind. It was "bullshit!" and so I said, *"BULLSHIT!"* Doctor Adams recoiled in shock, and as she shrank away from me, she exclaimed in a puzzled manner more to herself than to me, "Why, nobody ever spoke to me that way before..." (Incidentally, she hasn't yet welcomed us to the community. No doubt it was something I said.)

Well, after the break, Chairman Sugawara offered Berrigan an opportunity to respond to our charges. Berrigan attributed the errors in the first public notice to the "staff" thereby not taking responsibility for the product of his operation. He then granted that we had submitted revised plans but claimed falsely that, "...the square footage had remained essentially the same." (In actual fact we had reduced the area by 450 square feet.) With regard to the public notice for his second hearing Berrigan stated that, "...it wasn't until after the notice went out, and it may have actually been just at the public hearing, that I discovered that along with the landscaping plans they were submitting, the applicant had revised the square footage of the structure itself." (By this time the total reduction in area relative to the original submission was 700 square feet. In short, he had come to that hearing to make a ruling and had not done his homework.)

Next, Berrigan changed the subject, evidently hoping everyone in the room might have forgotten about the erroneous notice for the Supervisors' hearing. He returned to the visual impact issue, arguing that it was more important to protect the State Park view than the view from Highway One. Of course nothing in the Coastal Act nor the County regulations assigns a higher priority to park views over highway views.

Supervisor Henry then questioned Berrigan about the discrepancies in the height and size of the Corwin-Wolsky house. Berrigan responded with:

> "I can surmise what happened in terms of where the plans went.
> The Berlincourts came into the office, and they asked to review
> the address file, which contains building permit records, and we
> do not maintain plans for residential development after a certain
> period of time, so if anyone asked to review an address file, there
> will not be plans available unless it's a commercial structure. The
> plans are in the coastal permit file."

I attempted to interrupt at this point to make it clear that we had no knowledge of the County file system whatsoever, and that we had merely asked to see the plans. But Chairman Sugawara cut me off. I have to hand it to Berrigan for that cleverly-crafted evasive fabrication. He had falsely claimed that we asked for the wrong file, and he had avoided answering Supervisor Henry's query about the height and floor area of the Corwin-Wolsky house.

Supervisor Peterson, of the Fifth District (in which our parcel is located), then asked, "How does the County define stories?" Berrigan answered, "Outside of the town of Mendocino we go by the Uniform Building Code." I thought, aha, now we've got him. But Berrigan then proceeded to invent and state his definition, not the Uniform Building Code's definition! I could hardly contain myself knowing that Chairman Sugawara would not allow me to interrupt. Berrigan had pulled it off! It brought back memories of Hall's letter regarding the attached/detached issue. In the absence of clarity in the County regulations it was just a matter for determination by whatever Coastal Permit Administrator happened to be hearing the case. In short, Mendocino County does not offer equal protection of the law.

Evidently Supervisor Peterson had been well prepared for this hearing, if not by Berrigan (which would be an impropriety), then certainly by the anti faction. He next asked about the Elk County Water District issue. That issue is recounted in six and a half pages of the hearing transcript, which would bore you to death. Suffice it to say, the anti faction were trying to invoke the old western-movie-water-rights weapon all over again, even though we always had the option of drilling a well. So it was all beside the point.

There followed a lengthy discussion that included the Supervisors and the County Counsel. The gist of it was whether our proffered beach dedication and one-house-on-two-parcels vision could become a legitimate condition placed on their approval of our permit application. County Counsel Klein responded in the negative, just as we knew he would have to. Even so, Chairman Sugawara asked, "Is there any creative legal way of achieving the same result?" Klein responded,

> "Well, that's strictly in the hands of the applicant. But I would not like to tie that, quite frankly, into the decision-making process, particularly since the Pacific Legal Foundation is involved. This has been the Pacific Legal Foundation's bread and butter for years, our excessive exactions."

Now that sounded a lot like an admission of guilt didn't it?

When Chairman Sugawara called for public comment, Mary Pjerrou was the first to respond. She mentioned that her view would be impacted and wrongly claimed that, "all of the other structures in Elk are tucked away back into the highway, away from the ocean." Her closing shot was an accusation that this case, "...has to do with a developer's agenda in breaking the Local Coastal Plan and shutting people up," at which point she made an attempt at a dramatic gesture by sealing her lips with a length of scotch tape! (Duct tape would have been more effective.) We of course had no such grandiose aspirations, just simply wished to enjoy our retirement by the sea.

State Parks planner, Gary Shannon spoke next, expressing support for the Berrigan ruling and reiterating his previous two hearings statements and contents of the two opposition letters he'd authored. He was followed by Dean Wisdom who argued that the issue be decided on logical factors, that we had met and exceeded the code requirements, and should be granted our permit. Barbara McKnight seconded Wisdom's comments and added that she and her husband, Mac, had had great success planting trees on the two oceanfront parcels they built on one-half mile south of ours. I had earlier shown pictures of the tall trees which hid their 27-foot tall A-frame oceanfront home. Eleanor Lewallen then spoke in opposition to us, and she introduced a letter I'd written to her. In it I'd explained that, because she'd been harvesting seaweed on our beach for the past fifteen years for her sea vegetable business, it was quite inappropriate for her to be actively opposing our building on our bluff above. She interpreted that as a threat to her access to the beach. John Raffety, who owned three houses in Elk with views toward our property, spoke next, expressing his support for us and his "...hope that this isn't the way that this County is governed, in that we govern it by people signing petitions in the local store from as far away as London, England, to tell us how to run the housing on our coast."

Then RD Beacon, an Elk "old timer" spoke up. At about six-and-a-half-feet tall and approaching three hundred pounds, he's a commanding presence. Owner of several thousand acres across Highway One from our parcel, he once ran for Sheriff of Mendocino County. Beacon lives high atop a hill, where he looks down on our parcel, runs a bar, operates a radio communications business, tinkers with computers, and maintains his own fire department, complete with several fire engines and massive earth moving machines. All this, having had virtually no formal education. At one time Beacon had owned the State park property as well as our property, and he knew what would grow on them. He spoke forcefully in support of our project and chastised Shannon for his views on screening vegetation.

Bud Kamb added his voice in our support, saying that in his twenty years shepherding real estate projects through the administrative hurdles he had seen permits granted up and down the coast that were more visible compared to "...this little view that we're talking about from the State Park is absolutely, to me, ridiculous...there's terrible inconsistencies with what's going on here."

Ellen Saxe spoke next in opposition, attempting an analogy with the following flawed argument.

> "If one owns property with private roads on it, anyone who had
> their permission may drive on it, young children, persons under
> the influence, etc. If a person wants to drive on public roads,
> their actions come under the laws agreed upon by public or
> elected officials, because public driving affects many."

From this it would seem that she, like many of our antagonists, perceived our parcel as public property. However, we didn't seek to build on public property. Rather we proposed to build on our own private property.

Then Carole Raye attacked our project saying that it shouldn't be compared to the Corwin-Wolsky house, because, "You can't even see it [the Corwin-Wolsky house] from the road." Well, it's the same half-mile distance from the road that our house would be from the State Park. But then, perhaps her eyesight suddenly sharpens whenever she visits the park.

The next speaker began, "My name is Dr. Hillary Adams. I am also a retired professor." Uh oh! I knew where she was going. She continued,

> "I've taken no position on this. I've signed no petitions. I came here to listen, and after listening to the presentation and talking personally with Mr. Berlincourt, I have to say that I'm very concerned, both about the manner of presentation and about attitudes to our community."

Well, I asked for it. But her claim that she had taken no position was, well, *bullshit*. She had just finished telling me that she opposed our project. In fact I was to learn later that for years she actively opposed just about every coastal-zone project for miles around, and that many were subsequently approved by the Coastal Commission. So it was all downhill from there. Saying, "I'm a camera person," she proceeded to criticize the photos I had presented, nothing of any technical substance, just wild shots. Then she remarked that, "In the same way in the photograph, when we talk about a 12-foot bush in any way obscuring an 18-foot house, that distresses me." I had of course never claimed that it did, but it would obscure the lower twelve feet. In the rest of her four pages in the transcript Adams touched on wealth, community, design insensitivity, and government, ending with, "…our County government is a government of the people, by the people, and for the people."

Ella Russell followed, stating her opposition to our project and reading into the record letters of opposition from Elk Store proprietor, Ben McMillan, and bed and breakfast owner, Leslie Griffith Lawson. Mark Penn then spoke in our favor, and also expressed his concern as a taxpayer for what this could cost the County in terms of a legal battle down the road. Midge Denton, who lived in a rental property surrounded by the State Park supported our appeal. Alice Flores attacked our project and said that the Corwin-Wolsky house "…sticks out like a sore thumb." (She obviously has better eyesight than Carole Raye.) Resuscitating the "maid" issue Flores continued, "There's no way people in their seventies and eighties can maintain themselves without servants or whatever you want to call these people that they hire to help them."

After Thomas Neese expressed his opposition to our project, Mary (yet another Mary) Weaver, a local realtor, who would later write the novel, "A Mendocino Mystery", rose to voice her opposition, pretty much a repetition of that by others, except for the following:

> "...I have to say 'O.J.', that I feel O.J.'d a lot. And if you watched the O.J. trial, it's like I feel...today a little bit of the dream team is here. They're the ones that have the suits and ties on. They're the ones that have the intelligence and the facts and the photographs and the displays and the transcripts... but then you've got, you know, the citizens of the County...they can't afford to hire lawyers to come here and speak out. They can't afford to have these fancy displays made. It's just the little guy and the big guy again..."

At this point Supervisor McMichael remarked, "I think you just suggested that the rest of the County wasn't intelligent."

Final words of support came from former building inspector and contractor, Dave Skilton. With that Chairman Sugawara closed the morning session. As we broke for lunch, I was approached by a visiting tourist from Vermont who just happened to attend the hearing out of curiosity. He expressed his support for us and said he just couldn't believe how oppressive the County permitting process was and how uncivil our detractors were. Amen! Nevertheless, by my count, members of the public spoke ten to nine in favor of Berrigan.

When the hearing resumed after lunch, Chairman Sugawara permitted us to respond to the public comments. We certainly couldn't complain that we hadn't been allowed ample opportunity to make our case. Mike spoke first, correcting numerous erroneous statements that had been made by Berrigan and by the anti faction. I'll not mention all of them here, noting only that Mike attacked Berrigan on the two-story issue, as did Bob in his subsequent comments.

Following our architects' rebuttals there was lively questioning by Supervisors Peterson and Henry. They had by then reached the conclusion that the only significant issue to be resolved was that of building site location. In effect all of the other so-called issues raised by the planners and anti faction were mostly smoke screen. As the debate on location continued, Supervisor Henry picked up on Adams's criticisms of my photos, which illustrated the demise of our ocean views for different locations. She argued in effect that I should have taken them while standing on a ladder in order to take account of the height of the floor above the outside grade. (For our slab floor house this would have amounted to about nine inches at most. I had taken the photos at eye level while standing up.) That precipitated the comment from Chairman Sugawara that,

Figure 1: Scenic sea stacks offshore from Elk, California. This is a southward view from the Highway-One turnout at Cuffey's Cove. Our parcel lies shrouded in fog 1.6 miles to the south as the crow flies.

Figure 2: Northward view from our parcel across Greenwood Creek Cove. Our parcel extends 350 feet northward along this beach. Nevertheless, we voluntarily relinquished this view in order to spare beach visitors views of our home.

Figure 3: Northwestward view from our parcel toward the Elk sea stacks. More of the view we relinquished to spare beach visitors views of our home.

Figure 4: Southward view from our parcel. At left is the Crahan residence, which is situated on an immediately adjacent parcel.

Figure 5: The Duarte oceanfront residence viewed from Pine Beach south of Fort Bragg. The 28-foot height allowed by the County was an exception to the highly-scenic-area 18-foot limit.

Figure 6: The Duarte residence seen from the boundary of Jug Handle State Reserve, the closest public view point, 103 feet to the south. (Photographed with a 35 mm camera equipped with a 20 mm lens.)

Figure 7: The MacIver oceanfront residence on Chapman Point in Mendocino, as seen from the boundary of Van Damme State Park, the closest public view point, 64 feet to the south. (Photographed with a 35 mm camera equipped with a 20 mm lens.)

Figure 8: The Crahan residence, on an oceanfront parcel immediately south of ours, as seen from Highway One, the closest public view point, 109 feet to the east. (Photographed with a 35 mm camera equipped with a 20 mm lens.)

Figure 9: The spires residence, on the second oceanfront parcel south of ours, as seen from Highway One, the closest public view point, 50 feet to the east. (Photographed with a 35 mm camera equipped with a 20 mm lens.)

Figure 10: Our home viewed from the Highway One turnout, the closest public view point, approximately 800 feet to the southeast. (Photographed with a 35 mm camera equipped with a 20 mm lens.)

Figure 11: Our home viewed from the burner ring view point of the upper level of Greenwood State Beach approximately one-half mile to the north. (Photographed with a 35 mm camera equipped with a 20 mm lens.)

Figure 12: Our home photographed from the upper-level of Greenwood State Beach with a telephoto lens that increases its image size four times over that for a 20 mm lens. Yet, it's still much less conspicuous than images of the other four houses depicted in Figures 6 to 9.

Figure 13: Southward view from Cuffey's Cove. Our home and three neighboring homes are ever-so-faintly visible clustered about 2.5 inches from the right edge of the photo. Much more prominent are several structures in the village of Elk that appear about two inches from the left edge of the photo.

"Certainly, this is an adversarial setting, and there's efforts to
exaggerate, efforts to deceive, and this is on all sides, and we,
as decision-makers, you know, are stuck here trying to ferret out,
you know, what makes the most sense."

Supervisors Sugawara and Henry expressed the view that the opposing parties in this conflict should be sitting down together and negotiating a solution acceptable to all. Mike and Bob again pointed out all the concessions we had already made and that we did try to work it out. But there had been no concessions whatsoever on the other side, only escalations.

I then asked to speak, first expressing our thanks to our friends who made the trip over the mountains to express their support for our project. To those who might have felt O.J.'d, I noted that none of us were lawyers and that Margie and I, ourselves, had prepared all of the viewgraphs, exhibits, etc. Picking up on Chairman Sugawara's comment about exaggeration and deceit on both sides, I expressed how difficult it was for me as a physicist to function in that environment. Deceit and exaggeration are career ending in scientific circles. Unfortunately, they didn't appear to be in land-use disputes. (Clearly, I had no confidence that the Supervisors would ever ferret out the facts on their own and punish the exaggerators and deceivers.)

I again brought up the erroneous public notices, saying, "...not until after we had written to Mr. Hall [Berrigan's supervisor] certified mail, return receipt requested, did we finally get an improved, but still flawed, public notice... then to our amazement, the initial public notice mailing for this meeting again contained the old errors and had to be amended." After some shots at the anti faction for the false statements and unsubstantiated claims, I concluded with,

"Clearly their goal is not our compliance with legal requirements,
but rather unlawfully to establish conditions so onerous as to
render development of our parcel undesirable...[but] the facts
confirm that, as proposed, our project is in full compliance with
the legal requirements...I really appreciate your patience for
sitting through anything this long and difficult."

We were to hear next from the Supervisors. Perhaps because our parcel was in Supervisor Peterson's district, he was recognized first. His comments fill four pages of the transcript. He emphasized how special our parcel was, implying the need for very special protection (obviously at our expense). He questioned what he saw as a prevailing view by both sides, "...that the view available to the property is only the view from inside the house in the living room." Then he argued,

"Wherever this house is located, and whoever owns this piece of property, they retain and own the views from every square inch of this piece of property, whether they're in the living room, the bathroom, in the front yard, or standing on the ocean bluff."

In other words our home's access to scenic views was the very least of his concerns. From him, this was not unexpected. He continued,

"I am basically voting to see this thing closer from the highway and not from the State Park turnout and to pull it back off of the bluff point, because over and over and over again I have always felt that that is what if possible we must prevent from happening is the predominant points from being built on, and so my motion is basically with the Staff recommendation, but I do want to change that some way relative to being willing to accept the building height and size."

Thus the motion was placed before the Board. From our perspective, it would damage scenic views from Highway One, while providing no benefits to views from the State Park. We could take no comfort from Peterson's relaxation of Berrigan's illegal strictures on size and height.

Supervisor Henry seconded the motion. She went on to defend Berrigan and to say that she, "...hated to see some of the slings and arrows thrown at staff people..." and that she didn't, "...have as strong a view of property rights as the applicant." She concluded,

"I really think there could have been another way this could have been resolved, and I'm, sorry it wasn't, but...I will support our, the action of the Coastal Permit Administrator."

Supervisor McMichael disagreed with Supervisor Peterson's motion and the Berrigan denial, saying,

"I believe the project that was presented and the location that was presented is a good compromise for that site. It compromises for what the public would like to see, and it compromises for what the owner could do."

After additional expressions of support for our cause he remarked,

> "I am concerned that there were three successive erroneous
> notices posted, plus the Board of Supervisors, for this. That tells
> me that either we've got a very indifferent process or we've got
> a willful process, and I like neither."

Well said!

Supervisor Pinches then expressed his support for our appeal. He cited the regulations, which in effect showed equal concern for scenic views whether from a state park or from Highway One. He also remarked,

> "If the State Park felt that they had a problem that maybe in
> the future as to the view, then maybe they should have [had]
> a movement in the last 15 years to purchase this piece of
> property...I think that should have been the normal course of
> the State instead of coming to a hearing and protest it then. I
> think they're about 15 years late."

We were most grateful for the support from supervisors McMichael and Pinches, but we were troubled by the latter's mention of State Parks' power simply to take our property by eminent domain. We had of course been well aware of that possibility all along, but mention of it at our hearing just might activate Shannon to try to initiate the process in the State Parks bureaucracy. In any event, the vote on our appeal was now tied.

Chairman Sugawara would cast the tie-breaker vote. He began by complimenting us on our presentations, which was a wasted sop, because I knew damn well what was coming. He then mentioned his own electrical engineering education, which placed "...a high value on objectivity and rational thought processes." But then he stated that the matter at issue was subjective, and subjectivity had to be dealt with on a case-by-case basis. In effect, he declared that the ruling in such an instance might well be different near Elk as opposed to near Fort Bragg. (So much for equal protection of the law.) Then he remarked,

> "I couldn't help, you know, appreciating, and at the same time
> chuckling a little bit, about measuring the significances in terms
> of a view in terms of the proportion of the view. I was reminded,
> as a kid I had a pimple on my forehead. That was embarrassing
> enough, but had it been on the tip of my nose, it would have
> been disaster, you know."

Chairman Sugawara had obviously read Berrigan's findings and invented his own variation on the inapt analogy planted in Berrigan's mind by Pjerrou. (She must have been

124

ecstatic!) The Chairman of the Board of Supervisors then cast his deciding vote in support of the Berrigan ruling, concluding three hours and fifty-five minutes of deliberations.

The outcome came as no surprise to Margie and me. We had seen it merely as a formality that we had to endure to be eligible to pursue legal action. On the positive side, the hearing had provided additional documentation on the foul play of our opponents, thereby providing useful evidence in a lawsuit. But we certainly didn't feel good about the outcome. The condolences from our supporters were heartwarming, especially that comforting hug from Barbara McKnight. She and Mac have been the staunchest of friends from the beginning.

The minutes prepared by the Clerk of the Board of Supervisors duly reported the vote and stated,

> "IT IS ORDERED that the Board of Supervisors hereby rejects the appeal and upholds the decision of the Coastal Permit Administrator except as to those issues dealing with the height and size of the structure which the Board stated no opposition to."

Berrigan's triumphant "Notice of Final Action," issued the day after the hearing, cast still another shadow on his competence, for it failed to note the Supervisors' exceptions dealing with height and size, and it still listed Mary Stinson as Project Coordinator.

Later the same day of our hearing, Fetzer Vineyard's appeal for enlargement of their pitiful three-foot by four-foot window was heard by the Supervisors. Doctor Hillary Adams, Mary Weaver, and Kathleen Cameron had stayed around long enough to add their voices to those protesting the Fetzer appeal. Supervisor Peterson made the motion for denial and was joined by Supervisors Henry and Sugawara. Supervisors McMichael and Pinches dissented. All in all, it was a good day for Doctor Adams and her accomplices.

Bloomquist's celebration of our defeat would be less exuberant than theirs, for he was suffering his own setback. In his 11-16-95 column in *The Mendocino Beacon,* he duly reported the supervisors' rejection of our appeal in a single restrained sentence. But it was absent his usual scorn for us. It seems his criticism of us, of old timers, and of retirees had not been well received by many in Elk, and, in communications to *The Mendocino Beacon,* those offended had expressed their disapproval in no uncertain terms. The stage was thus set for Bloomquist's resignation. His last column appeared on 11-30-95. In it he declared that the column had "…ceased being funny and fun," and remarked, "…I want to especially thank my editor, Kate Lee, who invited me to try column writing over eight years ago and who gave me the freedom to hang myself however I saw fit." With that he passed the torch to Charlie Acker, who's been at it now for more than ten years.

Still, adverse coverage of our case continued elsewhere in the media. Louis Martin, whose *coastnews.com* beat extends from San Francisco to rural villages along the northern California coast, covered our appeal hearing at some length in several articles. And much later, on the internet, he displayed a telephoto image of our completed house, erroneously and derisively referring to it as "all 31,000 square feet of it." But, in that same article, he managed to get a few things right, referring to me as "a tall, thin man" and Margie (then age 67) as "small, a determined-looking woman, flawless in appearance." I wonder. Could that last factor have accounted in part for the zeal with which the female contingent of our detractors pursued their campaign against us? (Perhaps, although surely most women would be above such behavior, wouldn't they?)

As further illustration of our detractors' zeal, a follow-on item from our appeal hearing deserves mention. We came across it seven months after the hearing among documents the County provided in response to our lawsuit subpoena. Five days after the hearing, Mary Pjerrou had written a two-page, single-spaced letter to the supervisors (copy to Berrigan) explaining why she had put tape over her mouth at our appeal hearing. Excerpts follow:

> "...I was very upset about the Berlincourts' attacks on me, on others, and on our public process.
>
> At the August 24 CDP hearing, Marjorie Berlincourt stated that I and others had 'defamed' her, and had 'deprived' her of her 'civil rights,' in the Petition-Inquiry that is part of this record. I understood her language to mean that, if I didn't somehow recant the petition, the Berlincourts would sue me and others involved in the petition...
>
> I retained an attorney after the August 24 hearing, on behalf of myself and all potential victims of a S.L.A.P.P. (Strategic Lawsuit Against Public Participation). A copy of my attorney's letter to the Berlincourts is attached. While we have some protection against these sort of lawsuits in California, still, the threat of such a lawsuit, or the filing of one, even if it is eventually thrown out of court, can have a chilling effect on public comment. That is its sole purpose. And let me tell you, I felt such a chill when Mr. Berlincourt got up at the November 13 appeal hearing, and spoke about the 'MacMillan-Bloomquist-Pjerrou petition.'
>
> First of all, Mr. Berlincourt's invention of this new title, the "MacMillan-Bloomquist-Pjerrou petition" – words that did not appear as a heading on the Petition-Inquiry that was submitted

to the CPD – represents an attempt to target individuals for the public comment expression of many other people in this case, 161 other people. To assist the community in organizing a petition – and even to be a leader in that effort – does not mean that it is "your" petition, particularly when it is signed by 161 other individuals, presumably with minds of their own."

(two repetitious paragraphs omitted)

"As you know the Petition-Inquiry asks question and raises concerns about the Berlincourt project, and asks those who hold planning authority to answer these questions and concerns. The Berlincourts assert that all the questions and concerns are illegitimate, and even defamatory, because of certain minor inaccuracies in the description of their project in the early County Planning Department notice, and in the Petition-Inquiry."

(three more paragraphs omitted)

"As Mr. Berlincourt's testimony proceeded, I was thinking of the Berlincourts' many efforts to frighten and intimidate members of this community, and to bully our public officials - including visits to people's homes, personal letters, threats of retaliation, and the use of hostile language starting way back in June with the Berlincourts' description of Elk residents and visitors as 'trespassing' on a public beach.

And I just got fed up with these tactics, and threw my prepared testimony out the window - and put the tape over my mouth. I was suffering an emotional reaction to the threats at the hearing, and to all that had gone on before, and I couldn't articulate what I felt.

Several supervisors wondered why a compromise had not been reached on the location of the Berlincourt structure, that would satisfy the community concerns and requirement of the LCP [Local Coastal Plan]. Given the Berlincourts' tactics of threat and intimidation, and given their other land holdings on the Mendocino coast, and the involvement of the Pacific Legal Foundation, I don't think that such a solution was ever really possible. Perhaps that's why I got so upset - I finally realized that there was no solution, and I felt that we had all been tricked into thinking that there was…"

Yes, I admit to having left out a lot of that harangue, but you doubtless got the gist of it. It appears that Pjerrou was so totally engrossed in attacking us that she hadn't yet fully comprehended that the Supervisors had ruled against us *and in her favor!*

CHAPTER 11
OUR LAWSUIT AND A REVELATION

Well, we had exhausted the appeal process. We could (a) just give up and sell our parcel as distressed merchandise, which it surely was after Berrigan and the Supervisors had denied our access to the desirable view sites; (b) build in the despised envelope they had mandated; or (c) put up a legal fight. We never seriously considered (a) or (b), even though my cousin John Wingard, an attorney with Housing and Urban Development, a federal agency in Washington, DC, advised us that no matter how good our evidence might be, a land-use suit is always very, very risky. In short he thought a lawsuit wouldn't be worth the pain and expense.

But we were determined to keep that option open. During my earlier visit to Pacific Legal Foundation I'd learned that, in order to pursue a lawsuit, we'd have to obtain from the County a copy of the "administrative record" of our case. Accordingly, before leaving the Supervisor's chambers after our hearing, we submitted a verbal request. (It later took some correspondence and our check for $1,530 to get the process moving.) That telegraphed to the County our probable intentions. The administrative record would provide us with copies of pertinent documents related to our encounter with the County as well as a certified transcript of our hearing.

Early in the morning the day after the supervisors denied our appeal, we set out for Sacramento to visit the Pacific Legal Foundation. We were received graciously, and they kindly provided us with a list of law firms that specialize in cases such as ours. Most were located in the vicinities of Los Angeles and San Francisco, but one, Zumbrun and Findley, was situated immediately across the street from PLF. Moreover, Ron Zumbrun had co-founded and had formerly headed PLF. After earning a bachelor's degree in economics from Pomona College in 1957, he had entered Boalt Law School, University of California at Berkeley, and, in 1961, had received his law degree there. By the late 1960s he was serving under Governor Ronald Reagan as Deputy Director-Legal Affairs for the California Department of Social Welfare and later served in Washington, DC, as Special Counsel to the United States Department of Health, Education, and Welfare. But of most importance to us, in 1987, together with Robert Best and Timothy Bittle, Zumbrun had fought and won a historic property rights case, before the United States Supreme Court, viz., *Nollan v. California Coastal Commission*. Without hesitation we crossed the street.

At Zumbrun and Findley we briefly explained our situation to a young attorney, Neal Lutterman, who arranged for us to meet later with Zumbrun. That later meeting with Zumbrun gave us hope. He proved to be thoughtful and incisive. Though not flamboyant, he appeared fully capable of dealing in his own way with the most malicious of adversaries. We had prepared notes for the meeting, and Zumbrun listened carefully to what we had to say. He asked all of the right questions, and then laid out a battle plan. But he cautioned that it was all a roll of the dice. He made no promises other than to give it his best shot. We asked how long such cases normally take, and he answered one to three years. We asked what it might cost, and he estimated one hundred to two hundred thousand dollars. What a gamble! That was a long time and a lot of money. We could just be throwing good time and money after bad. But our anger toward our adversaries was now augmented with hope, and so we became his clients. (Incidentally, Zumbrun's high-end estimates of the required time and money would prove to be on the mark.)

Legal matters move glacially slowly. The County was allowed by law to take 190 days to produce an administrative record. How better to frustrate an adversary than to take the whole 190? Surprisingly we received the administrative record on 2-14-96, i.e., approximately 100 days before that deadline (but they should have been able to produce it in a couple of weeks).

Shortly thereafter, on 2-25-96, I left on another trans-continental round trip (my ninth in this quest), this time to develop additional evidence on the Berrigan-mandated building site and to confer with Lutterman and Zumbrun. On the coast I erected a graduated story pole at the Berrigan-mandated site and took photos from the State Park and from Highway One. This would enable me to develop more realistic photomontages illustrating our claims that that siting would be of no benefit to views from the park and would have a very negative impact on views from the highway.

While still on the coast, I sought a little diversion by undertaking an experiment designed to test Shannon's and Berrigan's claims that vegetative screening would not be successful on our parcel. I knew of course that it might take as long as fifteen years or so to complete the experiment and to have the satisfaction of saying, "I told you so!" But what I was going to do would be therapeutic. I bought a shovel in Fort Bragg and drove to Albion, where we owned a parcel covered with shore pines. I dug up a dozen or so little saplings one to two feet tall and threw them into the trunk. Arriving at our Elk parcel, I planted them in a staggered row perpendicular to the line of sight between our proposed house location and Cuffey's Cove. The soil appeared bone dry, and there would be little rain for several more months, and I had no way to water the saplings. No matter, it was therapeutic! Today a number of those trees stand fifteen feet tall. Clearly, Shannon was either incompetent or had deliberately sought to mislead in his letters and hearing testimony.

Next I drove to Sacramento, where I had very fruitful discussions with Zumbrun and Lutterman. Inundated with ammunition we were supplying, they were making good progress translating our complaints into legalese. They explained to me in some detail how the case was likely to unfold.

When I returned home we continued a lively dialog with Zumbrun and Lutterman by FAX. Margie and I made suggested changes and additions, and Neal incorporated them in legal terms. By early March his "Writ of Administrative Mandate" was a masterpiece. Don't be put off by that legal jargon. That's simply a history of our interactions with the County, a recital of the facts in the case, and our list of claimed violations of law and regulations by the County. In preceding chapters, you've already read most of what appeared in the writ. But there was one claim against the County, which we hadn't fully developed until participating in the preparation of the writ. In the writ that claim was boldly stated as follows:

> "Petitioners are informed and believe, and on that basis allege that the CPA and Planning and Building Services, in concert with the California Department of Parks and Recreation have denied petitioners their coastal development permit because the Department of Parks and Recreation intends to condemn petitioners' property at some unspecified point in the future through the use of their powers of eminent domain. Petitioners are aware that the Department of Parks and Recreation has attempted unsuccessfully in the past to condemn other property adjacent to Greenwood Creek State Park. The Department of Parks and Recreation, in an attempt to make condemnation at a later date easier and less costly to the state, has conspired with and aided Planning and Building Services to deny petitioners' application for a coastal development permit."

The writ continued by citing a section of the California Coastal Act, which specifically forbids such behavior. The first draft of the above claim was completed on 2-27-96. It had been developed with knowledge of

- o Erna Smith's letter,

- o Wishes expressed by Pjerrou and de Vall that State Parks would acquire our properties,

- o Supervisor Pinches' admonition to State Parks that if they didn't want a house on our parcel they should have acquired it years ago, and o   Information Dean Wisdom had recently provided describing how, about 18 years earlier, State Parks had sought to acquire a few small Elk parcels that were partially surrounded by park property.

That was all we had to back the above claim when our suit was filed with the court on 3-13-96. While it was enough to raise suspicions, it might not have been enough to make anything stick in court. What we needed was explicit evidence of State Parks interest in <u>our</u> parcels *per se*, and we didn't have it. Yet we just couldn't help feeling that we were being blind sided and that there had to be something behind all of the special attention we'd been getting, and so we kept digging.

Belatedly, I decided to follow up on some information Dean Wisdom had provided. Soon after the Supervisors denied our appeal, he had mailed me a copy of a letter he had written to Supervisor Peterson on 11-16-95. In it he asked why Peterson had not divulged the real reason he voted against our appeal. Puzzled by that cryptic comment, I telephoned Wisdom in late November of 1995 for an explanation. He told me that the State had tried to condemn Anna Daniels' parcels adjacent to the park in 1978, and that she had successfully sought intervention by then State Senator, Barry Keene. Wisdom said further that Daniels was told by the local park ranger, Kevin Joe, that, even if it takes a hundred years, State Parks will eventually get her property. That information provided encouragement for us to add the claim quoted above.

Nevertheless, four months went by before I followed up on that discussion with Wisdom. On 3-17-96, four days after our case was filed with the court, I telephoned Anna Daniels, former school teacher, mother of our ally, Don Daniels, and widow of a partner in the mill operation when lumbering was the lifeblood of Elk. She confirmed all that Wisdom had told me, and then, in an offhand way mentioned that, "State Parks must have spent a lot of money producing that elaborate plan for Greenwood State Beach." The next day it took me six telephone calls to State Parks in Sacramento and Mendocino to find someone who could provide us with a copy of the "General Plan for Greenwood State Beach." When we received it a few days later *it was a EUREKA moment, for it divulged that our two parcels, as well as our easement down to the beach across park property, had all been targeted by State Parks as "appropriate future additions!"* And the plan referred to an earlier "Preliminary General Plan for Greenwood Creek State Beach," which was described as listing additional properties of interest to State Parks. Well, our claim, which had been written before we knew anything about the State Park plan, was no longer mere suspicion. It now had fangs. Without doubt, our adversaries knew all along about State Parks' covetous plans, and that had undoubtedly helped fuel their opposition to our project from the very beginning. Suddenly it became crystal clear why we'd been receiving so much special attention.

On 3-28-96 the County of Mendocino was served with our suit's "Summons & Verified Petition for Writ of Administrative Mandate, Damages & Complaint for Declaratory Relief,

Monetary Compensation & Violation of Civil Rights." And it would only be a matter of time until State Parks was included in the suit. The County of Mendocino had thirty days to respond.

In the meantime we sought more information on State Parks' planning activities. In a 3-31-96 letter to State Parks' General Plan Project Manager, Robert Acrea, in Sacramento I cited freedom-of-information statutes as I requested a copy of the "Preliminary General Plan for Greenwood Creek State Beach" as well as the associated public notices and mailing lists. We received those materials on 4-22-96. In the Preliminary Plan our properties were listed as "Priority 1" for acquisition, *and* they were considered as "park resources," as if they were already park property. Other properties were also listed, but at lower priorities. Other local property owners had been aware of the park planning, had objected, and had succeeded in having their properties delisted in the final plan.

Our names were not to be found on any of the mailing lists for the park planning meetings. Why had we been kept in the dark? By law we should have received public notices of the planning meetings, which took place from 1990 until adoption of the plan on 11-4-94. Moreover, when protesting our project, State Parks had violated proper procedures by not disclosing their conflict of interest. Most interestingly, a listing of individuals who were active in the park planning process reads like a "Who's Who" of the opponents of our permit application. That list included:

> Berrigan, Gary (Supervising Planner, Mendocino County)
> Berry, Bill (District Superintendent, California Department of Parks
> and Recreation)
> Falleri, Alan (Chief Planner, Mendocino County)
> Hall, Raymond (Director, Planning and Building Services,
> Mendocino County)
> De Vall, Norman (Supervisor, Mendocino County)
> Joe, Kevin (Park Ranger, California Department of Parks and
> Recreation)
> MacMillan, Benton (Owner, Elk Store)
> Peterson, Charles (later to replace de Vall as Supervisor,
> Mendocino County)
> Pjerrou, Mary (Elk resident)

Among others who were informed of the park plan and opposed our permit application were eight individuals including:

> Bloomquist, Ron (Elk resident)
> Henry, Liz (Supervisor, Mendocino County)

It thus appears that our major detractors knew of, and surely approved of, the State Parks' expansionist plans. Moreover, they conveniently chose not to divulge those plans to us. It was now clear why they didn't subscribe to our vision of one house on two parcels. They had their own vision and hidden agenda, specifically, no house at all on two parcels! They had almost succeeded in keeping us in the dark.

Particularly disturbing is the fact that both Charles Peterson and Liz Henry are among those listed above, for this suggests that both of them, as Mendocino County Supervisors, had cast their votes against our Coastal Development Permit with full knowledge of State Parks' covetous designs on our properties!

It's pertinent that, if funds have already been appropriated for acquisition of a parcel by eminent domain, then, on that basis alone, a county can legally deny a Coastal Development Permit for that parcel. However, in the absence of appropriated funds, expressed plans for acquisition by a public agency are insufficient grounds to trigger such denial. In our case, funds had not been appropriated. Nonetheless, in their plan, State Parks officials openly identified our parcels and easement as "appropriate future additions." And they were careful to protect themselves by inserting in the plan the following disclaimer.

> "…comments regarding appropriate land additions are intended for long-range planning purposes only. This discussion does not represent a commitment to acquire such lands. Acquisition is dependent on many factors, including the willingness of an owner to sell and the availability of funds."

That disclaimer also tells County officials who are sympathetic to State Parks that they cannot deny the application by playing the "It's-going-to-be-condemned" card. But it's also an invitation to those sympathetic County officials to utilize overly-harsh interpretations of land-use regulations to keep the land undeveloped for easier acquisition by State Parks at a later date.

It was of course totally inappropriate for State Parks to write letters of opposition to our project without disclosing their interest in acquiring our property. It was also totally inappropriate for the County to quote from one of those letters in a Staff Report without revealing State Parks' conflict of interest. And it's reasonable to question to what extent the votes against our project by Supervisors Peterson and Henry were influenced by their knowledge of State Parks' interest in our parcels and easement. The actions of both State Parks and the County appeared designed to devalue our property to render it easy pickings for subsequent acquisition by State Parks.

Henceforth the specter of eminent domain would hang like a dark cloud over our plans, for at any time State Parks was at liberty to allocate funds to acquire our parcel. But we were committed to our project, and we didn't wish to make it easy for State Parks to intervene. And so we forged ahead, gambling that State Parks (caught with their hands in the cookie jar) would be unlikely to initiate eminent domain proceedings because of the probable adverse impact that would have on their position in our legal proceedings against them. Nevertheless, the possibility of eminent domain would continue to haunt us until such time as construction of our house was well underway.

While we had been gathering evidence against State Parks the deadline for the County to respond to our legal complaint had passed, and they were granted a twenty-day extension, which they also failed to meet. Lutterman telephoned to let us know that and remarked that we could declare victory, but a judge would undoubtedly let the County off the hook. Frank Zotter, Chief Deputy Counsel for the County, finally responded on 5-23-95. As expected, his response attacked all five of our causes of action. It took nearly six pages of legalese to say in effect that because we had the right to reapply on the County's terms we had not exhausted our procedural rights, and so we had no case, a totally ridiculous argument. He argued that our right to build was not disputed, "...the only disagreement is where and how large." (Actually, the supervisors had not disputed "how large," only "where.") Well, the wrangling would go on and on, and at the same time we would be demanding document production from the County and State Parks. And we would depose County and State Parks personnel.

The depositions would involve a new member of our legal team, Jeff Speich, an experienced litigator who was soon to join Zumbrun and Findley. Jeff earned a bachelor's degree in mathematics from the University of California at Berkeley in 1967 and then spent several years in the Air Force as a fighter pilot. In 1975 he received a J.D. degree from the University of California, Boalt School of Law and subsequently practiced and taught law. With a brilliant-mathematician-fighter-pilot-lawyer added to our side, we were prepared for combat!

In the meantime there was a lot of activity in Planning and Building Services that was pertinent to our case. On 12-13-95 Rita Duarte had submitted a Coastal Development Permit Application for an expansion of her house. The plans for the expansion had been developed by Mike and Bob. The project description read:

> "Add 2,169 square feet to a 2,078 square foot single story residence consisting of expansion of the first floor of residence and garage. The addition to the residence to include a 27' 9" high second story addition and a 23' 6" second story addition of the guest room over the garage, widen garage approach, add guest parking."

The house to be expanded was located on a one-acre, bluff-top parcel adjacent to Jug Handle State Reserve in an area designated as highly scenic. Visitors to the park would be able to view the front of the house from a distance of 103 feet. Visitors to Pine Beach, which lies below the bluff on which the house is situated, would view the back of the house from a distance of about 150 feet.

135

The Coastal Permit Administrator hearing for the Duarte project was to be held on 2-22-96, a mere two months after the application had been filed. Having suffered through our experience with us, Mike and Bob had conducted extensive research on the surrounding neighborhood for use in defense of Duarte's application. Duarte, herself, had engaged local attorney Jared Carter to bolster her case. Mike arrived at the hearing prepared to do battle and expecting to encounter fierce opposition from Berrigan. But, Berrigan wasn't there! Instead, Ray Hall, Berrigan's boss, traveled the sixty miles over the mountains from Ukiah to officiate as Coastal Permit Administrator. During the lunch break he visited the site, and when he returned to the hearing room he promptly approved the project. Suddenly it was a different planet!

Records we subsequently obtained revealed that Coastal Commission Planner Jo Ginsberg had written to County Planners expressing concern over the visual impact of the Duarte project. According to her,

> "It appears that the second-story additions would have a significant impact on public views from Mitchell Creek and from the beach [Pine Beach]. As such, Commission Staff is concerned that the proposed additions are not consistent with LUP Policy 3.5-3 or Zoning Code 20.504.015."

With the help of Figure 5, you can draw your own conclusion regarding Ginsberg's concern. That photograph was taken from Pine Beach after construction of the Duarte house was complete. At 28 feet in height the house is 10 feet taller than the County 18-foot limit and about 42% as tall as the bluff itself. County planners justified approval of that height because of a tall cupola on an adjacent house.

I've been unable to find any evidence that State Parks expressed any position whatsoever on the Duarte project, despite its proximity to, and high visibility from, Jug Handle State Reserve. (See Figure 6 for a photo of the completed house taken from the State Park boundary.) However, Duarte was not home free. It seems her neighbors had been having dry-well problems. One of them, Marion Timson, appealed the project to the board of Supervisors. On 3-25-96 Timson's appeal was denied by the Supervisors, 4 to 1, with Peterson dissenting. Duarte had triumphed in record time. She was free to expand her home, even though it would be ten feet taller than our proposed house, was allowed a three-car garage (which we were denied), would block ocean views, and would totally dominate views from the State Park and from Pine Beach. True, Duarte hadn't encountered the kind of fierce local opposition that we had, but there could be no doubt that we had not been accorded "equal protection of the law."

Yes, that phrase was included in our complaint against the County, and the Duarte case added still more fangs to it. It was most puzzling. Why had the County taken a course, which would be so obviously self-defeating for them in our impending lawsuit?

OUR LAWSUIT AND A REVELATION

And why didn't Berrigan officiate at the hearing? We would soon have an answer to that. On 3-4-96 we learned that Bob had telephoned Supervisor Henry to express his view that in light of the approval of the Duarte project, ours most certainly should also have been approved. The conversation was such that Bob concluded that Berrigan had been stripped of his Coastal Permit Administrator authority. That was both puzzling and not surprising. Puzzling because it could be interpreted as an outright admission by the County that he had handled our case improperly. That would place the County at a disadvantage in our lawsuit. But the County's move was not surprising, because they could ill afford that loose cannon on their deck. Indeed there'd been ample evidence that Berrigan's poor performance on our case was not an isolated instance. While we were relieved by the news, we couldn't be jubilant. After all, a formidable wall still stood between us and a Coastal Development Permit. To us, Berrigan had appeared to be guided purely by instinct. He clearly didn't want houses to be built in the coastal zone, and he invented his own set of laws, regulations, and word definitions to conform to his inclinations. But for now it appeared that (like Humpty-Dumpty) Berrigan no longer sat atop a wall (in this instance, the one between us and a development permit).

Still another Leventhal-Schlosser-designed house was proposed in a Coastal Development Permit application submitted on 1-30-96 by Bill and Sandra MacIver. The County's public notice for its 5-23-96 hearing by the Coastal Permit Administrator described the project, as follows:

> "Construct a 4,692 square foot single family dwelling with an attached 746 square foot garage, deck, patio, two accessory buildings (generator building and water storage building) of approximately 190 square feet each, driveway expansion, septic system and well."

The location was to be a five-acre, oceanfront parcel in the exclusive, Chapman Point development, a highly-scenic area across the bay from the village of Mendocino, which is designated a "Special Community" in the Local Coastal Plan. To the south, the parcel was bounded by Van Damme State Park. It was in fact the site for which the enormous Kenneth and Linda Rawlings project had earlier been proposed. The MacIver house would be highly visible from the State Park at a distance of only 64 feet. Moreover, it would obstruct public views to the ocean and would be partially visible from Mendocino across the bay. It was situated atop a knoll, the most prominent site on the parcel, even though it could have been moved back another 140 feet where it would be much better screened from public view by existing tall trees. How could this house possibly be approved after ours had been denied? The usual suspects, Joan Curry, Kathleen Cameron, Roanne Withers, and Ron Guenther (on behalf of the Sierra club), wrote letters opposing the project, but there were five letters of support as well. The

Coastal Commission did not respond directly to the County's referral for comments, but in 4-16-96 letters to Hall and to Falleri, the MacIvers claimed,

> "We have talked to Coastal Commission Planner, Jo Ginsberg, who has reviewed the application. Ms. Ginsberg stated that she found no problems with our plans and would not be filing a letter on our project."

Can you imagine such hearsay evidence being acceptable in our case?

State Parks did weigh in on the MacIver project and chose not to stand in the way. Bill Berry's 4-16-96 letter to the County Planners was signed by Berry himself, not on his behalf by Shannon. It included the following excerpts:

> "We suggested that the MacIver's help us with the planting of well planned natural screens on State Park Property directly to the south and east of the construction site. By creating a native screen with local trees, we can mitigate some of the visual impact of the residence and create a natural boundary, which will benefit both property owners. The lighting at the residence as shown Is not a concern."

> "The MacIver's plan on using native vegetation in their landscaping and are willing to allow our planners to review the types of plants to be placed on the site. This will reduce the possibility of any exotics escaping from the adjacent property onto the park property."

> "Finally the owners showed the same concern for the coastal bluffs that we have and are willing to take steps to prevent additional erosion to those sensitive bluff sites during and after construction. We will be happy to work with them throughout the process to ensure protection of the bluffs."

What could possibly have caused this remarkable transformation in the State Parks establishment? Is there any way they could have been more accommodating? Timing is everything. Note that Berry's letter followed by two weeks the serving of our lawsuit against the County (with its bold accusation against State Parks) and our freedom-of-information request to State Parks regarding the "Greenwood State Beach General Plan." Suddenly, both the County and State Parks were being very helpful to retirees wishing to build on the coast. However, it was of no benefit whatsoever to us.

Our Lawsuit And A Revelation

But to finish the MacIver story, the Staff Report had argued for a 25% reduction in the size of the MacIver project. At the hearing on 5-23-96 Bill MacIver responded to that recommendation with:

> "Considering the size of our parcel, five acres, and the cost of the land [uh oh!], we submit that the proposed size of the home is modest and scrupulously in keeping with the intent and spirit of the Coastal element. In fact the (Local Coastal Plan) allows a 10 percent buildout on our site which would allow construction of 22,000 square feet. Our residence covers one-fifth of the permissible buildout."

We know that argument wouldn't cut any ice with Berrigan, but his boss, Ray Hall, was now making the coastal-zone decisions, and, despite the project's very high visibility from the State Park and the fact that it would obscure public views to the ocean, he approved the entire 5,818 square feet at the County hearing. (See Figure 7 for an after-construction photo taken from the State Park boundary.) Very surprisingly, the "usual suspects" did not appeal it to the Coastal Commission. (That would have been free. The County Supervisors are the ones who charge a fee to hear an appeal.)

Speaking of the supervisors, beginning in 1996 our most ardent and articulate opponent on the board, Charles Peterson, had become Chairman of the Board of Supervisors. And he was making news. A 1-18-96 article in *The Mendocino Beacon* and another in *The Santa Rosa Press Democrat* on 1-21-96 featured Peterson, and he wrote a rejoinder in the "Community Forum" of *The Mendocino Beacon* on 1-25-96. An extreme liberal and staunch environmentalist, Peterson suffers from multiple muscular-skeletal birth defects. His position as Fifth District Supervisor was his first salaried employment as an adult. Then 48, he had been able to live on Social Security Disability Insurance during his adult life. Before his election he was a tireless advocate for political, environmental, and community causes. He viewed that as his way of giving back to the society that supported him. He viewed his board service in the same light. In order to perform his duties as Supervisor, Peterson required additional assistance with dressing, cooking, bathing, and page flipping, and he estimated that, during his first year in office, he had paid personal aides approximately $25,000 from his board salary of $31,000. His critics argued that, while earning a salary from the County, he should no longer be drawing social security payments, but that was a matter for the Social Security Agency to determine. Despite his physical disabilities Peterson managed to drive a car without any special equipment. This would lead to additional controversy. When his old car faltered he sent 500 letters to constituents asking for contributions of $5 to $250. He soon received $3,000 and was able to lease a new Toyota Tercel. The *Press Democrat* article on Peterson led off with a picture of a gleeful Peterson behind the steering wheel.

Having tangled with fishing, timber, environmental, agricultural, and property rights issues, Peterson announced that he would not run for another term, when his term expired at the end of 1998. An article written by Neil Boyle in *The Mendocino Beacon* on 5-22-97 reported his decision. Peterson was quoted as saying, "When I leave this job, I won't have a car...I'll leave with nothing except my life, the woman I love and my friends, which is more than enough." (Could that ordering reflect his priorities?) The article also stated, " A recent traumatic experience in Trinity County when he and his partner were held hostage and threatened by an ex-felon is not the basis for his decision." Rather, recent attacks from the environmental community made his decision easier to make. How he might have become cross-threaded with them I can't imagine.

Now, why have I paid so much attention to Chairman Peterson? Well, if our case were ever somehow to go back to the Supervisors again, we would have to face him yet another time. For Peterson, government had always been the solution, both personally and politically. And for him that apparently justified his arrogant attacks on private property rights. That same arrogance was apparent in his comment (quoted by Chris Calder in the 1-18-96 issue of *The Mendocino Beacon*) with regard to a ballot initiative to raise the sales tax by ¼ cent. Peterson remarked, "A new tax is good news!...I wish we'd asked for ½ cent." He clearly had no appreciation for the people who were paying the taxes to support the government that was supporting him. On the other hand, for us, the government was the problem, not the solution. We wanted nothing more to do with Peterson, and that influenced our stance on any settlement negotiations which might ensue.

CHAPTER 12

DOCUMENT PRODUCTION AND MORE REVELATIONS

Against that backdrop our lawsuit ground slowly onward. Fortunately, we were legally entitled to see all County and State Park records bearing on our case, and we were entitled to depose, or question under oath, anyone associated with it. We worked closely with Neal and Jeff to be as inclusive as possible as far as record requests were concerned. We named people to be deposed and provided long lists of questions that would be appropriate for each of them. On 6-23-96 I began my tenth transcontinental round-trip journey in quest of our permit, this time to participate in designating which of the documents produced by the County should be duplicated for use as evidence in our lawsuit.

At 9:30 AM on 6-25-96 Jeff Speich, Neal Lutterman, and I arrived for the County document production at a legal facility at 100 Manzanita Street in Fort Bragg. The building was locked. Operators of the facility had forgotten all about our appointment. Neal made a few telephone calls, and someone showed up at around 10:00 AM to let us in. Chief Deputy County Counsel Frank Zotter was even more tardy. He finally arrived at 12:30 PM, and he was not alone. With him were his twin daughters, age three-and-a-half, both of whom had become carsick from the infinity of curves and undulations of Route 20 as it snaked up and over the mountains between Ukiah and the coast. Although I had genuine sympathy for the little tykes, it pleased me to contemplate Zotter's predicament driving that twisting route with those little girls throwing up all over the inside of his car. Had he exploited his innocent young daughters to try to out-game us? Was this very unprofessional performance designed to telegraph how trivial and hopeless he thought our case was? Or was it just normal in Mendocino County to bring children to such legal proceedings, just as it's normal in Mendocino County to have dogs in the backs of pick-up trucks, or was it merely a case of Zotter's wife insisting on a little free time away from the kiddies? I don't know. Ask Frank.

In any event, the twins soon recovered, and amidst sounds of merriment from their frolicking in the next room, we attacked the County documents. We selected 2459 pages to be duplicated. A representative of Compex Litigation Services very efficiently copied each page. I was displeased by how hit or miss our search proved to be. There was just too much material to scan in too short a time. Also, we were trusting the County to come clean with all of the pertinent material, and, based on earlier experience, I had little trust in County officials. That proved to be justified, inasmuch as many documents we already possessed were not found in the County document production.

What of significance did we learn from the County document production that had bearing on our case? Well, a lot that indicated that County officials and the Elk anti faction were all well aware of State Parks' interest in acquiring our property (and were almost certainly complicit). Moreover, in passing judgment on our permit application, the County and State Parks officials involved had major conflicts of interest. In Washington, DC politics, decision-makers are usually more cautious about conflicts of interest. They're aware that inquisitive, vigilant, and brutal representatives of the media are scrutinizing their every move, and so decision-makers know that they're likely to get into trouble if they fail to disqualify themselves from rendering decisions in such instances. But this was Mendocino County. There's less press scrutiny here. Not only are the media less likely to discover a hand in the cookie jar, but they're less likely to consider it particularly improper if it is discovered.

During the planning process for the "Greenwood State Beach General Plan" from 1990 through 1994 there was copious correspondence among our Elk and Mendocino County opponents on the one hand, and State Parks officials on the other. Among the latter were Robert Acrea (Mendocino Coast General Plan Project Manager), James Doyle (Supervisor, Environmental Review Section), and Robert Ueltzen (Northern Service Center) all from Sacramento. They held frequent park-planning meetings, and a number of Elk residents even traveled to attend meetings of the California State Park and Recreation Commission (the statewide oversight body for State Parks) to make their views known. At those meetings Norman de Vall (then County Supervisor), Charles Peterson (then private citizen), and Mary Pjerrou spoke at length on their views regarding the plan for Greenwood State Beach. As already noted, other Elk residents had been hostile toward State Parks' having designated their properties as "appropriate future additions" in the preliminary plan. Aside from the issue of expansion, State Parks' planning had called for considerable development of the park so as to accommodate visitors more conveniently. That included spruced-up parking areas, picnic areas, and trails with interpretive signs. The locals wanted none of that. They simply wanted the park to evolve in its natural state. And they really didn't like the idea of more park visitors, which they thought would follow if the park were more developed. But they could agree with State Parks on the need for adequate restrooms. It seems that tourists seeking to use restrooms in local businesses had been a continuing annoyance.

Among other gems in the County document production were a number of items having to do directly with Berrigan. In a 10-24-90 letter to Doyle, Berrigan pointed out that Mendocino County regulations would have to be taken into account in the park planning process for Mendocino Coast State Park System Units. He concluded the letter with, "I am the contact person for this project and any questions may be directed to me." This left no doubt of Berrigan's significant involvement with park planning.

Even though Ruffing had been the first Project Coordinator for our permit application the document production revealed that Berrigan was fully involved from the outset, and in ways that can only be judged as improper. A post-it note attached to the 7-21-94 receipt which Berrrigan executed for our payment of our application fee, bore the words "Refer to DPR," i.e., Department of Parks and Recreation. Under those words was the name "Bob Acrea" and the latter's Sacramento address. As a kind of afterthought in small letters on the right he wrote "Mendo Dist." and its address. It would appear that, on the very day the County received our permit application, Berrigan had scrutinized it, and his first thought was to notify Acrea, who was in charge of the Greenwood State Beach General Plan, that we intended to build on a parcel of prime interest to State Parks. That was further reinforced by information on the worksheet for the interested agency referral notice that Berrigan (not Ruffing, the Project Coordinator) filled out on 7-22-94, the day immediately after the day of our application for a Coastal Development Permit. The worksheet lists 35 agencies which may be selected, and then has several blank spaces where the names of other interested parties may be added. Berrigan added "Dept. of Parks & Rec." in both Mendocino and Sacramento, the latter obviously with Acrea in mind. Berrigan also added de Vall, which must have been what prompted Supervisor de Vall's (illegal by my standards) 4" x 6" note to Ruffing. On the second page of the worksheet Berrigan circled "Special Communities," an incorrect designation for Elk. In notes taken by Berrigan at the Supervisors' 11-13-95 hearing of our appeal he referred to Peterson and Henry as Charles and Liz, while referring to the other three Supervisors only by their last names. That might be interpreted as indicating that he had a more familiar relationship with Peterson and Henry. Other evidence suggests that as well.

Other revelations from the document production deserve mention. On 5-4-95 a referral for comments on our case was sent (whether by Stinson or Berrigan I was unable to determine) to supervisor Peterson along with a copy of our permit application, eight of our exhibits, and a copy of de Vall's 4" x 6" comments on our project. That may have violated the Brown Act, because the other four Supervisors were not similarly informed, and because, as indeed it turned out, Peterson would later sit in judgment of our case. We found no record of a response from Peterson. Perhaps, unlike de Vall, he was shrewd enough not to submit written comments to County planners, thereby avoiding jeopardizing his eligibility to vote against our proposed project at our appeal hearing. On 5-8-95 a referral for comments was also sent to Shannon. Recall that State Parks had not met the 15-day deadline nearly a year earlier. Shannon's belated (year later) 6-6-95 response on behalf of Berry was undoubtedly prompted by this referral and probably as well by communications he received from a County Planner (Stinson or Berrigan) regarding the contents of the soon-to-be-publicly-released Staff Report. In actual fact, the County Planner fed Shannon critical comments to put into his letter and then quoted Shannon's letter in the Staff Report!

To our surprise, one of our own letters (not addressed to the County) turned up in the County's document production. On 8-5-95, prior to our second hearing before Berrigan, we had sent a letter to all residents of Elk, friend and foe alike, explaining our plans. After all, we couldn't trust the public notices from the County to portray our project faithfully. One of the letters found its way to Shannon, whose office and home were far, far away in Duncans Mills and Santa Rosa respectively. Possibly he obtained it from Park Ranger Kevin Joe, a resident of Elk. However the interesting point was that, on 8-15-95, Shannon had faxed a copy of our letter to Tony Navarro, at that time the only remaining County Planner reporting to Berrigan in Fort Bragg. It would thus appear that the State Parks-County intelligence network was operating very efficiently.

The next phases of our lawsuit took place in early July. Both Margie and I boarded a jet on 7-6-95 (my eleventh transcontinental round-trip journey in our quest for a permit) to participate in the document production by State Parks and to attend depositions of Berrigan, Berry, Shannon, and Hall, all of which were to take place in the same Manzanita Street legal facility in Fort Bragg. However, before proceeding to Fort Bragg, we stopped in Sacramento for preparatory conferences with our attorneys.

Unfortunately, the timing of the State Parks' document production was very poor. It took place early on 7-10-96, the day following the end of Berrigan's deposition and immediately prior to the depositions of Berry and Shannon. As a consequence there was no opportunity to question Berrigan about items uncovered in the State Parks' documents that related to him, and there was little time to review the State Parks' documents prior to the depositions of Berry and Shannon. Nevertheless, I was impressed by how skillfully Jeff and Neal integrated information from the newly obtained State Parks' documents into their questioning of Berry and Shannon.

The State Parks' document production exploited a technique we had earlier seen depicted in a David E. Kelley television show about a fictional legal battle. In that instance the document production by the accused consisted of a mountain of irrelevant material in which pertinent documents were "concealed," making it less likely that the incriminating ones would be discovered. Similarly, State Parks presented us with about six cubic feet of documents, most of which had no bearing at all on our case. We had no choice but to sort through all of them to try to uncover pertinent ones. Fortunately there were four of us, and, although we may have missed some significant evidence, we managed to uncover numerous documents which ultimately placed both State Parks and the County at considerable disadvantage.

At the very beginning of the search, Margie picked up a letter from atop one of the stacks of documents and began to read it. A State Parks attorney had written to a higher-level park official pointing out that, based on evidence in our lawsuit against the County, State Parks was very vulnerable and highly likely to become a defendant along with Mendocino County. Before Margie could read further, a State Parks attorney (most likely Peggy Dalton) suddenly snatched the letter and snapped, "You're not supposed to have that!" Apparently, she had absent-mindedly left the letter atop a stack of the subpoenaed documents and then turned her back, not fully aware that the search had begun. That incident brought some satisfaction to us, for it meant that upper levels of the

State Parks hierarchy were being informed of the Berry and Shannon transgressions, which could cause considerable embarrassment to State Parks.

As we probed the mountain of documents, we came across a good number that were pertinent, and many that were highly significant. One State Parks study dated 6-15-78 was a "Negative Declaration" (a claim of no harmful environmental impact declaration) for "Land Acquisition - Greenwood Creek Project." At that early date State Parks' sights were set on the land currently comprising Greenwood State Park plus the land now comprising our two parcels plus the parcel to the south of ours where Elizabeth Crahan now resides, a total area of approximately 76 acres. That was clearly indicated on a map outlining all parcels totaling 76 acres. The acquisition that actually took place in 1978 did not include what are now the Crahan parcel and our parcels. The records accessible to us provide no information on why the purchase by the California Department of General Services was ultimately limited to the approximately 47 acres that now comprise Greenwood State Beach.

Nevertheless, State Parks' continued interest in the three additional parcels remained, and this was evident in a State Parks report entitled "Greenwood Creek Project" published in 1980. In that report it referred in part to,

> "Size: ...Proposed acquisition involves 20 more acres along the coast southward."

> "Ocean frontage: This State-acquired land encompasses 3,000 feet of ocean beach and cove. Proposed acquisition would add about another 3,000 to 4,000 feet of beach and bluff shoreline."

> "Vista Points: -- There are two vista points: one is on State Land south and west of Elk overlooking Wharf and Casket Rock in Greenwood Cove; the other lies at the south end of Greenwood Cove outside of the State boundary, but within the acquisition plan. Both sites will have to be evaluated in terms of pedestrian or vehicle access."

The report included in "Proposed Developments,"

> "Day-use parking: 50 vehicle spaces on the southern bluff at the potential vista point."

Those quotes from the report indicate continued planning for the entire 72 acres. To obviate any doubt, the included map showed the entire 72 acres shaded. The issue of development of overnight facilities remained to be determined. That and the 50-car vista point on our parcel would no doubt have encountered extreme opposition from Elk residents!

The other State Parks documents of even greater interest were 43 pages of internal email communications. That means of communication was new to State Parks, and they were enjoying the ease with which they could now communicate internally with their new toy. I quote some of the email below, and, as you read them, it will be obvious to you that it must never have occurred to them that their email might be vulnerable to subpoena in a lawsuit.

6-23-95 Bill Berry to Shannon
Subject: Re: communications
"OK Dude, We're on line and ready to rock. Got all your stuff from
Berlincourt. Wow. Did he have a lot of not much to say. Sorry
you had to endure his wrath. Give me an update as to how you
felt the meeting went."

That was written the day after our first hearing before Berrrigan. It appears that Shannon had obtained, from Berrigan, and passed to Berry a copy of the text of the remarks I made at that hearing. Shannon' email response follows.

6-26-95 Gary Shannon to Bill Berry
Subject: Coastal Permit Hearing - Berlincourt
"…The county did not approve the permit and sent it back to
the applicant (owner) to have them revise it. The County wants
Berlincourt to modify their site plan so there is minimal visual
impact from Elk and the State Park. The architect has been
directed to work with us on taking measures to reduce visual
impact."

6-29-95 Bill Berry to Gary Shannon
Subject: Coastal Permit Hearing - Berlincourt
"Is there anything I need to do with respect to this permit? If so,
send me a note. What was Berlincourt's reaction to the process?
Was he mad? Will we be able to work out a compromise this
is our best interest? Just some questions which come to mind.
Thanks."

6-29-95 Gary Shannon to Bill Berry
Subject: [none]

"...Berlincourt was upset. He thought everyone was out to get him, and I was a California conspiracy. We don't need to do anything. We will be asked to review the Berlincourt's revised plans before another scheduled hearing..."

7-30-95 Gary Shannon to Bill Berry
Subject Re: A variety of things
"I met with the architect and the landscape architect to review proposed screening plans. These folks will propose to plant shrubs and trees on the bluff between the proposed house and the park, as a means to reduce the visual impact. These guys think that this will do the trick. I don't think so. It will help the situation, but it's not black and white. They had the balls to tell me that there is enough existing shrubs on the site that will effectively screen the house. I almost puked, but held myself back. They want to go ahead with screening to keep everyone happy. I need to go back on the site and look around a little more. It was foggy when we were all out there and couldn't see too much."

"...He (Mr. B) wants to be able to see the ocean crashing on the rocks below from his living room...My feeling at this time is the house should be pushed back to a low point or back into the existing vegetation."

"...Let me know how it goes with Mr. B on tuesday morning..."

It must indeed have been very foggy, for Shannon had apparently been unable to discern the thriving twelve-foot-tall brush barrier already existing between the proposed building site and park viewpoints!

7-30-95 Bill Berry to Gary Shannon
Subject: (not available)
"...I agree with all your thoughts on this one. Ted is being very stubborn on this issue. We need to hold firm with the view that the view will be impacted. That is that!"

8-1-95 Bill Berry to State Parks subordinates Gary Shannon, Renee Pasquinelli, Karl Poppelreiter, and Kevin Joe (park ranger and resident of Elk).
Subject: Berlincourt.

"I met with Ted Berlincourt this morning at 0700 in Elk. Looked at the property on the point where he wants to build his house. Brought an assortment of photographs and renditions depicting the house built on the bluffs to the south of the beach. Ted's argument is that whether the house is overlooking the bluff or set back 45 feet, there is the same impact. After looking at the bluff from the kiln picnic area it was clear to me that no matter where on the bluff you place the house it will have the same general impact on the view. It really does not matter as viewed from parks where the darn thing is placed unless we could have it placed at an elevation below the horizon. With that in mind I suggest that we look into a strategy to have Mr. Berlincourt deed some of his land to us and guarantee that he will do no additional developments on his two properties to the south of Elk. We should try to get him to underground the telephone poles on his property. Ted is interested in working with us on this and I believe we may be able to get a better deal than having the house set back on the bluff 45 feet. What are your thoughts regarding such a strategy?"

Actually, the Staff Report envelope would place the house about 60 feet (rather than 45 feet) further east, but the important point in this email is that the State Parks' Mendocino District Superintendent was agreeing with us, not the County on the visual impact issue. At public hearings Shannon had been agreeing with the County.

8-?-95 Kevin Joe to Bill Berry.
Subject: Berlingcourt.
"I think moving the house will lessen the intrusion of the building even if it won't eliminate it from the horizon. Undergrounding [the telephone lines] would be great, but it would cost $200,000+ to get PacBell to do it from Berlingcourt's property, through the beach and tie in behind town. They would actually reroute it behind town on an existing easement. If Berlingcourt could get PacBell to re-route the entire cable it would be worth working with him. I'm not sure if he owns the bluff all the way to the beach, we don't actually own the south bluff and probably 50-100' of the beach, but its definitely a public easement and not critical for us to purchase."

In 1995 professional surveyors determined that the southern 350 feet of Greenwood Cove beach falls within the boundary of our eleven-acre parcel.

Subject: Re: Berlincourt Property

"I have seen copies of the Planning Dept. applications, Coastal Com. Applications, etc, in the Elk store, along with petitions, etc. I have also seen young "activist" looking individuals looking out at the property in question discussing it and pointing. They did not seem to want to talk to me about the situation, and just said they were looking at the beach. I think the general concensus is that the town of Elk does not want anything build on that bluff area."

"I don't know for sure that there will be that much opposition, but given the history of this county, and our history within the town of Elk, I can see us taking a black eye no matter what we do."

8-5-95 Bill Berry to Kevin Joe
Subject: Re: Berlincourt Property

"When we get a chance we should look at that property together and discuss strategy for the future. As a whole what actions can we take to reduce the effects of development to the south? Berlincourt has tremendous leverage because of his ownership of two developable lots. With that in mind we need to establish a plan to keep the development to a minimum and reduce the effect of poles, roads, etc. Food for thought."

8-18-95 Gary Shannon to Bill Berry.
Subject: Berlincourt upcoming permit hearing.

"Attached is a letter I believe we should be sending the County. It basically recommends that berlincourt move his house to the east. I know this is different from what you wanted to do. I think we need to have a different strategy."

"This project has a good chance of being denied, as proposed, at the county level. The County is not happy and has some problems about it, the community of elk doesn't like it, and we don't like it. If the project is not approved, Berlincourt is going to be mad as hell and worried. You can bet they will appeal to the state coastal commission. Berlincourt will see this as their last resort to get what he wants. If it goes to the state commission, chances are it will be approved no matter what the opposition. These guys have approved every appeal that I have seen go through in mendo county. The time to work with Berlincourt is during the time before any state coastal commission hearing. I think he will be frightened from the denial at the local level, and be more willing to deal with state parks. I don't believe [he] understands that the coastal commission approves everything."

"At this point we would do better to bond with the local community, score some points there, then deal with Berlincourt later. Your thoughts please. The permit hearing is schedule for Thursday 8-24. I want to send this letter to the county on Tuesday 8-22."

In this email Shannon was referring to his second State Parks letter to the County just prior to our second hearing before Berrigan. That letter repudiated the agreement Berry had reached with me. Because Berry later denied to me having seen that second letter until he later returned from vacation, it appears that Shannon had knowingly usurped Berry's authority. Or, had Berry been confused? I don't know. In any event, Shannon was wrong about the appeal process. We could only appeal to the County Supervisors. In the last paragraph of the email it appears that Shannon rather liked the idea of conspiring a bit with the Elk anti faction don't you think?

> 8-25-95 Gary Shannon to Bill Berry (and three others). Subject: Greenwood Creek S.P. - Berlincourt house proposal. "Yesterday, at the county coastal permit hearing, Mendocino [County] denied the coastal permit for this project. As you can imagine, the Berlincourts and their architects were very upset. On the other side, some of the residents of elk were very elated."
>
> "In about a month from now the county will issue its findings on the project. This is essentially the reasons why the permit was denied and what specific options would then be available to the Berlincourts. At that time, the Berlincourts can appeal the decision to the County Board of Supervisors, or to the State Coastal Commission. They will also be granted the opportunity to resubmit their application. If they choose the latter, they must comply to the conditions and criteria established in the findings report."
>
> "The hearing went very well for DPR. We made some comments against the proposal as written, but basically supported the county permit conditions. The county had many concerns that went beyond what ours were. Thanks for all your input and help."

I think Shannon was very pleased with the denial and his own performance. Note the royal "We" in "We made some comments…"

9-20-95 Bill Berry to Gary Shannon
Subject: Various Things
"I got a letter from Ted Berlincourt - "For my eyes only". He was pretty upset with the letter to Berrigan. We need to talk about our strategy for the upcoming appeal meeting with the supervisors."

I certainly was upset. That letter repudiated the agreement Berry had made with me at the park view point on 8-1-95.

9-22-95 Gary Shannon to Kevin Joe.
Subject: Berlincourt Hearing.
"I'm curious if there is any around town gossip following this hearing. If so what, and is there any change in how the locals see the state parks."

9-26-95 Kevin Joe to Gary Shannon
Subject: Re: Berlincourt Hearing
"The Berlincourt issue has brought out the two main factions in town: the relative new comers/ex-hippies vs. the old time families/ conservative retired folks. Ron Bloomquist wrote in his weekly column in the Mendocino Beacon about "retirement fortresses" being built and ruining the coast, which pissed off a lot of retired people in town. Also, some who had been against projects next to their own property, were suddenly for peoples being able to do what they want with their property. So, I would not say that our involvement has helped us change the way locals look at us. You should read the Beacon and Mendonesian and the ICO [*Independent Coast Observer*] regularly to keep up on what's happening, I don't read any of them regularly, but when I do it's rather interesting. Send me any articles of interest from any of those papers if you start subscribing to them."

11-8-95 Gary Shannon to Bill Berry
Subject: Berlincourt
"I found out today that the appeal hearing secheduled for Monday, Nov 13, in Ukiah is a public hearing. The Board of supervisors will basicly re-hear the berlincourt saga. Only this time your buddy Ted has armed himself with sharper pens

spewing all kinds of conspiracy theories between DPR and the County. Gary Berrigan says we need to be there. I will plan to go and restate our position. Only this time, I would like to oppose the project as proposed. And support the counties recommendation for relocation of the house. Any comments, thoughts or words of wisdom?"

To me, this is one of the more interesting emails. Shannon disparages our suspicion of a conspiracy between DPR and the County in one sentence, and in the very next states that Berrigan (who is supposed to be an unbiased County employee, who is not supposed to discuss the merits of the case with anyone outside a public meeting) "says we need to be there." Might that not be an unequivocal confirmation of my "conspiracy theory?" Then Shannon expresses his desire "this time" to oppose the project as proposed. I was rather under the impression that that was precisely what he had done in his two letters and at the two previous hearings before Berrigan! But, of course, the main purpose of Shannon's email was to get Berry's concurrence for him to side with Berrigan's mandate of a 300-foot increase in setback. He would have it in 43 minutes.

> 11-8-95 Bill Berry to Gary Shannon
> Subject: Re: Berlincourt
> "As stated by the county, the relocation area would be in the best interest of the visitors to the state park. In that area we could support the county's plan. Ted told me that the house was only going to be located 45 feet back from the location he originally showed me. The location the county picked would reduce the visual impact as viewed from the state park and as such would be in our interest. If we want to take that position, I support it."

Obviously Berry was totally confused by this time. He failed to understand that the setback I had discussed with him on 8-1-95 was what was demanded in the Staff Report by Stinson, and that, only much later, Berrigan had demanded the 300-foot increase in setback in his findings adopted on 9-28-95. With the final sentence of his email, Berry completed his transformation from high-level park manager to willing puppet atop his subordinate's knee!

All factors considered, the document production had been highly revealing, providing evidence that would be highly damaging to the County and to State Parks in our continuing litigation.

CHAPTER 13

DEPOSITIONS OF COUNTY AND PARKS OFFICIALS

As noted in the previous chapter, Margie and I had flown to California on 7-6-96 for the State Parks' document production and to witness the depositions of County and State Parks officials. The depositions were scheduled to commence on 7-8-96 at 9:30 AM, but, again, Chief Deputy County Counsel Frank Zotter was late. At least this time he was only half an hour late, and he didn't have his twin daughters in tow. (This was serious business, and he evidently didn't want any distractions.) The depositions began with Jeff Speich interrogating Gary Berrigan, Mendocino County Supervising Planner, age 46. Zotter sat protectively at Berrigan's side. Every word was recorded by licensed certified shorthand reporter, Loretta Simons, from the Ukiah firm, Adair, Potswald, & Hennessey. With time subtracted for meals and breaks, Berrigan's marathon deposition would last approximately ten hours over a two-day period. Jeff's performance was most impressive. How he had gained such extensive knowledge of, and insight into, our case in such a short time was truly remarkable. He seemed almost flawlessly to have absorbed everything Neal and we had thrown at him, and we kept throwing it through breakfasts, lunches, and dinners.

In the beginning of the interrogation Jeff asked Berrigan a series of "friendly" personal questions, evidently to try to put him at ease (and off guard). But Berrigan would have none of that. He was nervous. He couldn't remember the year of his college graduation, although that could have been a ruse concocted by Zotter to trick us into thinking he simply had a bad memory and so should be excused for the infinity of "I don't remembers" and "I don't knows" that were to follow. (Well, it wasn't really an infinity, just somewhere between 100 and 200 depending on how they're counted.) When asked where he lived and if he had children, Berrigan became very agitated. Zotter asked if he wished to go outside for a conference, and he did indeed. When he returned Jeff asked if he had some concern over revealing personal information, and Berrigan replied that he didn't know that his children had anything to do with this case. Then Berrigan volunteered that I had been seen photographing the building in which his office was located, and that during the County document production I had photographed his truck. (If the latter were true, it would have been purely by chance, for I had no idea what kind of vehicle he had. That day I had taken two pictures of the Manzanitas facility. In one of them there are three cars, and in the other there are three cars and two pickup trucks.) The day of our hearing before the Supervisors I had photographed the Supervisors' chambers, inside and out, as well. (I guess Berrigan was unaware of that.) Berrigan went on to express his concern for his own and his family's safety. Zotter cut him off with, "I think you've answered the question." Jeff then explained that the relevance of his question was,

> "...because you exercise considerable discretion with regards to my client's property rights, is to try to understand you perhaps a little better. What your perspectives are in life the common things of your life, having children, owning property, living on the coast. Things of those nature which I think are relevant to decision making. So my questions I meant innocently and I apologize if I caused you any concern. Let me know if I get into those areas and I'll try to be sensitive to yours."

It turned out that Berrigan did not own the house he lived in.

After the personal matters were covered, Jeff asked Berrigan questions about 57 exhibits, most of which had been obtained from the County document production. In each case Jeff asked if Berrigan remembered seeing it, or if he was familiar with it, or if he knew what it contained. Most often, Berrigan would answer either "I don't remember" or "I don't know." At one point Jeff asked if any rough drafts of the Staff Report had been made, and Berrigan responded, "I would assume some were made," at which point Zotter interrupted with, "He's only asking what you know." Berrigan then replied, "I don't know or I don't remember." It was evident that Zotter had prepared Berrigan intensively and had burned those two classic evasive answers into Berrigan's brain. Zotter's intent would have been for Berrigan to state either one answer or the other, but Berrigan had parroted them together. Berrigan often had to concede that even though he didn't remember seeing a particular document, it was nonetheless in the County file, and so he must have seen it, because he would normally have reviewed the file prior to a hearing. He didn't even remember seeing a number of documents that had notations on them in his own handwriting.

As noted earlier, prior to our second hearing, Berrigan had not reviewed the revised plans we had earlier submitted. He admitted that again, and he again argued that there had been no cover letter to advise him that revised plans were being submitted. Yet Mike's 8-8-95 cover letter addressed to Berrigan clearly listed among the enclosures "Two sets 24 x 36 revised drawings of the project consisting of pages A-1 (Site Plan), A-2 (Floor Plan), A-3 (Exterior Elevations), and L-1 (Landscape planting Plan from Satre Associates)." Also, in Berrigan's 9-20-95 memorandum to Hall, his boss, he had stated, "There was no clear indication from the agent that the project had been reduced in size." From all of that it would appear that Berrigan was either incompetent, or he consciously intended to mislead (or possibly both).

Berrigan's memory proved to be highly selective and mostly unreliable. He remembered a transmittal letter dated 10-11-75 from State Parks' (Sacramento) Robert Ueltzen that forwarded "Comments and Responses for the Greenwood Creek State Beach Preliminary Plan." But all he remembered was the incorrect date, which should have been 10-11-94 instead of 10-11-75. He didn't remember that the comments and responses prominently addressed "Appropriate Future Additions" in the plan. Nor did Berrigan remember having written the post-it note on the receipt for our permit application fee, the one on which he had written Acrea's name and address. Later, after Jeff had concluded his questioning of Berrigan, Zotter tried to repair the damage. He attempted to dissociate the post-it note from the receipt, but he only made it worse. He asked Berrigan, "Were these two documents prepared simultaneously?" Berrigan replied, "No, they weren't." So far they were on safe ground. Literally, "simultaneously" would only be possible if Berrigan could write with both his right hand and his left hand at the same time. Under further questioning from Zotter, Berrigan said that the post-it would have been prepared "sometime later" just before the referrals would have gone out. He further came clean and recalled that he, himself, not a Project Coordinator, had filled out the worksheet for the referral to interested agencies, and that he had listed both the Sacramento and Mendocino offices of State Parks. (Of course he hadn't told us anything we didn't already know.) What he did not divulge (and what we also knew) was that the referral worksheet was dated 7-22-94, just the day after the date of our application and the date of the receipt, and so it appeared that, when he received our application, he just couldn't wait to get State Parks working against us.

With further regard to memory, Berrigan claimed to remember only a portion of what he had written in his findings on our case. Asked if he could recall his first hearing on our case, he replied, "Yes, vaguely." Then, when asked if he recalled that Shannon was the only one to oppose our project at that hearing, Berrigan responded, "No, I don't recall who was at the hearing. Well I do recall that Mr. Leventhal was there...I don't recall what Mr. Leventhal said." Asked if he recalled that Shannon spoke in opposition to our project at the second (8-24-95) hearing, Berrigan replied, "No, I don't." Questioned about whether or not he had attended the coastal permit hearing on the MacIver project, Berrigan replied, "I really don't remember..." even though that hearing was held on 5-23-96 only 47 days prior to his deposition.

The foregoing are but snippets from a mountain of "I don't knows" and I don't remembers," but they illustrate the problem. Was Berrigan's memory really that faulty; was he just being evasive; was he incompetent; or was he an undecipherable admixture of all of the above?

Jeff's interrogation of Berrigan followed a number of other directions. One had to do with the relationship between the Coastal Permit Administrator and the Project Coordinator. We had earlier been critical of that relationship. There had been no proper separation of powers. In Mendocino County the former supervised the latter. (Would you approve if the district attorney who is prosecuting your case were supervised by the judge who would be ruling on it?) Berrigan himself confirmed the necessity for an at-a-distance relationship with the Project Coordinator. Berrigan claimed he never gave written instructions to Ruffing or Stinson. He noted that,

> "You have to walk a fine line, because you want to make sure
> that the various issues have been addressed, but you also can't
> make changes that are modifications to the substance of their
> recommendations."

Asked specifically about discussions with Stinson regarding our case, Berrigan recalled that,

> "...at some point Miss Stinson came to me and said, 'I don't
> know what to do with this,' or something of that effect, and I
> said, 'I can't help you. You have to make a recommendation.'
> Because I, you know, could not go in and discuss with her any
> part of what she should do, but I do recall that she seemed
> somewhat perplexed or just unsure of herself in some way as
> to what her recommendation was going to be, and I told her I
> couldn't help her, that she was going to have to make her own
> recommendation."

At another point Berrigan stated that transmitting information on a case outside the department is, "...a responsibility of the Project Coordinator, because that's part of the referral."

Despite all of the above, Berrigan's fingerprints were all over aspects of our case that should have been handled by the Project Coordinator. He executed our application fee receipt, filled out the referral worksheet, followed up on an archaeological issue, communicated with Chief Planner Falleri on our case (and was the addressee of Falleri's memo that was highly critical of our project), followed up on a botanical survey issue, told Stinson from what locations photos should be taken for our photomontages, passed judgment to Stinson on our photomontages, and traveled to Elk to be certain notices had been posted. And there could have been a lot more we just hadn't been able to discover. Moreover, for approximately four months he served as both Project Coordinator and Coastal Permit Administrator for our project. Despite what Bob had heard in his telephone conversation with Supervisor Henry, Berrigan testified that he was still a Coastal Permit Administrator, and the reason he was not hearing cases was that he was all alone in the Fort Bragg Planning Office and so had to perform Project Coordinator tasks (as if he hadn't been performing both tasks simultaneously all along).

In another line of questioning, Jeff sought to explore Berrigan's relationship with State Parks. Recall that in a 10-24-90 letter to State Parks' James Doyle, Berrigan identified himself as the County "contact person" for matters having to do with the General Plan for Mendocino Coast State Park System units. Despite this, in his deposition Berrigan sought as best he could to distance himself from State Parks. After our accusation on this issue you can be certain that all four County and State Parks employees deposed by us had been well coached on this matter by their attorneys. And Berrigan's memory in this area was no better than in the areas discussed above. Yet he did admit to knowing that Acrea, "...was the manager for the General Plan for the Mendocino Coast." Berrigan also conceded that, at the time he wrote Acrea's name on the post-it note, he knew that Acrea might have an interest in our project. Berrigan also said that he had discussed the park planning activity with Falleri, but, because de Vall, then a County Supervisor, was active in the park planning, they decided to keep a low profile. Berrigan allowed that he might have attended one of the planning meetings where parking-lot considerations were discussed. He also recalled having seen and "skimmed through" the "Greenwood Creek State Beach Preliminary General Plan." Asked if he had reviewed the section on "Appropriate Future Additions," Berrigan said, "I could have," and was interrupted by Zotter's, "'Do you recall?" That was of course code for Berrigan to respond with, "No I don't recall," which he did, right on cue. A little later Jeff asked if at any point he learned that our parcels had been designated as Priority 1 for "Appropriate Future Additions." Berrigan responded, "I don't recall it. No I don't." Jeff continued, "You never heard that from any source?" Berrigan conceded, "Well, I must have seen it in the plan. There's a lot of stuff in the plan." But under direct questioning Berrigan never admitted to discussing the "Appropriate Future Additions" with Berry or Shannon. (Too bad we didn't yet have the State Parks' email. Confronting Berrigan with that would have been devastating. Most damaging would have been Shannon's email to Berry just prior to our hearing before the supervisors. In it Shannon had remarked, "Gary Berrigan says we need to be there.")

Jeff also questioned Berrigan about his designation of the south and east siting mandate in his findings. His mastery of interrogation was beautifully demonstrated in this arena, so I'll quote at length.

Jeff: "Did you ever ask the Berlincourts or anybody else to do a photomontage of how their parcel would look if [the house were] constructed where you thought it more appropriate to construct?"

Berrigan: "No, I don't think I did."

(irrelevant interval omitted)

Jeff: "Did you make any conclusions as to whether or not their home would be subordinate to the character of the property [setting] if located where you suggested it be located?"

Berrigan: "I don't recall what those findings were. The decision that I made was to deny it and the basis for that denial is in the record and in those findings. I don't recall specifically what that was at that time."

Jeff: "Well, by denying the project, as opposed to approving it with conditions, the Berlincourts would have to go through the public review process all over again if they wished to construct any house on the portion of the property that you thought it should be located on. Correct?"

Berrigan: "Yes."

Jeff then had to repeat his next question three times in slightly different forms before Berrigan was willing to respond to it. The last version was as follows:

Jeff: "After you rejected their application, albeit without prejudice so that they could file within a year, and if they went forward and, in fact, had their home redesigned to make it significantly smaller and to place it where you had suggested in your findings, there still would be nothing to prevent an Elk resident or anybody else from objecting to the newly designed project on the basis that it impacted their view from Highway one, correct?"

Berrigan: "Correct."

The point of this of course was to demonstrate that Berrigan had pulled the site mandate out of his hat rather than having developed hard evidence in support of it.

Next to be deposed was William Bud Berry, Junior ("Billy," as he signed his emails, and "Smokey Bear" as Jeff derisively referred to him) age 44, State Parks Superintendent III, responsible for overall management of seventeen park units in Mendocino County. Berry was resplendent in his California Department of Parks and Recreation uniform, complete with ranger hat, holster, pistol, *bullets*, and handcuffs, all doubtless carefully designed to create an aura of authority and respectability. For his additional protection, State Parks attorney Peggy Dalton and Chief Deputy County Counsel Frank Zotter flanked him. Again Jeff was doing the interrogation, ably assisted by Neal, who fed him exhibits prompting various lines of questioning. The date was 7-10-96.

In contrast to Berrigan, Berry had been deposed previously, was very self-assured, and seemed genuinely to enjoy Jeff's inquiries into his personal life and employment history. Berry gave the appearance of having a good memory. There were relatively few "I don't knows" and "I don't remembers." Interestingly he revealed his home address on Headlands Drive in exclusive Little River. State Parks was providing him with an oceanfront house, with white-water views, adjacent to Van Damme State Park, and overlooking Little

River Cove. It seems that the good life he was enjoying was not much different from what he was intent on denying us.

Under intense questioning Berry denied ever having talked about the "Greenwood State Beach General Plan" with any County employee except Supervisor de Vall. In that instance he claimed that the discussion was only about the public hearing process for the planning, not the substance of the plan. Berry acknowledged that he had had correspondence with Berrigan on earlier matters, but not regarding the general plan. Berry also acknowledged that he had participated in the development of the general plan, but claimed to have attended only one public meeting. Regarding his involvement, Berry said that,

> "…as Superintendent, I met with general plan staff, provided advice, asked questions, gave input about our operation, worked with assigned staff to assist the general plan team with the completion of the plan, and reviewed the plan on occasion as portions of it became available for review, and made suggestions and comments."

From that it would certainly appear that he was being a very effective manager, keeping close tabs on the development of the plan for one of the park units under his jurisdiction. When asked by Jeff if he had received and reviewed a copy of the "Greenwood Creek State Beach Preliminary General Plan," he answered in the affirmative on both counts. But when asked if he had participated in the development of the portion entitled "Appropriate Future Additions," he responded, "No, I did not." Imagine that! A possible 50% enlargement of the park was of such little consequence to him that there was no need for him to have any involvement with it. Questioned further by Jeff, Berry acknowledged that he learned from Acrea that members of the Elk community were upset by the "Appropriate Future Acquisitions" section of the plan, and so, according to Berry, "…we had eliminated the whole idea of this acquisition process from our final general plan." Well, not by a long shot! Our two parcels and our easement were still designated as "appropriate future additions" in the final plan as Jeff showed him in a copy of the final plan.

Was this simply a matter of faulty memory on Berry's part or was it a clever evasion? I don't know. Obviously, if he claimed (erroneously) that the "Appropriate Future Additions" section had been entirely eliminated from the final report, then he could, as he indeed did under questioning, deny knowing that our parcels and easement were still being covetously regarded by State Parks. I believe that Dalton and Zotter had prepared him very well for this deposition. But Berry claimed that only after questioning by Jeff in this deposition did he come to associate our properties with what were designated as "Appropriate Future Additions" in the general plan. Nevertheless, earlier in the deposition he claimed to have been aware of that "…six to eight weeks ago."

According to Berry, he and his supervisor, Robert LaBelle, had collaborated in creating Shannon's staff position about a year earlier with the intent that Shannon would handle land-use matters, subject of course to their review. Nonetheless, as is apparent in State Parks' email, Berry was very much involved in our case. At his deposition he claimed that he even argued our side (was devil's advocate) in debates with Shannon to try to arrive at the best solution for State Parks. But at the time of his deposition Berry was still very much confused over the setback issue. He failed to understand that the increase in setback (whether 45-foot or 60-foot) that I had discussed with him on 8-1-95 was what was demanded in the 6-22-95 Staff Report by Stinson, and that Berrigan had demanded the far-greater 300-foot setback increase much later in his findings adopted on 9-28-95. Berry was under the impression that the County-required setback increase had been 300 feet all along and that I had deceived him with talk of the lesser setback increase at our 8-1-95 meeting. There can be no doubt that that played an important part in Berry's repudiation of the agreement we had reached. Shannon was surely aware of the facts, but evidently never tried to set Berry's mind straight on the setback issue, because it would have exonerated me of having deceived Berry. Interestingly, at the deposition Berry was still unable to understand why I'd been angry with him with regard to the second Shannon letter to the County, the one which abrogated the agreement Berry had reached with me. And he claimed to be "hurt" by the anger I'd expressed.

With regard to the two opposition letters to the County that Shannon wrote and signed over Berry's signature block, Berry insisted under questioning that they were merely suggestions and opinions, not opposition. Those letters speak for themselves, and clearly indicate opposition. Berry claimed not to have seen Shannon's first letter until he returned from travel. With regard to the second letter, Berry remarked under oath, "...I was aware of this letter and Gary and I talked about it." Also, under oath he said, "Gary sent me the letter. I didn't like the wording of it. We dickered around about the wording and sent the letter that we sent." Yet, in a 9-18-95 telephone conversation with me he said that he, "...didn't get a chance to review it" before he left on vacation, and further that it "...didn't come out the way I thought it should." In his deposition, Berry admitted telling me that "...Shannon was under pressure from the County." Then he attempted to repair this by describing it as merely pressure to meet a deadline, not pressure to oppose our project. However, in his telephone conversation with me, Berry had made the comment in defense of the position Shannon had taken on our project. There had been no reference to any deadline. Berry did tend sometimes to talk a little too much for his own good. Jeff asked Berry, "Did you ever advise Mr. Berlincourt that it was State Parks policy to oppose any development adjacent to State Parks?" Berry replied, "No I didn't." Both my memory and my telephone notes are in clear conflict with that denial, and, as I mentioned earlier, my son-in-law's letter asking the Director of State Parks for clarification of that matter provides further evidence. Berry's deposition had lasted about four hours.

Next to be deposed on 7-10-96 was Gary Patrick Shannon, State Parks Landscape Architect, a week shy of his 42nd birthday, and again Jeff conducted the interrogation.

I seem to recall that Shannon was in his State Parks' uniform at our hearings and also at his deposition, but, unlike Bill Berry, he was probably not armed (and he didn't look resplendent). Shannon seemed less guarded than either of the two preceding deposees, but he had some difficulty recalling when some events took place. He said he'd not been involved in the planning process for the "Greenwood State Beach General Plan," but he was certain he'd seen the final plan and was not certain whether of not he'd seen the preliminary plan.

With regard to Shannon's interactions with Stinson after receiving her 5-8-95 referral for comments (i.e., her follow-on referral after getting no response to her year-earlier 7-22-94 referral) Shannon remarked, "…I was in contact with Mary Stinson maybe two or three times before we sent the June 5th response." That response was the first of State Parks' opposition letters. This was a major admission, although I don't think Shannon realized the significance of it at the time. His first letter contained information he could have obtained only if he'd had access to Stinson's Staff Report prior to its public release, or if Stinson had earlier fed him some quotes to include in his letter. Either would be highly improper. Later in his testimony, and, prompted by State Parks' attorney Dalton, he denied that Stinson fed him phrases for the letter. Contradicting this was his statement earlier in his deposition that, "She [Stinson] or someone else from the county put together a report that was part of the referral." That would seem to confirm that he'd seen the Staff Report prior to its release.

In another contradiction, Berry had thought he'd seen Shannon's first (6-5-95) letter to the County only after the fact, but Shannon claimed, "I either read it to him over the phone or I emailed it to him," and, "he agreed." Before sending the first letter, Shannon had described our project to Berry as a "serious threat." State Parks in general and Shannon in particular, had the habit of referring to the view toward our parcel as a "*park resource*," as if State Parks owned the views over surrounding parcels and hence had jurisdiction over them.

Shannon acknowledged that, between writing his two letters, he had frequent discussions with Acrea regarding our project, but answered "no" when Jeff asked, "Did you ever learn from any source that Parks and Recreation had any interest in the future in acquiring the Berlincourt property?" Obviously he had to have learned that at some time, but he clearly didn't want to acknowledge having discussed it with Acrea or Berry. In Berry's deposition, Berry had told of receiving a telephone call from Acrea regarding our project after we had made our freedom-of-information request for the general plans and associated documentation.

For some reason, under questioning, Shannon expressed the belief that he had not spoken at our first hearing before Berrigan. In fact he'd been quite voluble, pretty much reiterating what was in his letter and then later making seven additional comments. I wouldn't characterize any of them as having been friendly. Apparently, Shannon's first acquaintance with Berrigan was at that hearing. Nevertheless, I recall being highly annoyed at break time as I watched the two Gary's walk out of that hearing room together talking animatedly like two comrades in arms. I knew then that our quest for a permit was going to be difficult to say the least.

Under questioning Shannon readily acknowledged having had several discussions with Stinson and Berrigan regarding his concerns about our project, but he denied discussing our case with any other County officials. Yet his first letter (on behalf of Berry) to the County was addressed to Hall, his second to Berrigan. Shannon testified that some time after our first hearing and before his 7-28-95 meeting on site with our architect and landscape architect, he had called the County to talk to Stinson and had been referred to Berrigan, because Stinson had left. Jeff asked, "He [Berrigan] was acting, you know, as project coordinator, at least for a time?" Shannon responded, "Uh-huh, or at least my contact for the County." There can be little doubt that for about three or four months Berrigan acted both as Project Coordinator and Coastal Permit Administrator, i.e., as both prosecuting attorney and judge.

Despite having expressed his "concerns" about our project to Berrigan and Stinson on many occasions, Shannon was reluctant to admit under oath that he opposed it. Jeff asked him, "…did you ever express to Mr. Berrigan whether you opposed or supported the Berlincourt project?" Shannon responded, "No. No." Without question, State Parks felt very vulnerable on that issue. Both Berry and Shannon had obviously been coached by their attorneys *never, never, never* to admit that they opposed our project. Were they to do that, it would give substance to our charge that, by opposing our project, they were trying to realize State Parks' "appropriate-future-additions" expansion. But both State Parks and the County were trapped by the former's email, which explicitly expressed opposition to our project. Moreover, the day after Berrigan's denial of our permit application, Shannon had reported by email that, "The hearing went very well for DPR." And just prior to the hearing of our appeal by the Board of Supervisors, another Shannon email stated, "Gary Berrigan says we need to be there." The State Parks' email also revealed scorn for me personally to such an extent that it would be impossible to conclude that they did not oppose what I had proposed.

Shannon's testimony with regard to landscape screening was most revealing. Regarding the existing brush height north of the proposed building site in the direction of the State Park, Jeff asked him, "Do you think it's as low as one or two feet?" Shannon replied, "Uh-huh. Yes. I do." It's hard to imagine that he had ever visited our parcel. Existing brush there rose at least to twelve feet, and today a number of the shore pines I planted there in 1995 are fifteen feet tall. Unfortunately his two letters and three testimonials at hearings had all expressed the view that landscape screening would not be successful. It was his word against that of our professional landscape architect, Sara Geddes (and, importantly, also against the evidence of tall stands of trees on similar nearby points). At the beginning of Shannon's deposition he had recited his experience as a landscape architect. At the time he wrote his opposition letters and testified at our hearings he'd had approximately one year's experience dealing with landscaping on the Mendocino-Sonoma coast, whereas Geddes had more than ten and could point to significant accomplishments at the exclusive Sea Ranch development, which extends for nearly nine miles along the adjoining Sonoma County Coast. Under oath Shannon acknowledged that he'd never seen Geddes's plantings at Sea Ranch. Could Shannon's scorn for me simply have overruled his professionalism?

Zotter next took over the questioning in an attempt at damage control. He tried to downplay Shannon's role in land acquisition. However, by coincidence, the State Parks' emails included information beyond that for our project alone, which indicated Shannon's heavy involvement in at least two ongoing land acquisitions. Shannon's deposition had lasted approximately three hours.

The next morning, 7-11-96, Raymond William Hall, Director, Mendocino County Department of Planning and Building Services arrived for his deposition. Hall was of average height and build, about 42 judging from the date he graduated from high school. His college majors were geography and planning. He spent a year and a half with an engineering firm before joining the County in 1978. By 1985 he had become Director of Planning and Building Services, suggesting that he was endowed with some political savvy. In Mendocino County land use was a political minefield, and, despite that, Hall had ascended to his lofty position in only seven years.

Surprisingly, Hall answered many of Jeff's questions at first as if he were on our side. Then, after interjections by Zotter, he "justified" his answers in ways which tended to support the County position. One might say he was adept at taking both sides, perhaps to distance himself from the inappropriate actions of his department. His answers to Jeff's questions about the relationship between Project Coordinator and Coastal Permit Administrator are illustrative. Jeff asked, "Have there ever been instances where the people acting as the Project Coordinator has also served as the CPA [Coastal Permit Administrator]?" That was of course one of our charges against Berrigan, and Hall had to have known of it, yet he answered, "Not that I'm aware of." Jeff continued, "Is there a reason for that?" After some clarification of the question, Hall replied, "I'd just say in discussions of potential conflict of interest and *ex parte* communications that would occur outside of a hearing." Jeff asked, if any County procedure had "...been established to maintain the integrity between the Coastal Permit Administrator who was going to act on a permit and the Project Coordinator?" Hall responded that there was no written procedure, but that "the general operating procedure is enough knowledge of the law that says you should, you know, separate those functions..." Under questioning about when a Coastal Permit Administrator would normally start "...assimilating information to get ready for a hearing..." Hall responded that if he were the Coastal Permit Administrator on the case, it would be, "...when I receive the Staff Report." Yet he maintained that there would be nothing wrong with a Coastal Permit Administrator consulting the project file prior to that. A little later Hall revealed that the "project planner" prepares the referral worksheet (green sheet) with its project description. That surely rang an alarm bell for Zotter, because, later in the day, at the very end of Hall's deposition, Zotter asked him, "You said normally a Project Coordinator prepares that [green sheet]..." Earlier, Hall had not used the word "normally," which Zotter was inserting here as an escape hatch. Zotter continued, "would there be anything inappropriate in your view as a Department head about say Gary Berrigan preparing a green sheet on a case where he will act as a Coastal Permit Administrator?" Hall replied, "Unfortunately, given the size of the office, it may be a reality. At that point I would say no, because you haven't entered into the discretionary review process..." Thus Hall attempted to rationalize his department's disregard for proper separation of powers.

At one point, the question of Berrigan's fitness to serve as Coastal Permit Administrator on our project was addressed by Jeff. Hall's document production had yielded an 8-2-95 memo he had received from Berrigan. Its content follows:

> "I'm writing this to document the behavior of Mr. Berlincourt. At about 8:00 a.m. today, Mr. Berlincourt was parked across the street from our office taking photographs of the building and at least one employee (Tony Navarro) entering the building. Mr. Berlincourt's demeanor when dealing with this office had been cold and somewhat hostile. As such, this activity is peculiar and disturbing."

Jeff asked, "Did you ever in your mind have any doubts after having received this memo from Mr. Berrigan that he was sufficiently objective to serve as the Coastal Permit Administrator with regards to the Berlincourt application?" Hall's response was, "I don't recall that that issue came up."

It should have. A quick search through the 20,000 photos in my 70 photo albums revealed that I took one photo of the Planning office that morning. No person is pictured in that photo. Now, who might have 20,000 photos organized well enough to be able to retrieve that photo taken eleven years earlier? A scientist of course. Scientists organize information and analyze it. They make associations. Can't help themselves. The date on Berrigan's memo to Hall? 8-2-95. Yes, wasn't that the date someone in Berrigan's office (who might it have been?) placed the Fort Bragg police on my tail under suspicion of a hit- and-run fender bender with a BMW? Sure enough, my correspondence with the Fort Bragg Police Department confirms that that was indeed the date. Had Hall had the whole story he might well have questioned Berrigan's objectivity as Coastal Permit Administrator on our project. Too bad I didn't have that information for Jeff during the depositions.

But back to our story. Jeff's further questioning of Hall revealed that, upon his first opportunity to review Stinson's Staff Report, Hall determined that there were some fundamental problems with it. He "...thought that the condition stating to relocate the dwelling, you know, without any specifics as to the exact height or size was inappropriate and possibly contrary to law." (We had of course made this same point in our complaint.) Asked if he had discussed these comments with anyone, Hall responded, "I might have made them to Mary [Stinson]. I don't recall. I have made them to Alan Falleri, and I have subsequently made them to Gary Berrrigan." With regard to the former, Hall said, "I discussed with Alan how I thought it was inappropriate, the conditions, you know, regarding relocating a structure, downsizing it without specific standards was inappropriate." With regard to his having discussed it with Berrigan, Hall remarked,

> "Yes I did talk to Gary Berrigan about it, before he took action on the Coastal Development Permit. I said that, you know, once he has taken action I wanted to talk to him about the staff recommendation, but I specifically stated I didn't want to go into any details at that point, because I didn't want to influence his decision. Subsequent to his action, I spoke to Gary and said I agreed with his decision and that I thought it was inappropriate to have a condition, approve a project, with a condition that provides no direct guidance."

At the end of Hall's deposition Zotter tried to repair damage from this testimony by posing questions which amounted to implying that it was appropriate to deny our application because of the inappropriate special conditions which the County had imposed. I don't think Zotter was taught that kind of logic in law school!

At one point Jeff told how Berrigan's "Notice of Final Action" stated that his findings on our case had been upheld by the Supervisors, whereas in fact the Supervisors had accepted his findings *except* for being "...willing to accept the height and size." Jeff referred to that as a "major procedural discrepancy that we have to deal with." Both Hall and Zotter appeared baffled over how to deal with that, and so they simply didn't. But Jeff had entered it into the record so it wouldn't be a disallowed surprise in court.

Aspects of Hall's testimony with regard to matters of visual impact also proved helpful to us. His annotated copy of the Staff Report was included in the County document production. Hall's marginal notes had been made prior to Berrigan's ruling. In a note, next to the report's claim that our house would be highly visible from Cuffey's Cove, Hall asked, "How can it be highly visable [sic] based on picture on p. 25? [approximately] 2 miles to the north?" Thank you, Mr. Hall! On page 25 were 200 mm and 400 mm telephoto photomontages. Even with their extreme magnification, Hall did not agree that our house would be highly visible from Cuffey's cove. Incidentally, at other times in his testimony Hall scorned the use of magnified photomontages as not "...relevant to any issues I had in front of me." So it was evident that the magnified photomontage approach was a Fort Bragg Planning Office innovation, whether by Berrigan, Ruffing, or Stinson, or some combination of them.

Hall saw nothing in the Coastal Act or County regulations which would favor views from a State Park over views from Highway One. Asked by Jeff, "How do you resolve the conflict in terms of priority, or do you?" Hall answered, "...I would probably consider, you know, numbers and the numbers of people that would utilize a particular area compared to, you know, another area." As a matter of fact motorists greatly outnumber Greenwood State Beach visitors.

Hall denied that he'd participated in the generation of the "Greenwood State Beach General Plan," although he had discussed it with Falleri. Hall said further that he'd never met Acrea, although he knew of him (and we knew that Acrea had written to him about the planning activity). Hall also said he'd never met Berry or Shannon. (Of course, Shannon's first letter to the County regarding our proposed project had been addressed to Hall.) Hall did recall having read a copy of the "Greenwood State Beach General Plan" but claimed not to be aware of any park interest in acquisition of additional properties until the day of his deposition, when Zotter told him, "...that the initial preliminary plan identified properties in this zone of interest..." (Of course, so did the final plan.) Hall either didn't remember, or chose not to divulge, that in a 10-24-94 memo to Supervisor de Vall he had stated, "I have briefly reviewed the Preliminary General Plan and your comments." Hall's memo, which we had obtained in the County document production, went on to comment on both the plan itself and de Vall's comments on it. Hall had read the plan carefully enough to make comments on it. How could he possibly have missed the blatant "Appropriate-Future -Additions" map on page 108?

Early in Hall's testimony, Jeff asked, "Is it one of the functions of the Project coordinator to bring to the attention of the applicant all relevant information that may relate to the application?" Hall replied, "...yes, you should let the applicant know of issues so they can address those." But, when Jeff asked why then had we not been notified of Chief Planner Falleri's highly-adverse comments in his 8-10-94 memo to Berrigan and of Supervisor de Vall's likewise highly adverse 4" x 6" note to Ruffing, Hall rapidly backpedaled. His response was, "Again, I think it is the responsibility of the applicant to review the file for that information." Hall did however allow that if a supervisor does make comments on a project (presumably to staff), he must divulge that at any hearing where he sits in judgment. Hall claimed that Supervisor de Vall had in fact disqualified himself in some other instances.

Other issues remained with regard to Supervisor de Vall. After leaving office at the end of December, 1994, his interest in our permit application continued very much unabated, and, when the Public Notice and Staff Report for our case were released, Berrigan sent him copies of those documents as well as exhibits for posting in Elk. Jeff asked if that was irregular or unusual, knowing full well that it was. Hall replied, "...just that it would be sent to an individual [de Vall] rather than [County] staff performing that function." In fact, Berrigan was making every effort to assure that the Elk anti faction would not overlook our project.

On 8-22-95 de Vall had sent a four-page letter to the planning office. In it he suggested that our parcel be acquired by State Parks. Hall denied any knowledge of the letter and of that suggestion. de Vall's letter also stated that, "In addition, no development permit should be issued unless and until the subject parcel is contained within the Elk County Water District." Stinson's Staff Report special condition thirteen had contained that same requirement. I strongly suspect that de Vall (perhaps even while he was still a Supervisor) made certain that special condition thirteen would be inserted into the Staff Report. I just can't imagine that, on her own, Stinson, a resident of Mendocino, would have thought of anything that specific to the politics of Elk. Jeff asked Hall if he was, "...ever aware that former Supervisor de Vall had made such a statement to the Planning office." Hall answered, "No." After three hours of intense questioning Hall's deposition ended.

By the conclusion of the depositions we were much encouraged, because we had learned a great deal that would be useful in court. But we had obtained no admissions on one critical point. It seems that all four of our deposees had read copies of the Greenwood State Beach General Plan, but their comprehension was faulty. All were unable to recall details of the part about "Appropriate Future Additions," let alone make the association of the southern headlands of Greenwood Cove with our property. And to think, all four were college graduates! Can our educational establishment really be that ineffective, or was it perhaps a case of lawyer-induced amnesia?

Although not a part of the depositions, telephone records obtained later as a part of the subpoenaed document production from the County cast interesting light on the depositions. They reveal telephone traffic between County planners and State Parks greatly in excess of what was admitted by County and State Parks deposees. Whereas telephone records do not divulge explicitly who actually talked to whom, nor what was said, they can be used highly effectively to guide questioning in subsequent depositions. Telephone calls originating from County planners in Fort Bragg and directed to Shannon's Monte Rio office telephone number between 5-8-95 and 4-1-96 were eleven in number and totaled 77.7 minutes. Coincidences of those calls with significant events provide a basis for suspicion of conspiratorial relationships between County planners and State Parks. A 2.1 minute call from Stinson (?) on 5-8-95 possibly alerted Shannon (?) to the referral she was directing to him approximately one month prior to her issuance of her Staff Report. A 9.5-minute call on 5-15-95 from Stinson (?) to Shannon (?) would have allowed ample time for her to prompt him on suggested content for State Parks' letter of opposition to our project. An 8.5-minute call on 8-15-95 from Berrigan (?) (Stinson had resigned) to Shannon (?) probably solicited the second State Parks' letter of opposition dated 8-21-95. A 9.5-minute call by Berrigan (?) on 11-8-95, just prior to the 11-13-95 Supervisors' hearing of our case, to Shannon (?) was probably the one Shannon recounted in his email to Berry in which he said, "Berrigan says we need to be there." An 8.1-minute call on 4-1-96 from Berrigan (?) to Shannon (?) doubtless informed him that the County was served with our lawsuit summons and complaint on 3-28-96. It should be kept in mind that the above eleven calls lasting 77.7 minutes comprised perhaps only one-half of the communications between County planners and Shannon, inasmuch as we had not subpoenaed records of calls to County planners that had originated from Shannon's telephone. Thus it would appear that County planners and Shannon had a great deal more to say to each other than they were willing to divulge in their depositions.

Also of interest are six telephone calls totaling 17.1 minutes between County planners in Fort Bragg and Supervisor Peterson's home telephone. Berrigan would almost certainly be the caller, for no Supervising Planner would be likely to tolerate his subordinates going around him to telephone a member of the Board of Supervisors. One 7.3-minute call on 6-7-95 might be a discussion of Stinson's Staff Report issued the day before. A 6.9-minute call on 3-1-96 occurred around the time we learned that Berrigan would no longer hear cases as a Coastal Permit Administrator. Could that have been Berrigan pleading with Peterson to intervene on his behalf so that he could retain his Coastal Permit Administrator authority?

There were six telephone calls totaling 31.4 minutes from the Fort Bragg planning office to Hall from 7-21-94 to 4-22-96. The first, lasting 3.0 minutes, occurred on 7-21-94, the very day of our initial application for a Coastal Development Permit. Could that have been the topic of a call from Berrigan to Hall?

CHAPTER 14

LAWSUIT SETTLEMENT NEGOTIATIONS

The depositions of County and State Parks officials and their document productions provided us with a wealth of ammunition for reinforcement and expansion of our claims. Those disclosures were bad news for County and State Parks officials, and the second round of depositions we were planning would likely yield additional bad news for them. Accordingly, even before Jeff had completed a draft amended complaint, we received settlement overtures from the County. A 9-16-96 letter from Zotter expressed a willingness "to discuss possible resolutions informally before anyone makes a specific proposal." It continued, "I am sure you recognize, of course, that the requirements for public hearings on at least some potential resolutions limit the Board's range of options."

So as not to make it seem as if the County was too eager to settle, Zotter had allowed himself to be interviewed a few days earlier by *Mendocino Beacon* reporter, Neil Boyle. In the latter's 9-19-96 article, Zotter was quoted as saying, "… it [our project] was a geological hazard…" That was only one of seven factual errors in the article. Jeff had declined comment for Boyle's article but did provide him with a copy of our complaint, which Boyle could just as well have obtained from the County or the court. In a telephone conversation with Zotter a few days later Jeff remarked, "…the timing of the article in the *Beacon* was unfortunate since it demonstrated, once again, the County's publication of false information arguably to generate public support against the project." Because Zotter never sought a retraction of his quote in the *Beacon* he had exposed himself to becoming a witness if our case went to trial.

In any event, we were underwhelmed by the County's settlement overture, especially in view of Zotter's misrepresentation of the facts in the local newspaper. But we did let Jeff know that we would consider settling, but only for a coastal development permit on our project as submitted and County reimbursement of our legal expenses. In the meantime we demanded from the County the long distance telephone bills from the Fort Bragg Planning Office for the period 6-1-94 to 3-31-96. As noted in the preceding chapter, they provided interesting circumstantial evidence to the detriment of the County and State Parks. On 9-23-96 we submitted a claim against State Parks for damages, a necessary step to bringing the State of California into our lawsuit.

Unfortunately, from this point onward the settlement negotiations went on and on and on. It would be nearly two-and-a-half years from the date we engaged Zumbrun and Findley until we and the County signed a settlement agreement. The County sought above all to save face and not have to admit having erred in any way whatsoever. They knew that above all we wanted a permit to build without devastation of our ocean views. It was a poker game. The County possessed the authority to grant us the desired permit. We had the ability to embarrass the County in court. We wanted the permit immediately. The County could stall and stall and stall. But they had to fear that our patience would be exhausted and they could end up in court. A recitation of the infinity of proposals and counterproposals that were put forth during that two-and-a-half-year period would be out of place here, and so I merely add a very incomplete timeline listing but a few highlights.

12-23-96 - Our very harsh settlement demand letter is mailed to the County. We seek a permit for our building site and legal expenses of $92,000. Our letter lists County offenses.

1-1-97 - A new Mendocino County Board of Supervisors is seated under the Chairmanship of Charles Peterson, a staunch opponent of property rights. One other carryover Supervisor, John Pinches, is a supporter of property rights. Two new Supervisors, Patti Campbell and Michael Delbar are both supporters of property rights, and the third new Supervisor, Richard Shoemaker is said to be middle-of-the-road with regard to property rights. The composition of the new board appears to be more favorable to us.

1-16-97 -Our amended complaint is mailed. It names both the County of Mendocino and the California Department of Parks and Recreation, but State Parks is not yet served with the lawsuit. The causes of action are increased from five to seven.

1-29-97 - The new board is evidently less supportive of property rights than we had hoped. A letter from Zotter reports the Supervisors' rejection of our settlement demand. By telephone Zotter says the Supervisors decided to "back their staff."

2-5-97 – We're advised by our attorneys that, although our prospects in litigation are good, the courts don't issue permits. In short, if we win the lawsuit we might collect legal fees and damages, but we still wouldn't have a Coastal Development Permit. We consider reapplication, forsaking legal fees and damages, but subject to a number of constraints on the County, many of which appear in the final settlement agreement. The most important one is that denial of our reapplication would automatically reactivate our lawsuit.

LAWSUIT SETTLEMENT NEGOTIATIONS

2-11 to 22-97 - We travel to California (my twelfth transcontinental round trip on this quest) to meet with Jeff. Then Jeff meets with Zotter and Hall to discuss our conditions for settlement. Then we meet again with Jeff for his report on those discussions. At this stage we're so disgusted that we consider abandoning settlement discussions to return to active litigation. We spend five days touring the Oregon coast looking at completed homes on the market. Had we found an interesting and affordable one we would have bought it and reverted to litigation.

4-30-97 - Following consultations with our architects, we propose a refined approach to settlement in which we would reapply proposing two plans, the first at our originally-proposed site but with the house lowered two feet by digging into the western rise, and the second with the house in a swale 48 feet farther south, the lowest buildable site on the marine terrace. The latter site would degrade our western and northern views, while modestly improving our southern views. With these plans, decreases in the visibility of the house viewed from the upper level of Greenwood State Beach would amount to approximately 20% and 40%.

4-30-97 - Jeff recommends delaying serving State Parks with our lawsuit until after a settlement agreement is reached with the County. His logic is that, during the reapplication process, our lawsuit would be in abeyance, and, therefore, were State Parks to oppose the reapplication they would be increasing the probability that they would be defendants in a reactivated lawsuit.

5-7 to 13-97 - I travel to California (my thirteenth transcontinental round trip in this quest) to meet with our architects and perform additional surveys of the Berrigan-mandated site.

1-20-98 - Jeff receives a FAX from Zotter with five pages of counterproposals prepared with the collaboration of Hall. We review them and fax Jeff, saying in part, "First of all, if we make a counter offer, we want you to inform Zotter that we expect an answer in five days or less, not five weeks, as in this most recent instance (and not five months as in our 1996 offer). Secondly, we long ago established that Hall is incapable of impartial, unbiased, professional administration of the laws and regulations with regard to our case. He has his own personal agenda. As such, he is incapable of creating, maintaining, and managing an organization that will perform in an impartial, unbiased, and professional manner. All the bullshit in Zotter's letter is clearly designed with Hall's collaboration in order to try to make Hall look good. We are not trying to reach a settlement with Hall. The whole point of considering a settlement is to go beyond Hall, reach a settlement with the Supervisors (not Hall) and seek a fair hearing by the Supervisors. We believe that you should make that point to Zotter...Finally, Zotter's asinine comment about our 'preparing to fight the last war' completely missed the mark. In case he didn't notice, the war hasn't ended, and it won't until we have a coastal development permit on terms acceptable to us, and we aren't demanding anything more than our rights under the laws and regulations! If anybody is trying to fight the last war it is Zotter, for he wants to involve the old files, and the old combatants, viz., Berrigan, Ruffing, and Stinson. It wouldn't surprise us if Lynch [who would be the County's Project Coordinator if we were to reapply] has already been poisoned by them and by Hall, and so Zotter is trying to legitimize that in hindsight..." Judging from this, it wouldn't appear that we were getting close to a settlement with the County, but then sometimes it takes strong language to reach an agreement!

2-26-98 - Seventeen-and-a-half months after the County's first settlement overture, we and the County agree on the terms of our reapplication.

3-20-98 - The California Department of Parks and Recreation is served with our lawsuit.

3-26-98 - We pay a reapplication fee of $970 to the County.

5-28-98 - Our lawsuit is placed in abeyance pending outcome of our permit application.

The complete text of our lengthy settlement agreement with the County is quoted in the Appendix. Here, I quote the most significant excerpts.

> "It is the desire and intention of the parties to this agreement to settle and resolve the claims and causes of action alleged in the Berlincourt lawsuit. The settlement of the controversies existing between the Berlincourts, the county and the board is, however, expressly conditioned upon (1) issuance of a coastal development permit with conditions subjectively acceptable to the Berlincourts and (2) the right of the Berlincourts to withdraw the reapplication for any reason at any time prior to the issuance of an acceptable permit and to then prosecute the Berlincourt lawsuit. It is the further desire and intention of the parties that the reapplication shall not prejudice or affect in any way the Berlincourt's prosecution of the Berlincourt lawsuit in the event that action is subsequently prosecuted for any reason. It is the further desire and intention of the parties that this settlement shall not prejudice or affect in any way any rights, remedies, or causes of action the Berlincourts may have in the future with respect to the reapplication."

> "Within 90 days of the date that this agreement is executed, the Berlincourts will file the reapplication with county's Department of

Planning and Building Services (PBS). Concurrent with the filing of the reapplication, the Berlincourts will pay PBS the normal filing fee for a coastal development permit application."

"PBS shall assign the reapplication to Frank Lynch as the project coordinator...."

"The reapplication shall be evaluated initially by the project coordinator independently of the Berlincourt's prior application. Only after the reapplication is initiallly evaluated by the project coordinator may the project coordinator:

a. have access to information existing in PBS's file or files related to such prior application except insofar as such information is included in the reapplication or is subsequently introduced by the Berlincourts, or

b. discuss the reapplication with Gary Berrigan, Mary Stinson, or employees in PBS' Fort Bragg office including, but not limited to Linda Ruffing."

"The project coordinator shall memorialize in writing and include in the reapplication file any discussion he may have in person or on the telephone with any person relevant or related to the reapplication. The project coordinator shall include in the reapplication file all evidence of communications bearing on the case, whether in person or by telephone, letter, facsimile, electronic mail, etc."

"Prior to filing the reapplication, the Berlincourts and PBS will agree how the project defined in the reapplication will be described in any referral or public notice related to the project. Thereafter, PBS, county and board shall consistently describe the project as agreed."

"Any referral or information relevant to the reapplication that is directed or communicated by the project coordinator to any member of the board shall be directed or communicated to every member of the board."

"The project coordinator shall make all information in the reapplication file readily available to the Berlincourts or their designated representative. On request, the project coordinator shall transmit to the Berlincourts via priority mail copies of all documents placed in the reapplication file."

"Upon determination that he is ready to prepare a staff report relative to the reapplication, the project coordinator shall:

a. give the Berlincourts and their representatives fifteen (15) days' notice in writing of his intention to prepare a staff report, and

b. direct to the Berlincourts and their representatives in writing any comments or concerns that the project coordinator may have relative to the reapplication so that the Berllincourts and/or their representatives may respond in writing to such comments or concerns."

"Thereafter, the Berlincourts may submit to the project coordinator additional information relevant to the reapplication. Upon written request made within the 15-day notice period, the Berllincourts, or their representatives may request, and the project coordinator shall grant, up to an additional forty-five (45) days to submit any such additional information. In no event shall the project coordinator prepare the staff report before receiving and considering such additional information submitted by the Berlincourts and/or their representatives."

"The reapplication shall not be heard by a coastal permit administrator. Instead, the reapplication shall be heard in the first instance by the board."

"Except as expressly provided in the following paragraph, the parties shall not prosecute the Berlincourt lawsuit while reapplication is pending and shall take any and all action appropriate and necessary, including an application to the court in the Berlincourt lawsuit, to stay or hold such litigation in abeyance without prejudice to any party."

"Upon issuance of a coastal development permit with conditions subjectively acceptable to the Berlincourts, the Berlincourts shall dismiss the Berlincourt lawsuit with prejudice. At any time prior to issuance of a coastal development permit with conditions subjectively acceptable to the Berlincourts, the Berlincourts may, for any reason, withdraw the reapplication and prosecute the Berlincourt lawsuit. Notwithstanding, the Berlincourts acknowledge that by entering into this agreement County has not agreed that it will issue a coastal development permit or that, if it issues such a permit, the permit will contain conditions subjectively acceptable to the Berlincourts."

"In the event that the Berlincourt lawsuit is subsequently prosecuted for any reason by any party thereto, such litigation shall in no way be affected or prejudiced by the reapplication including, but not limited to, any effect caused by any staff report prepared by the project coordinator or action taken by the board; in all respects, the Berlincourt lawsuit shall go forward as if no reapplication were made. Notwithstanding the foregoing, the Berlincourts will and do retain all rights, remedies and causes they may have in the future with respect to the reapplication independent of rights, remedies and causes of action they are asserting in the Berlincourt lawsuit and unaffected in any way by this agreement."

"The purpose of this agreement is to settle claims which are denied and contested or are potential, and this agreement is the result of a compromise. Nothing contained herein shall be deemed as an admission by any party of any liability of any kind to any other party, all such liabilities being expressly denied."

"The parties hereto agree to bear their own attorney's fees and costs incurred in connection with the Berlincourt lawsuit or the resolution of matters reflected in this agreement provided the Berlincourt lawsuit is not subsequently prosecuted."

"Each party hereto recognizes and acknowledges that this agreement is not intended to and shall not release any of the parties hereto from any liability or damages, if any, caused by, or arising out of, the failure or refusal to perform any or all of the acts required on their respective parts to be done, as per the

terms and conditions of this agreement. In the event of any
breach of this agreement, the party aggrieved shall be entitled
to recover from the party who breaches, in addition to any other
relief provided by law, such reasonable attorney's fees and costs
as may be incurred by the non-breaching party in enforcing this
agreement."

The settlement agreement was signed by the County on 2-24-98 and by us on 2-26-98. The assignment of Planner Frank Lynch, from the Ukiah Planning Office, as Project Coordinator was dictated by the fact that he had not participated in processing our original application. The bypass of a Coastal Permit Administrator and initial hearing by the Board of Supervisors instead was necessitated by the fact that both Coastal Permit Administrators Hall and Falleri were on record as opposing our original application. Many of the requirements in the agreement merely dictate that the County must follow proper procedures that should have been followed all along, but were not, during our original application. Importantly, the agreement allowed us to deal with contentious issues prior to issuance of the Staff Report. Most of the provisions of the settlement agreement are no more than every permit applicant is entitled to and has the right to insist upon. Obviously the most essential feature of the agreement was our right to reactivate our lawsuit without impairment at any time of our choosing. That presented the County with two possibilities. They would either have to approve our reapplication or face us in court.

CHAPTER 15

COASTAL DEVELOPMENT PERMIT REAPPLICATION

During the year and a half we haggled with the County over the settlement agreement there was a lot of other pertinent activity. Some of the principal characters in our saga changed employment; the County approved other nearby much-more-highly-visible projects; we worked closely with our architects to develop reapplication plans; and, as those plans were developed, we met with Elk residents and officials from State Parks and the Coastal Commission to keep them informed. As expected, the most difficult part of our reapplication experience was trying to achieve agreement on the facts with Project Coordinator Frank Lynch. Obviously, he'd been placed in a difficult position between our lawsuit and his superiors (Hall and Falleri), who opposed our project. All of the foregoing topics are addressed in turn in this chapter.

After the depositions in July of 1996, we were told, but have been unable to verify, that Berrigan took a leave of absence from the Fort Bragg Planning Office for several weeks. Then, on 11-7-97, he left permanently for a position as Environmental Planner with the Eureka Office of the California Department of Transportation. In the 11-6-97 issue of *The Mendocino Beacon*, tribute was paid to Berrigan by Linda Ruffing, who had been the first Project Coordinator on our case. She'd been rehired in the Planning Office specifically to assist the County in fighting our lawsuit. Ruffing was effusive in her praise of Berrigan, saying:

> "With 10 years experience working for the Coastal Commission before he came to work for the county building inspection department [more likely "planning department"], Berrigan has mastered the legal complexities involved in coastal land use issues. He knows the details; the history that he has is just irreplaceable."

We dearly hoped so!

In the spring of 1997 Neal Lutterman left Zumbrun and Findley for another law firm. He had very effectively launched our lawsuit and handed it off to Jeff Speich. Then in August 1998 Jeff Speich reduced his relationship with Zumbrun and Findley to part time and assumed new duties with Hatch and Parent, a Santa Barbara law firm. From our perspective the transition was handled seamlessly, and both Jeff and Ron Zumbrun continued to provide us with outstanding legal representation until the conclusion of our case.

Early in 1997, Bill Berry was honored by the Mendocino Rotarians with their "Outstanding Citizen Award." He was cited for a number of accomplishments including "…acquisition of the Spring Ranch property." (So it was evident that he did indeed participate in acquisition activities and could hardly have been disinterested in State Parks' designs on our two parcels.) Then in June 1997, Berry announced that he was being transferred to Riverside County to serve as Superintendent for the Los Lagos District of State Parks. Brian Hickey filled in behind Berry until January 1998 when the new Mendocino District Superintendent, Greg Picard, arrived. Picard would figure prominently in our reapplication activities.

In late 1997 and early 1998 we watched with amazement as County Planners rapidly approved Coastal Development Permits for the two parcels immediately to the south of ours. The first to apply for a permit was Elizabeth Crahan, a gracious octogenarian from Los Angeles, who possesses a degree in architecture, but worked for many years as a medical librarian. She owns the three-acre, oceanfront parcel immediately to the south of our parcel, and she had provided the County with a letter of support for our project. Her two adult sons, Charlie and Steve Acker have been longtime residents of Elk.

Mrs. Crahan's application for a permit was filed on 8-11-97. Linda Ruffing served as Project Coordinator. Seven months later, after modest concessions on project size, Mrs. Crahan received approval for a 4,000 square foot house plus a 500 square foot garage. At her hearing Ray Hall served as Coastal Permit Administrator. The house proper rises 18 feet above average grade and 21 feet at its highest corner, but the 17-foot wide chimney rises a few more feet. The buildable space on the long thin parcel is very limited, and so the house lies only 109 feet from Highway One and blocks views to the ocean. Ruffing's Staff Report betrayed her puzzlement over how to handle the "subordinate" requirement of the Coastal Act and the Local Coastal Plan, for by no reasonable judgment could the proposed structure be said to be "subordinate to the character of the setting." Nevertheless, she wrote, "Whether or not the residence is 'subordinate to its setting' is a difficult judgment to make…a smaller house might be more subordinate…" In reality, the Coastal Act's "subordinate" criterion breaks down completely when a legal parcel possesses only a very constrained building site. This is recognized in the Local Coastal Plan, Section 3.5-4, which states that, "Nothing in this policy shall preclude development of a legally existing parcel." It is also recognized in the Zoning Code, Sec. 20.540.005, having to do with variances, which states that:

> "A variance is an exception from zone restrictions granted by the
> Coastal Permit Administrator upon application, when, because
> of special circumstances applicable to the property, including

size, shape, topography, location, or surroundings, the strict application of the zoning ordinance deprives the property of privileges enjoyed by other property in the vicinity and under identical zoning classifications."

These provisions were doubtless derived from the United States Constitution's equal-protection-of-the-laws clause. Instead of expressing her puzzlement over the "subordinate" issue, Ruffing might better have rationalized her recommendation in terms of the above-cited County regulations.

In any event, we were very pleased to learn of the approval of the Crahan application, for, after approving such a visually prominent house, how could the County possibly deny our reapplication? I should interject that Mrs. Crahan's house and landscaping have since proved to be unobtrusive and in exceptionally good taste. (See Figure 8 for a photo of the completed Crahan house taken from Highway One. Note that, while the artificial berm and landscaping are rapidly concealing the house from public view, they are also obscuring public views to the ocean.) Interestingly, the Elk anti faction offered no opposition whatsoever to the Crahan project. We considered adopting Mrs. Crahan's adult sons, Charlie and Steve. But we thought better of it, because of their wives' active opposition to our project.

Next to apply for a nearby permit were Jeff and Patricia Spires, a delightful couple whose oceanfront parcel lies immediately south of the Crahan parcel. For many years they operated a vacation rental on the oceanfront parcel immediately to the south of the one on which they now wished to build. They filed for a Coastal Development Permit on 2-14-98, and, three-and-a-half months later, their application was approved by Ray Hall upon the favorable recommendation by Coastal Planner Doug Zanini. Their project consisted of an 1,879 square foot, 23.5-foot-high, full two-story house, plus a 576 square foot garage on a 0.37-acre lot. Unlike Ruffing, Zanini completely avoided the use of the word "subordinate" in his Staff Report and simply recommended approval. In this instance the buildable site was even more constrained than in the Crahan case. The Spires' house is located only about 50 feet from Highway One, and it blocks public views to the ocean, and so could not by any reasonable judgment be considered "subordinate to the character of the setting." Nonetheless, it's done in good taste and is rapidly being screened with landscaping (see Figure 9 taken from Highway One). Hall was particularly accommodating in his remarks at the Spires' 5-28-98 hearing about the prospect for effective landscape screening. He volunteered,

> "I put Leylandi cypress on my own property... they do grow fast. They're easy to put in...you almost put them down and they just take off...I know cypress grow very fast. I put mine in maybe five years ago, and they're probably already up at 25 feet."

Could this be the same Raymond Hall that questioned the prospects for success of our landscape screening? The Elk anti faction was equally accommodating, raising no objections whatsoever to the Spires project.

It was significant that in the Staff Reports for the Crahan and Spires projects the County was careful to point out that neither project would be visible from Greenwood State Beach. That was a card they could still play against us. But they failed to mention as well that the Crahan and Spires houses would, like ours, be visible from the Cuffey's Cove view point. Whereas visibility of our house from that very distant vantage point had been unacceptable to the County and the anti faction, visibility of the Crahan and Spires houses was evidently not a problem to them.

In preparing for reapplication we worked very closely with Bob, Mike, and Jeff. The revised plans were quickly developed, because the only changes were to dig in the southern section of Plan 3 and to relocate the house for Plan 4. Another task was to do a more extensive survey of the Berrigan-mandated site, because we anticipated that the County would continue to advocate it. That site proved to have a 13% downward slope from east to west. According to our architects a sloping-terrain structure meeting the 18-feet-above-average-grade height limit would,

> "...rise 23 feet above natural grade at its western face, and, in addition, it would be necessary to excavate up to 5 feet in depth around the eastern half of the structure. That excavation and provision for drainage, septic field, and firebreak would entail significant removal of existing vegetation. The result would be a much-more-prominent profile for the sloping terrain structure when viewed from Elk, from the State Park and from Highway One. In addition, more time would be required for added landscaping to obscure the taller structure."

With our assistance, our architects developed an illustrated brochure discussing the many diverse aspects related to our reapplication. It was to serve as a "Coastal Development Permit Application Addendum" and was entitled "Architectural Study of the Proposed Berlincourt Residence, Elk, California." This highly professional 69-page addendum brochure listed our architects' as authors, distancing it from the admittedly highly belligerent notebooks Margie and I had prepared for the Supervisors on our first encounter with them. The topics addressed included location, site analysis, public viewshed considerations, proposed sitings, photomontage representations of Versions 3 and 4, siting strategy, mitigation measures, public input on plans, efforts by applicants to mitigate impact, landscape screening and Its prospects for success, house design considerations, the parcel and its setting, precedents for approval, and conclusions.

Most of the points included in the addendum brochure have already been covered in this account, but a few issues merit further discussion. At one time Hall had disparaged completely the use of photomontages. Then later he narrowed his distrust to the ones I had prepared. The addendum brochure included a photomontage for Plan 4 prepared by Bob and Mike. Their work further verified the process I had used in preparing the earlier photomontages.

Also in the addendum brochure we expressed our willingness to donate our northern beach property (approximately 1.75 acres) to the State of California. This was of course conditioned on our obtaining a permit from the County immediately following the Supervisors' hearing. Because of the legal expenses we'd incurred we were no longer willing to place a no-development deed restriction on our five-acre parcel.

Well in advance of reaching any settlement agreement with the County, we undertook "public relations" initiatives to test the waters. We understood of course that our interaction with the County was like picking our way through a minefield, and we were working that problem as best we could. But what kind of reaction might we expect from the Coastal Commission in response to a referral from the County regarding a reapplication from us? Also, was there any possibility of *rapproachement* with the anti faction in Elk? Don't laugh! Well, we really didn't think so either, but Jeff urged us to try. That way we could tell the Supervisors that we had made the effort. Moreover, aside from trying to make peace with the anti faction while in Elk, we could further strengthen relations with those who'd been supporting us all along. The time was appropriate for another visit to California. Through friends in Elk we learned that an informal planning group had been established in the village, and that we were welcome to meet with them both in session and at a Town Meeting. We were pleased to accept that offer, and on our way we planned to call on the Coastal Commission as well.

On 11-4-97 Margie and I flew to San Francisco (my fourteenth transcontinental round trip on this quest). Ms. Jo Ginsberg, Coastal Planner with the California Coastal Commission in San Francisco had granted us an appointment at 2 PM that same day. We explained that, after having been denied a coastal development permit by the County of Mendocino, we had initiated a lawsuit, that a possible settlement agreement was pending, and that we might be submitting a reapplication based on modified plans. If so, she would doubtless receive a referral from the County soliciting comments, and we wanted to describe our plans to her so that she would be fully informed in that eventuality. We showed her maps, Plans 3 and 4, photomontages, and pictures of a number of comparison precedents (some of which she had earlier commented favorably on in response to referrals she had received from the County). We discussed mitigation measures, landscape screening, and how we had voluntarily relinquished the most desirable northern view site at the outset. Upon learning that our house would not be visible from the beach level of the State Park, Ginsberg expressed surprise at State Parks' opposition to our project. We described some aspects of our lawsuit so she would be aware of State Parks having designated our properties as "Priority 1 Appropriate Future Additions" and also aware of the County's erroneous public notices. She appeared to grasp fully the inappropriate implications of the magnified-view photomontages required by the County. We hastened to point out that, seemingly chastened by the revelations of their document production, depositions, and email, both the County and State Parks were showing signs of mending their ways. Berrigan had no longer been hearing cases as a Coastal Permit Administrator and would soon transition to the California Department of Transportation; magnified-view photomontages were no longer being required of permit applicants; a number of projects, all more-highly-visible than ours would be, had subsequently been approved, and the County had urged us to reapply even using the same plan. Ginsberg mentioned that she was following the Crahan application, which was pending at that time. It was her view that there was not much that could be done about it because of the small amount of space available for building. It was evident that she recognized that applicants with large parcels faced much greater difficulties.

Overall we believed that our meeting with Ginsberg had gone quite well, although there had been no doubt that she could be a formidable hurdle. But she had listened attentively, spoken knowledgably, and had allowed us an hour and twenty minutes to make our case. Most importantly, the atmosphere had not been charged as it had been with County officials.

We were not looking forward to our encounter with the Elk anti faction, but we had made extensive and careful preparations. We had composed a one-and-a-quarter-page handout describing the status of our project, and we had distributed it ahead of time to our supporters. We planned to distribute it to our opponents as well during our Elk visit. It expressed our regret at having had to resort to a lawsuit, and it noted that the County was encouraging us to reapply even with the same project, although we had developed alternate plans. In order to establish the facts, we described our alternate plans in some detail. We explained that, to assist us in planning our future course, we would be spending ten days in the area during which we would meet with individual Elk residents, participate in the Town Meeting, and meet with the newly formed Greenwood/Elk Community Advisory Group (GECAG). In all instances we would make available extensive additional material on our alternative Plans 3 and 4. We listed our vacation rental telephone number and encouraged telephone calls from interested parties.

In advance of our meetings with individuals we had reviewed all of the opposition letters, and we had prepared a listing of names, addresses, and telephone numbers of all who had either written opposition letters to the County or had signed the petition opposing our project. We began by simply going door to door calling on people. In some instances we were graciously received, and people carefully viewed our plans and illustrative materials and listened attentively, asking pertinent questions. In a few instances we might have made some progress toward *rapproachement*. But in most instances we were coolly received and allowed but a few minutes at the door. It was clear that most of the anti faction simply believed that our parcel should never be built on. In some instances we were immediately rebuffed with unconcealed hostility. But our task was not for the faint hearted, and we persisted, even when it appeared in remote areas back in the hills that we might be stumbling into the territory of the local drug culture. In hindsight we were probably foolish to go as far as we did along those dark lanes deep in the forest.

In instances when knocking on doors produced no responses we telephoned in the evenings to attempt to set up appointments. Again responses were mixed. One was particularly memorable. Earlier in the day we had stopped by the residence of Zelda Ralston in the woods up in the hills above Elk. There had been no response to our knocking. The area was like a junkyard. Odd, discarded, and rusting items were scattered all over the landscape. If ever there was an assault on the environment this was it. That evening when I reached her by telephone, I gave my name and asked if we might meet with her to discuss our proposed project. I had scarcely uttered those words when she shouted, "How dare you telephone me? You can't build that monstrosity on our coast!" Although the receiver was firmly pressed against my ear, Margie could hear her shouting on the far side of the room. Obviously, there was no point in trying to meet with her. Overall, we had to conclude that our door-to-door, person-to-person campaign had been a waste of time and a most unpleasant experience as well.

Our meeting with the GECAG on 11-10-97 was more civil. That group, also dubbed the "Elk Visions Committee," had been established informally by Supervisor Peterson several months earlier, presumably to provide advice on the future of Elk and environs and to provide Elk citizens a forum for discussion of changes that were taking place. I haven't been able to find a written charter for the group, but I think the goal was to try to establish a more civil way for people to deal with differences that arose regarding future development. The group had no official status or authority, and I have no idea how its initial members were selected. The GECAG voting membership included Leslie Lawson (Chairman), Joan Gates (Treasurer), Kay Curtis (Secretary), Ken Call, and L.T. "Mac" McKnight. Alternate (non-voting) members were Polly Green, Kirk Handley, and Karen Keehn. Lawson, Curtis, Green, and Handley had actively campaigned against our project, while Gates, McKnight, and Keehn had supported us.

In our meeting with the GECAG we presented pretty much the same material we had covered in our meeting with Ginsberg. We emphasized that, if we decided to reapply, we would propose alternative Plans 3 and 4, and that the project would not be the same as our original proposal. Rather, we had eliminated a bedroom and a garage bay. The maximum height would be within the 18-foot limit, and the average height would be only 12.9 feet. And we told of additional surveying which revealed the lowest buildable site on our parcel to be the swale site, where Plan 4 would be located. From there, the house would have minimum visual impact seen from Elk and the State Park. We reminded them that in neither case would our house be visible from the beach level of the State Park. We provided the GECAG with a large collection of descriptive materials on our proposed projects. Then we took them on a tour of our parcel, where both Plans 3 and 4 were staked out so they could see the alternate locations first hand. This also provided them an opportunity to see the existing vegetation that would provide partial screening initially. I doubt that any GECAG members had changed their minds as a result of this meeting, but at least they had had ample opportunity to question us in depth so they wouldn't have any surprises.

The next event was to be a "Town Meeting" sponsored by the GECAG and held in the Community Church on 11-13-97. We were scheduled to make a presentation on our plans, and Bob was standing by to provide assistance; Charlie Acker would make a presentation on his mother's (Mrs. Crahan's) project, which had recently been filed with the County but not yet acted upon; and Jeff Spires would describe the project he and Patricia would soon submit to the County. About 40 people were in attendance including GECAG members. The presentations on the Crahan and Spires projects were uncontroversial and elicited little discussion. Our presentation was pretty much a repeat of what we had told the GECAG. A few people spoke in support of our project and a few spoke against it. Ben MacMillan, proprietor of the Elk Store and cosponsor of the anti faction's petition opposing our project, was very curious about our lawsuit. He seemed to be worried that he might be named, but I assured him that our suit was against the County and State Parks, not anyone in Elk. The majority of attendees favored our project. I suspect that Barbara McKnight had diligently worked the telephone lines to encourage attendance by our supporters.

Much to our surprise, at the end of the meeting, GECAG Chairman Leslie Lawson called for straw votes on our project and the Crahan project. It appeared to be a spur-of-the-moment act on her part, one she would later regret. With regard to our project, there were 21 votes in favor of both Plans 3 and 4, 3 votes in favor of Plan 4 only, 2 votes against both Plans 3 and 4, and 8 votes undecided. With regard to the Crahan project there were 23 votes in favor, 3 against, and 5 undecided. As you can imagine, this caused quite a stir as news of the vote ricocheted around Elk over the next few days. The opposition screamed, "Foul!" Not unexpectedly, Charlie Acker's next Greenwood/Elk column in *The Mendocino Beacon* on 11-20-97 allocated space for a disclaimer from GECAG Chairman Lawson. She emphasized that the votes, "...should in no way be construed as being a reflection of how the general population of Elk feels about projects..." And she added that the meeting was billed as a "Public Forum," not a "Town Meeting" and was announced only a few days earlier. She stated that for a "real vote" to be taken, it would have to be announced well ahead of time that a vote was indeed to be taken. Moreover she noted that a significant fraction of the attendees were themselves project applicants or related to project applicants. Judging from letters to the editor that followed in the local weekly newspaper, debates about GECAG continued for about four more months, and then GECAG was consigned to oblivion.

The bottom line to our visit to Elk was that if we reapplied, we could expect that the anti faction would continue to fight us tooth and nail. Nevertheless, we'd had some good times during our extended visit to Elk. Also, while there, we learned that both Pjerrou and de Vall had been renting out parts of their homes in violation of the single-family zoning regulations that apply to their residences. More pertinent to our lawsuit, Postmaster Erna Smith mentioned that the mystery man from the County Planning Office, who'd shown our plans to her in a disparaging manner at the Post Office two years earlier, had graying hair and a pony tail. And so it appeared that that individual was indeed Berrigan, despite his denial under oath. Jeff reported this development to Zotter in a letter dated 12-8-97.

State Parks was another very important target in our campaign to clear the path for approval of our reapplication. In this instance Bob Schlosser would serve as intermediary. He already had some friendly acquaintances within State Parks. Moreover, he's both articulate and charismatic (whereas Mike and I can be a bit abrasive). On 4-28-98, two months after our settlement agreement with the County became effective, and a month after State Parks was served with our lawsuit, Bob telephoned the new State Parks Superintendent, Greg Picard, for an appointment to describe our proposed project. Picard remarked that he had reviewed the file on our project the day before, that he looked over the application and couldn't understand why all the fuss, and the thing he was most interested in was to "...get the Berlincourts into their house!" Was he so cooperative on his own, or had State Parks' attorneys, Dalton and La Franchi, told him how to respond should he receive such a call? Whatever, it was a clear sign of movement in the right direction.

On 5-8-98 Bob met Picard and Shannon at the former's office and went through the 69-page "Reapplication Addendum" with Picard page by page, finally leaving him a copy. Then they traveled to our parcel where Bob pointed out the existing brush screening barriers, which refuted what Shannon had claimed in the two letters he'd written over Berry's signature block. This elicited a grudging admission of error on Shannon's part. Bob pointed out the building sites for Plans 3 and 4, noting that, no matter which one might be actually built, it would make but little difference to public views. Pointing out the greater slope at the Berrigan-mandated site, Bob explained why a house built there would be more prominent. Next, moving to the burner-ring view point at the State Park, Bob used the photomontages of Plans 3 and 4 to illustrate the visual effect. Leading Picard and Shannon part way down the path to the beach, Bob showed them how our house would not be visible at all from the beach level of the park.

After seeing the whole picture, Picard expressed the view that we had not been asking for anything unreasonable. Asked by Picard why we were suing State Parks, Bob told him how our parcels had been targeted for acquisition without our being notified, and that evidence uncovered in our lawsuit implied collusion between the County and State Parks in the denial of our application. It would appear that Picard had not been made aware of Shannon's and Berry's obstructive activities. And you can be certain that Shannon had not been about to enlighten him.

The next day Picard's 5-8-98 letter responding to the County's referral for comments expressed a preference for Plan 4, stating that, "'Version 4' of this proposal offers a very reasonable compromise in addressing our concerns for the visual impacts to the State Park." All along we had of course fully expected that Plan 3, which we much preferred for its better views, would have to be a sacrificial lamb. Interestingly, a couple of months later Bob went on a camping trip with a group, which included a State Parks official. The latter confirmed State Parks' embarrassment over its highly incriminating emails, and stated that

State Parks was keeping its head down while our lawsuit played out. By then our suit had been placed in abeyance while our reapplication was being processed.

The final topic of this chapter has to do with our interactions with the County's Project Coordinator, Frank Lynch. He was of course in a difficult position. If he granted points of fact upon which we insisted, he would actually be conceding points on which the County and State Parks had differed with us in our original application. Yet, at this stage we were in a position to insist that agreement be reached on the facts or we would revert to the litigation. In short, there was no point in his writing and issuing a Staff Report until we all agreed on the facts of our case. As is so aptly and so often stated in acrimonious political confrontations, both sides are entitled to their own opinions…but they're not entitled to their own sets of facts.

Jeff, Bob, Margie, and I debated how best to interact with Lynch during what we knew would be a long and contentious battle over the facts. We concluded that our articulate "good cop," Bob, should always be our interface with Lynch. Thus, Bob had the unenviable task of trying to turn Lynch around when his perspectives differed from ours. Bob was not to grant concessions to Lynch on his own. Rather, he had first to debate them with Jeff, Margie, and me. We can well imagine that Lynch was similarly constrained by Hall and Zotter. Only in the rarest of circumstances, when things appeared to be at an impasse, would we resort to negotiations between Jeff and Zotter to try to reach agreement. Clearly, it was going to be like negotiating the settlement agreement all over again, except this time the debates would address the facts of our application rather than the rules of the reapplication game. As we saw them the facts were as follows:

> Both Plan 3 and Plan 4 would consist of a 3125 square foot single family dwelling with a mezzanine in the living room, a 640 square foot guest quarters, and an attached 989 square foot two-car garage.
>
> According to the Uniform Building Code, a mezzanine does not constitute a second story. County regulations are silent on that issue.
>
> Even if our proposed house were said to be a two-story house, it would not be in violation of the County regulations.
>
> The height of our proposed house above average grade would be 18 feet.
>
> The average height of our proposed house would be 12.9 feet.
>
> Plan 4 would be situated in a swale at the lowest buildable site on the parcel.
>
> The most prominent and best-view building site on the parcel would have been the northern one that we voluntarily relinquished,

because the house would have been visible from the beach level of the State Park.

Both Plan 3 and Plan 4 houses would be subordinate to the character of the setting.

A house placed at the Berrigan-mandated site would be at least as visible from the State Park as our proposed house, but would be much, much more visible from Highway One.

Regarding protection of public views the regulations state no preference between State Parks and Highway One.

Initially our house would be partially screened by existing brush ranging up to 13 feet high.

Additional vegetative screening would be provided by 66 trees and shrubs specified in our landscaping plan.

Tall and dense growths of trees on points immediately north and south of our parcel confirm that vegetative screening of our house will be successful.

Our proposed house will not be visible from the beach level of the State Park.

Our proposed house will not obstruct public views to the ocean.

As stated in the "Greenwood State Beach General Plan," "Greenwood State Beach lies within the town of Elk." From the marine terrace of the State Park some 70 structures are visible, most at very close range. At least 23 are visible from the beach level of the State Park.

Our goal was to arrive at agreement on the facts and to debate the inferences and opinions *before* the issuance of a Staff Report and prior to the Supervisors' hearing. We didn't want a repeat of the previous Supervisors' hearing, where Chairman Sugawara expressed his dismay that he was stuck with trying to figure out which side to believe. We viewed it as inappropriate to expect the Supervisors to make sensible spur-of-the-moment rulings on an intuitive basis, when the rightful resolution of conflicts may well require extensive field work and exhaustive analyses to arrive at the facts.

As we had anticipated, our reapplication got off to a rocky start. Prior to our actual reapplication, callers to the County Planning Office in Fort Bragg were being told inappropriately that we had already reapplied. Our actual reapplication became effective only after we signed the settlement agreement and submitted a new Coastal Development Permit application. However, two weeks before the settlement agreement was finalized, Lynch had reviewed the information that would accompany our reapplication in order to determine if it was complete. The facts as he saw them were put into writing and reached us via Zotter and Jeff. Lynch erred in his estimates of the setbacks from the northern bluff edge, claimed Plan 3 was 19 to 20 feet tall and exceeded the 18-foot limit, described the mezzanine as a "second story loft," and exaggerated the guest quarters floor area as 700 square feet, rather than the 640 square foot limit in the regulations. That last error alone would have provided convenient grounds for denial. He didn't like our version for the project description, because it mentioned the existing 7 to 13 feet high vegetative screening. We promptly prepared a very diplomatic, but firm, response for review by Jeff and Bob prior to Bob's negotiating the points of difference with Lynch. Bob prepared an even more diplomatic and articulate version of that response and sent it to Lynch on 2-18-98. In order for accord to be reached on the project description it took still another very diplomatic letter from Bob to Lynch. In that 3-23-98 letter, Bob covered a number of points, one of which bears repeating here to illustrate the general tenor of his rebuttals.

> "Unfortunately, the Owners' current project must overcome the unhappy history of their originally proposed project and the incorrect information circulated about it in a variety of sources. For example, in letters to Planning and Building Services, at the County's public hearings, and in internal email, State Parks Department officials alleged that vegetative screening would not be feasible in this location, that there was no significant existing vegetative screening, and nothing but grasses would grow out on the point. Their remarks were even quoted extensively in the original Staff Report, and so this is the way the public remembers the project."

The project description was thus agreed upon, but there were still bumps in the road ahead. The County had not agreed that Lynch would *automatically* keep us informed of communications, written and spoken, that he received regarding our project, and so each week Margie faxed a request to him for such information. Lynch would have to deal with 28 such requests. More troubling to us, in early April 1998, *before* Lynch had completed his preliminary review of our case, he revealed to Bob that he was reviewing the file on our original case. Thus, Lynch had violated a significant requirement of the settlement agreement. It was not possible at that time to judge what damage that may have caused, but later events would suggest it was significant. Regarding the addressed and stamped letters to interested parties that applicants are required to provide the County for dissemination of the public notices, Lynch wanted envelopes for all 188 "interested parties" that were to be found in the original file. We objected to making our case an international event, and the County pared the list to 97 residents of Elk and vicinity.

Coastal Development Permit Reapplication

Lynch made his site visit to our parcel on 4-21-98 accompanied by Bob. All corners for Plans 3 and 4 were staked. In addition Bob showed him the northern bluff site we'd voluntarily relinquished at the outset. And, because Lynch had already inappropriately reviewed Berrigan's findings on our original application, Bob showed him the Berrigan mandated site. While we'd reached accord with Lynch on the project description, it remained for him to make a determination regarding the visual impact of structures constructed in accord with Plans 3 and 4. This would be the real litmus test of whether the County was willing to give us equal protection of the law. To make certain Lynch understood this issue clearly we provided information for a letter that Bob sent to Lynch on 6-12-98 providing comparisons pertinent to the visual impacts of our proposed projects relative to those for the recently approved neighboring houses under construction by Mrs. Crahan and by Jeff and Patricia Spires. The letter noted that:

> "(a) The Crahan and Spires projects will present larger facades to public views than will the Berlincourt project,"

> "(b) The Crahan and Spires projects will be taller than the Berlincourt project will be,"

> "(c) The Crahan and Spires projects will obscure large regions of the ocean from public view, while the Berlincourt project will not obscure public views of the ocean at all, and "

> "(d) The Crahan and Spires Projects will be 8 and 18 times closer respectively to Highway One view points than will be the Berlincourt house; they will be 26 and 55 times closer to public view points on Highway One respectively than will be the Berlincourt house from Elk and State Park view points; and so in comparison, they will stand out far more prominently in public viewsheds..."

On 6-23-98 we received good news and bad news from Lynch in the form of positions he was considering adopting for his Staff Report. He expressed his inclination to recommend approval of Plan 4, although he planned to make no recommendation for or against Plan 3. And, of the several facets that were negative, only a few will be mentioned here. Lynch remarked that, "...the proposed project may be considered inconsistent with the applicable goals and policies of the Local Coastal Program...," which was strange (perhaps a typographical error?) because he cited no such inconsistencies, and this statement was in conflict with his favorable recommendation on Plan 4. A more troubling aspect was his assertion that, "There are other locations on the property, such as the previous staff alternative, which would make the project invisible." That of course was ridiculous, but if it appeared in the Staff Report it would be used to great advantage by the opposition. Finally, Lynch intended to discuss the history of our previous application at considerable length. We considered that to be out of place, because his Staff Report should be all about our present application. We didn't reapply for the privilege of fighting our original application a second time!

Attempts by Bob to resolve the above points of disagreement with Lynch were not successful, and on 7-13-98 Jeff discussed several of them in a letter to Zotter. There were subsequent telephone calls and other communications signifying nothing other than delay after delay. While our case dragged on, Lynch took three vacations, and Zotter took one. In the interim, in an effort to vent my anger, I composed a 14-page draft Staff Report the way I believed it should be written. I don't recall that anything ever came of it other than my having sent copies of it to Jeff and Bob. Finally, on 9-21-98 more than two months after Jeff's letter of objections was sent to Zotter, the latter got around to discussing the problems with Lynch, who responded with a revised and improved set of positions. But troubling aspects remained. Most significant was the one having to do with The Berrigan-mandated site. This time Lynch claimed that, "There are other locations on the property, such as the previous staff alternative, which would clearly make the project less visible from the town or State Park, however those locations would make the project more visible from other areas, e.g., Highway One." This was more dangerous than his earlier claim of invisibility, which was so obviously ridiculous that it could be easily discredited.

In an attempt to resolve remaining issues, Bob telephoned Lynch late in September and mentioned some of the points at issue. Unfortunately, he failed to make any progress on the alternative site issue, and so that issue would have to remain a disputed issue. Our survey and analysis would have to be judged in opposition to his very subjective evaluation. Although Lynch did not say so in as many words, Bob sensed that he was greatly annoyed by the intervention which reached him through Zotter. That's of course understandable, given that County Project Coordinators have doubtless become accustomed to formulating their opinions on cases without being second guessed by anyone, especially by lawyers!

After making a few minor changes in his positions, Lynch was ready to write his Staff Report. It would include a project description upon which both we and the County had reached agreement. To our surprise, in the process of negotiating that project description with us, Lynch had at one point omitted the square footage of the garage. We thought that to be strange, but, because we had other more contentious issues to resolve, we decided not to argue that matter. On 10-13-98 Lynch issued his Staff Report. We still had problems with some facets or it, but at least there were no surprises! The "Notice of Public Hearing" was mailed the next day to 97 recipients. Our hearing was scheduled for 10-26-98, this time at the Board of supervisors' Chambers in the elegant new County Administrative Building in Ukiah.

CHAPTER 16
BOARD OF SUPERVISORS HEARING II

Knowing that we could expect fierce opposition from the Elk anti faction during the reapplication process, we knew that it was important to rally our supporters early in the game. Accordingly, on 5-3-98, long before our 10-26-98 hearing before the Supervisors, we wrote to our supporters giving them an update on our plans, and we informed them that we had provided the McKnights with a copy of our 69-page "Reapplication Addendum," which they could consult for additional information. We mentioned that Frank Lynch would be the County's Project Coordinator, and, for those who might be willing to write letters supporting our project, we provided his address. We also informed our supporters that the Board of Supervisors would rule on our case, and so we provided the Board's address as well. So as to avoid any accusation of being sneaky, we had also written earlier, on 4-2-98, to Leslie Lawson, Chairman of the Greenwood/Elk Community Advisory Group (Visions of Elk Group) providing her with knowledge of our reapplication, with a copy of the "Reapplication Addendum," and with knowledge that Lynch would be the Project Coordinator, and the Board of Supervisors would rule on our case. We anticipated that Lawson would post the addendum in the Community Center for all to see. We also anticipated that she would activate the anti faction, for she was of that persuasion herself, but, surprisingly, the only anti-faction contact with the County at that early date was a lone telephone call from Ben MacMillan to Lynch seeking information. On the other hand, our supporters wrote 14 letters of support to Lynch and 8 to the Supervisors. Months later, on 10-14-98, twelve days before our hearing, we again wrote to our supporters expressing our hope that some might be willing to make the trip over the mountains to Ukiah to speak on our behalf at our hearing before the Supervisors. We included a list of five talking points and related rationale. We hoped that this would be the last time we we'd be bothering them.

During the seven months while we'd used intermediaries to argue with Lynch, Hall, and Zotter over the facts of our case, the anti faction had slumbered. But they would soon be awakened. The alarm that triggered them was the County's 10-14-98 "Notice of Public Hearing" which was mailed to 97 recipients. Outraged, the antis managed to get 14 letters to the supervisors, five of which were dated 10-26-98, the day of the hearing. They also managed to gather 22 signatures on a "Petition to Protect Coastal Views" and

30 signatures on a "Petition to Delay." Of course, the usual suspects had signed both petitions. (Incidentally, political scientists might find it interesting that, among Elk residents who registered their opposition to our project at one time or another during our long battle and who also declared their political party affiliations in the 11-5-02 Elk polling precinct tabulation, 49 were listed as Democrats, 8 as Greens, and none as Republicans. Despite that heavy representation of Democrats among the opposition, 17 registered Democrats supported our coastal development application.)

Ex-Supervisor de Vall sent two letters to the supervisors, one attacking aspects of our project, the other attacking the legalities of our settlement agreement and the fact that our case was to be heard by the Supervisors instead of a Coastal Permit Administrator. Included with one of de Vall's letters was a copy of a letter he'd sent to an Attorney, Mary Hudson, in Oakland, CA. He'd also sent her a copy of our settlement agreement with the County and had requested an opinion on its legality.

Many of the protestors claimed that insufficient information had been provided and that the public had not been given enough advance notice of the hearing. Yet, the County had provided the statutory advance notice, and, moreover, we'd provided full information to Elk residents during our ten-days-of-November-1997 visit to Elk, and we'd also provided Leslie Lawson, Chairman of the Greenwood/Elk Community Advisory Group, with our 69-page addendum in early April 1998. Perhaps, as that group imploded, she simply failed to activate its measures to publicize information on coastal development matters in the vicinity of Elk.

Interestingly, my files revealed no letter of protest from Doctor Hillary Adams, although the latter's husband, the Reverend Henry Schaeffer, did submit a letter of protest. Nor could I find a letter of protest from Mary Pjerrou, although she was said to have composed one in collaboration with Judith Hale. Perhaps they were so busy inciting others and managing the petitions that they just didn't have time to write letters on their own. Or perhaps my files are incomplete. But, most likely, the opposition had decided by then that their time was best spent preparing an appeal to the California Coastal Commission, which would surely follow any approval of our project by the County. Also, in hindsight, we now know that in this same time frame Pjerrou was in the throes of launching her "Save the Redwoods – Boycott the Gap" campaign, and so she would have had a lot on her plate.

Most of the letters of protest had nothing at all to say about whether or not our plans conformed to the regulations, and some were very abusive personally to us. To cite but one example, I'll quote from one from Zelda Ralston, the first of the antis to respond. You'll no doubt recall my having mentioned earlier the plethora of junk littering her yard, and, how, when I telephoned her to seek an appointment to describe our plans, she had scolded me. Her version of that November 1997 telephone discussion appears in her 10-16-98 protest letter, a portion of which follows.

"...Mr. Berlincourt actually telephoned me in my home and verbally harassed me. He shouted at me for signing a public petition trying to stop him, over the telephone. I told him I would not change my mind and that I considered his invasive behavior unconstitutional. He persisted to tell me how I was '...ruining his wife's view from their new summer home.' He also said he '... didn't care what the community thought.' I made it clear to him that he was not to contact me again. He had taken a copy of our petition from the Elk Store and telephoned all the 'nays' to personally argue with our decision to stop his projected plan..."

As Jack Benny used to say, "Well!" All I did was ask politely if Margie and I could meet with her and describe our plans. Beyond that her account is pure fiction. We came to Elk that November to win converts. You don't achieve that by harassing people. Our house was never intended to be a "summer home." And we didn't take a copy of the petition from the Elk Store. We had requested and secured a copy from the County.

Incidentally, nine years would go by before we would again be aware of Zelda Ralston, and in this later instance the mystery of her addiction to junk would be clarified to some extent. Touring the Elk Studio Gallery recently we came upon two color photographs depicting rusting junk. Zelda Ralston's name immediately sprang to my mind, and, sure enough, she had taken the photos. To my surprise they were actually quite interesting, not overwhelming like the excess of junk surrounding her home. Still later I happened upon an exhibit of some of her photographs of coastal landscapes (sans junk), which were more to my liking.

But to return to the main theme, on 10-20-98 Margie and I again boarded a jet bound for California (my fifteenth transcontinental round trip on this quest), this time to prepare for, and appear at, our second hearing before the supervisors. On our way to Fort Bragg, we stopped in Ukiah to request copies of any late-arriving protest communications. By then only the abovementioned letter from Ralston had been received. We happened upon Lynch, and he told us of a telephone call from Doctor Hillary Adams, who wanted to see story poles on our parcel. After our many months of using intermediaries to wrangle with Lynch over the facts of our case, we were surprised to find him to be quite civil with none of the personal hostility so evident in our interactions with Berrigan and Hall. Most surprising, as we were departing, Lynch remarked that he hoped we would get our permit. By recording this for posterity, I'm not doing him any favor. Indeed it could be the kiss of death for his career at the Mendocino County Department of Planning and Building Services. If so, Frank, please accept my apologies.

When we arrived at our motel in Fort Bragg, we made some telephone calls to offer the opposition more information as well as tours of the building site. There were no takers. There was no response at the Adams-Schaeffer residence and so Margie left a message on their answering machine. Two additional messages left on succeeding days also failed to evoke a response.

During the several days prior to the Supervisors' hearing we met with our architects a few times to plan and rehearse presentations. We planned to include a lot of visual displays for our project as well as comparisons with projects that were recently approved by the County and were (or would be) much-more-highly-visible than our project would be. Because I'd been the focal point for most of the ire from the opposition and the County, and Mike possessed an edge every bit as incendiary as mine, we all (including Jeff by telephone vote) decided that Margie would make some opening comments, Bob would make the principal presentation, hitting the high points of the 69-page addendum, and Sara Geddes would provide assurances on the efficacy of vegetative screening. There'd been a possibility that Jeff might attend our hearing to look out for our interests from the legal perspective, but in the end he concluded that it wasn't necessary. Was he really that confident, and was he that trusting of Zotter, or did he simply have bigger irons in the fire elsewhere?

But to return to the story-pole issue, Lynch had informed Adams that he had not required story poles, and so it was up to us. A letter from MacMillan to Lynch, and copied to the supervisors, soon followed also complaining about the lack of story poles and arguing that the hearing should be postponed to a later date. Zotter was informed of that either by Lynch or by the Board and sent a copy of the MacMillan letter to Jeff and to Bob. Zotter expressed the opinion that it was not a problem, citing a legal precedent in which the plaintiff's complaint was the absence of story poles. The case had been dismissed. Of course on four previous occasions we had erected story poles, but, nevertheless, to defuse that complaint, we decided to put one up anyway. With a helping hand from Mac McKnight, that task was soon accomplished. Much to our surprise, in this story-pole incident, Zotter had offered a helping hand to us. Evidently the County didn't relish the prospect of facing us in court! And so maybe there was no need indeed for Jeff to participate in our hearing.

At the County Planning Office in Fort Bragg Margie learned that our case file had been consulted on separate occasions by Pjerrou and by MacMIllan, as well as by "Mendocino Coast Watch" activist Roanne Withers, who also had ties with the Sierra Club. We had contacted Withers earlier offering to meet with her and provide information on our project, but she'd rebuffed us with a terse letter to the effect that she never meets with "developers." Yet we had a copy of a chummy three-and-a-half-page, single-spaced letter she'd written to Charlie Acker in response to his having provided information to her on his mother's proposed project, i.e., the Crahan project. In it, Withers, a resident of Fort Bragg some 25 miles to the north, revealed that some Elk residents had expressed to her their objections to Charlie's mother's project. It was as if they expected Withers to register a protest for them, in effect by proxy, so that they, themselves, wouldn't be seen as protesting their neighbor's mother's project. On the other hand, the anti faction basked righteously in the notoriety of their opposition to our project. After all, we were easternseaboard aliens without kin in Elk! Now there's an interesting facet of human nature. In any event, the County received no protest letters at all regarding the Crahan project.

Two days before our hearing we left four copies of the Staff Report with MacMIllan at the Elk Store and offered him a tour of the site. Later, by telephone message, he declined our invitation, saying he had no time to meet with us. That was not surprising. We'd previously arranged for appointments with him, which he failed to keep.

Most of the last day before our hearing we spent on our parcel on the chance that members of the anti faction might arrive for a tour. None did. Had they shown up and been informed they couldn't complain at the hearing about not having been adequately informed.

Attendance at our 10-26-98 hearing in the new and elegant Supervisors' Chambers in Ukiah was sparse. The 60-mile drive over the mountains to Ukiah had taken its toll. Our supporters in attendance were RD Beacon, Mac and Barbara McKnight, John and Ruth Raffety, Dave and Audrey Skilton, Tricia Spires, and Dean and Rae Wisdom. We were particularly touched by Audrey's attendance. In spite of her delicate health she had chosen to make the journey "for principles she believed in." The opposition in attendance included Doctor Hillary Adams, Judith Hale, Mary Pjerrou, Ellen Saxe, and Roanne Withers. (Now, isn't that interesting? Half of our supporters were women and half men, whereas all of our opponents were women.) Charlie Acker was also present, but, as the Manager of the Elk County Water District and Columnist for *The Mendocino Beacon*, he had to be neutral (at least in public). Notable by his absence was Shannon, our old adversary from State Parks. It would appear that, recognizing their vulnerability to litigation, State Parks had put a muzzle on him this time around.

Conservative Supervisor, John Pinches, opened the hearing. He had become Chairman after Supervisor Peterson's term as Chairman had expired. Pinches called for Frank Lynch's presentation. It was pretty much a repetition of his Staff Report, complete with the history of our original application, a description of our presently proposed plans, and a recommendation for approval of our Plan 4. We were pleased that he expressed less advocacy for the Berrigan-mandated site than had been evident in the Staff Report and during the months we wrangled with him over the facts. He concluded by citing communications, both pro and con, that he had received from the public.

The normal procedural sequence of the hearing was then interrupted as Supervisor Peterson asked that legal issues be resolved before proceeding. Accordingly, Chairman Pinches read quotes from one of de Vall's letters of protest in which he asserted that the settlement agreement had been drafted by our attorney, and the hearing should be postponed. Zotter explained that de Vall seemed to have the impression that the County had not been involved in drafting the settlement agreement, which was not the case. In fact Zotter mentioned that County Counsel had gone through rather lengthy negotiations with us to arrive at the agreement, and that he didn't see anything in the agreement that would be objectionable and require the hearing to be postponed. He then offered to address specific concerns if anybody had any.

Doctor Hillary Adams had of course been straining at the bit for that opportunity, and she was fully prepared. She requested, and was allowed, the opportunity to attack the validity of our settlement agreement with the County. She asserted that she and others in the opposition had taken legal counsel, and, reading from her prepared text in her best imitation-of-a-lawyer tone, she began attacking the agreement point by point asserting that each was "possibly illegal." She asked if the Supervisors were aware of the agreement [they were]; argued that the agreement had all the earmarks of a SLAPP [Strategic Lawsuits Against Public Participation] suit "meant to harass and intimidate" [not so; our target was not public participation, but rather illegal County Government behavior]; argued that the agreement was not legal because it was not signed by a judge [indeed it was not signed by a judge, but agreements willingly entered into by two opposing parties enjoy full legal status]; asserted that the Board's signature was not a valid one [not so]; argued that we had chosen our own Project Coordinator sympathetic to our cause [not so], had dictated what documents the Project Coordinator could see and when [true, so he would judge this application, not the original application], had dictated what other planning staff he could talk to and when [true, so that he would not be influenced by County employee participants in the earlier conflict], had been allowed to write our own project description [it was developed in negotiations between the County and us in keeping with provisions of the Coastal Act], and had been allowed to respond to the planner's comments before the Staff Report was written [shouldn't every applicant enjoy that opportunity?].

Adams was particularly peeved that all communications with the County regarding our project should be made known to us. She objected for two reasons, the first having to do with convenience. She complained, "We have to travel long distances in order to access these records, while the Berlincourts and their representatives receive weekly reports by mail." Of course, she could simply have faxed Lynch once a week requesting copies the same as we did. Secondly, she considered it an invasion of her privacy that we should learn of her contacts with the County. Adams then pointed out as an aside,

> "I may say that when I called… and asked that story poles be erected on the Berlincourt's site so that members of the public could judge visual impact from public places, I received within a short time a telephone message from the Berlincourts, and repeated messages thereafter, offering me a personal tour of the site. I have not asked for a personal tour of the site. I do not want a personal tour of the site, and I consider it an invasion of my privacy to be harassed in my own home on my own private property in this manner."

Evidently it never occurred to her that, through her campaign against our project, she might be harassing us on our "own private property." Adams was also very peeved by having to travel 60 miles to Ukiah to attend the hearing. Clearly, she was not at all concerned that she and her cohorts had caused us to make innumerable transcontinental journeys. Capping her tirade, Adams requested that our case be removed from the agenda and that our reapplication be processed through the normal and established County procedures.

Zotter responded, saying, "The simple reason why the agreement does specify Mr. Lynch is that quite frankly we ran out of other people." That comment elicited a burst of laughter from attendees. Zotter then went on at some length enumerating how the other County planners and Hall had been involved in the earlier case one way or another and how, fortunately, Lynch had not, and, in addition, was knowledgeable in coastal matters. Zotter also explained the legal legitimacy of the agreement, making several points. Our suit was still on file in the court and could be reactivated at any time at our discretion, and so he said, "It's always easier and less expensive to settle than to litigate." However, so as not to give the impression that we had the upper hand, he claimed that the County had a good case, and he was "prepared to defend." He remarked that, with Hall's participation, he had negotiated the terms of the agreement for the County and had presented it to the Board, which had approved it. He added that because, in the end, the Board would be sitting in judgment of our project, it would have been inappropriate for them to negotiate the terms of the settlement agreement. Zotter expressed the view that if the agreement were to be challenged, it would prevail, and he told the Board, "I feel quite comfortable if the Board wishes to proceed today." The Board concurred with his recommendation and called for our presentation.

Margie was first to speak on behalf of our project. She began by thanking the many Elk residents who had been our faithful supporters, and she noted our close association with the Mendocino coast for a period of nearly 50 years. She mentioned our sacrifice, at the outset, of the most desirable northern building site and pointed out that we'd had five separate surveys in order to arrive at our present plans. She emphasized how little difference there would be between public views of our two proposed plans, while indicating how our ocean views would be much poorer for Plan 4. Margie also enumerated the changes we'd made since the original application and spoke at some length about our many meetings with Elk citizens and our attempts to reach accord with them. She concluded by asking the Board to approve both of our plans and "allow us to enjoy our property as our neighbors enjoy theirs."

Bob spoke next, providing architectural perspective. He covered aesthetic, visual, technical, and regulatory aspects. He followed very closely the content of the 69-page "Reapplication Addendum," which I've already mentioned. But in several instances he augmented it. While covering vegetative screening he included a photograph of one of the shore pine seedlings I'd planted three years earlier at a location where Shannon had scornfully predicted that nothing but grasses would grow. The tallest of them had reached about seven feet in height, and, in the photo, Margie appeared diminutive alongside it. In his inimitable fashion Bob had set the Supervisors at ease, and they were even chuckling at times.

Bob was particularly effective in describing how our 1998 situation differed from that in 1995. He explained that the Plan 4 site was 50 feet further from view points in Elk and the State Park and was at the lowest buildable location on the parcel. He noted that, while Plan 3 would utilize the earlier location, the building would be lowered by digging it down into the slope. Bob pointed out that this time County Staff and State Parks had endorsed plan 4, and no concern had been expressed by the Coastal Commission. Also, he explained that our substantial reductions in size and height had been significant concessions to visual impact concerns of State Parks and Elk residents with whom we had made every effort to communicate regarding our project. Back in 1995 Berrigan had expressed concern that our project would set a precedent for development of the two vacant parcels south of ours. Bob noted that projects for those two parcels had recently been approved by the County, and so in 1998 those projects comprised precedents for ours. Finally, whereas in 1995 State Parks had questioned the prospects for success of our plan for vegetative screening, Bob quoted their1998 perspective on this important issue, which was that, "The additional number of plants available for screening, and the plant maintenance specifications shown, represent the best solution for achieving an effective revegetation effort."

Sara Geddes spoke next. After mentioning her ten years' landscaping experience on the Mendocino/Sonoma coast, she expressed her firm conviction that our vegetative screen would be effective in as little as ten years. She showed viewgraph photos of successful growths of evergreens up to 50 and 60 feet tall at Sea Ranch, at a few State Parks, and on nearby points north and south of our parcel. According to her the existing brush growing on our parcel would help our newly planted trees get off to a good start. Sara also showed the photo of Margie standing beside a seven-foot-tall shore pine I had planted as a seedling three years earlier near the western edge of our parcel. The repeated use of this photo was intended to discredit totally Shannon's contrary comments in his 1995 letters to the County.

The meeting was next opened for public comment, and Charlie Acker rose to comment on issues that had been raised regarding Elk County Water District service to our project. He provided assurance that service to our project had been properly authorized. Then, pressed by Supervisor Peterson to state a position on the project before the Board, Acker responded,

> "I could speak to both sides of it, but, you know, I think it's better
> that, being I am manager of the water district, that I just stick
> to doing my job. I figure there's plenty of voices on both sides
> of the issue…but I will say this, that both my mother and I look
> forward to having the Berlincourts as neighbors."

Board Of Supervisors Hearing II

To the sounds of laughter, one of the Supervisors added, "You should run for public office." (Of course, what Charlie hadn't mentioned was that both his wife and his sister-in-law were very much opposed to having us as neighbors!)

Then, words of support for both of the proposed versions of our project were offered by John Raffety, who continued, "...I think possibly the Berlincourts' property rights have been trampled upon for a long time now, and I think it's time they were granted their desire..."

Again, Doctor Hillary Adams asked to be recognized. She added another 14 minutes to the seven minutes she'd already spent voicing her opposition to our project; said she was speaking under protest because she believed the settlement agreement to be illegal; argued that, because of the adverse visual impact of our house, it would threaten the livelihoods of Elk bed-and-breakfast inns; claimed that our parcel was subject to such extreme gale winds and salt air that vegetative screening would be ineffective; proposed that our house be placed at the southeastern Berrigan-mandated site and insisted that his 1995 "Findings" to that effect be entered into the record of the current hearing; expressed her shock regarding the high visibility of the story pole we had erected, and complained that no information had been provided on its location (even though she had repeatedly rebuffed our offers to meet with her on the parcel to provide such information); expressed her dismay that she'd only had access to reduced-size architectural drawings (as opposed to 24" x 36" working drawings) and hence had been unable to check the height, square footage, setback, and other features of our proposed project; criticized the Staff Report for not stating more stringent requirements for the installation, maintenance, and replacement of vegetative screening; and said that others would talk about the "so-called citizens' approval," but added nonetheless that the State Parks Superintendent had told her that,

> "Part of the reason he had approved site 4 was because the Berlincourts had told him there was strong citizens' approval of these sites out of the town of Elk. The other problem of course was that the Berlincourts took a law suit against the State Parks just as they took a lawsuit against you."

(It's pertinent that neither Margie nor I ever had any contact with State Parks Superintendent Picard.) About a third of the Adams presentation was devoted to an attempt on her part to discredit our photomontages. In effect she granted that we had expertise in photography, but were using it to deceive. Her own discussion of "what the eye sees and what the camera sees" was without technical foundation.

Next to comment was RD Beacon, rancher, ranch fire department chief, communications-business operator, bar keeper, computer tinkerer, probably the biggest man physically in the vicinity of Elk, and provocateur of the antis. Launching an attack against them, he said,

"Some people that are protesting this project are, I guess, professional protestors, and they're retired and they've got nothing else to do with their time. I myself gave up about 900 to 1000 dollars worth of my day to come here and speak to this project and I believe it's a good sound project."

RD had cleverly placed a higher dollar value on his opinion than it appeared likely that the antis could muster for theirs. He went on to tell how there had been big trees on our parcel and that he'd removed them more than once for previous owners in order to keep the fire hazard down. Thank you RD!

Next to comment was Ellen Saxe, who denied that she was a professional protestor and said that, in order to testify, she'd given up only a little of her day job, which was looking after other people's children. With that she trumped RD. Everyone would surely have to agree that children are of much greater value than RD's 900 to 1,000 dollars! Referring to us by name, she cautioned the supervisors, saying,

"Ted, Marjorie, Bob, Michael, and Sara, whom I'm fond of, you guys are so smart, but tend to get a little tricky with the site 3 and 4 thing, so I want to ask all of you supervisors to be very careful when you consider this project."

We had just been complimented and insulted....I think. She went on to rate the view from Highway One to be of less importance than that from the upper level of the State Park. This would seem to imply that she was going to express a preference for the Berrigan-mandated site. But to our surprise, she urged the Supervisors, "Please do not approve version 3!" Did that imply her acceptance of version 4? Perhaps the "site 3 and 4 thing" had been a little tricky in ways we never intended.

Next, the issue of the favorable vote on our project at the "so-called Town Meeting" was addressed by Judith Hale, a local artist. She too was testifying under protest because of provisions of the settlement agreement. And testify she did, taking nine minutes to say that the GECAG-sponsored meeting had not been a "Town Meeting" and arguing that it had not been widely enough publicized, nor had it been announced that votes would be taken, and that for those reasons the vote was meaningless. (Her arguments were of course valid, but then we hadn't initiated the voting. Rather, it was requested by Leslie Lawson, a staunch opponent of our project, who, as GECAG Chairperson, chaired the meeting.) Hale then extolled the creation of the Greenwood/Elk Community Advisory Group and complimented Chairman Peterson for having established it. Basking in praise, Chairman Peterson described his rationale for creating the group.

Then, in two brief sentences, Dean Wisdom expressed his support for our project. He was followed by Roanne Withers, who submitted a brief and cryptic letter of opposition to our project, which she'd signed on behalf of Mendocino Coast Watch, and which Ron Guenther had signed on behalf of the Sierra Club Mendocino/Lake Group. She neither read from the letter nor criticized our project. Rather, she told how she had been invited to Elk to speak to the Greenwood/Elk Community Advisory Group, but as she continued,

> "The group was immediately disbanded, and I was told that
> the group had turned into a rather rambunctious very pro-
> development group, and anyone who had any other concerns
> was simply voted from the group, and I was sorry to hear that."

Perhaps the true depiction of the GECAG lies somewhere between those of Hale and Withers. But how could anyone ever have expected a happy marriage between the two divergent factions in the GECAG? I have no knowledge of the date of the disintegration of the group, but it appears that it must have predated our April 1998 mailing of voluminous information on our project to its chairman, Leslie Lawson.

Dave Skilton then spoke briefly in our support, mentioning the need for a level playing field. Evidently referring to the Spires project, he said that a house 35 feet from the highway had been approved, and that that was OK. But so is the Berlincourt's project OK.

Then it was Mary Pjerrou's turn, and she wasn't about to tape her mouth shut at this hearing. She was indignant and pugnacious, yet plaintive at times. Unfortunately, print fails to portray her strident tone and the sharpness of her exchanges with Zotter and Pinches. Also unfortunately, because the combatants were striving to be heard above each other at times, come of their words could not be recovered from the audio tape. Here is what could be recovered:

> "My name is Mary Pjerrou. I'm a native of California. I disagree
> with Bobby Beacon that he is the person most affected by this
> project. I live right in the middle of Elk, and this project is right in
> my view, but it isn't really my view that I'm so concerned about
> as the Cuffey's Cove view, which I think the Berlincourt's speakers
> deliberately ignored.When you're coming down to Elk from the
> cemetery and stop at the Cuffey's Cove outlook, you're looking
> at the most beautiful view of any coast in any state, in any
> country, in the world. It is the most spectacular breathtaking
> view. It is why people come to Mendocino. This project is going
> to be right smack dab in the middle of that view. That's going to
> change it forever. That's why I skipped a doctor's appointment
> today, even though I'm very sick, to come here, because this is
> so important. *[Then looking toward Frank Lynch]* I didn't like your
> attitude when you said it's easier and less expensive to settle than

to litigate and you agreed to this, because you discussed it with parks *[Zotter tries unsuccessfully to interject]* this whole settlement agreement that is based on evidence that is not in the record. *[Zotter: 'You should be addressing me, because I was the one who negotiated the settlement, not Mr. Lynch.']* Now who said this about the agreement? Who said it was less expensive to settle than to litigate? We're talking about ourselves. We're talking about our views. Where do you live? You're all over here *[Ukiah]* making settlements about what we're going to look at for the rest of our lives. With an agreement that excludes the coastal permit office *[in Fort Bragg]* and it doesn't have a coastal hearing that we can attend without spending our entire day in Ukiah. I resented your rushing the public speakers, John *[Supervisor Pinches]*, you didn't say anything about the time during all the presentations today until we got up to speak, and then you shot somebody down. She didn't finish what she was still saying. *[Pinches: 'No I , no I let every speaker go and say everything they wanted to say.']* You interrupted her twice John. *[Pinches: 'Normally, we have the right to limit talkers to three minutes which is the rule that we have on all, but sometimes even the comments got totally off the subject, but we kind of let it go on, you know. It's after six o'clock, so that's the reason that I'm trying to get the focus back onto the project at hand.']* Frank you also said there's a lot that is subjective about highly scenic areas and that is just what you gave away in that agreement. All matters subjective are decided by the Berlincourts not by the people we pay to make those decisions. I think you've been railroaded and I'm very upset with you. I support the Berlincourt's right to build on this property. They were told where they can build so that this structure will not be seen by the millions of people that come to the coast, and they refused to do it, and they were turned down and then they came back with these compromised projects that nobody on the coast had had a chance to study."

Pjerrou had been justifiably eloquent in her praise of the view from Cuffey's Cove, but she had grossly overestimated the impact our house would have on that view. And she had never registered any objection to the Crahan and Spires houses, which would be about equally visible from Cuffey's cove. Today if you pause to admire that magnificent and spectacular view you won't even notice those three houses unless you search them out with your binoculars or telephoto camera lens. You'll note also in the above quotation that, like Adams, Pjerrou judged the 60-mile trip to Ukiah to be an enormous imposition (and you could be certain that she was also quite unconcerned about the additional transcontinental travel she had inflicted upon us). Listening to her, I also concluded that Zotter must have been terrified at the thought of facing us in court. Otherwise, why would he have been willing to endure the tongue-lashing he received from Pjerrou over the settlement agreement? Interestingly, Pjerrou had been so busy chewing out Lynch, Zotter, and Supervisor Pinches that she'd made only scant mention of Margie and me, a slight that caused us no distress whatsoever.

Mac McKnight spoke next, advocating approval of our project and telling of the success he'd had establishing trees on his bluff-top parcel just a half-mile south of us. His neighbor to his north, Patricia Spires, also spoke on our behalf, and she told of the success she and her husband had enjoyed growing screening trees on their nearby bluff-top parcel. The last to speak on our behalf was Ruth Raffety, former water-board member and wife of John Raffety. She had an interesting perspective on our situation. In her mind the conflict was not about our project so much as it was about who (or what) was going to be in charge in the village of Elk. That seemed to make sense to me. Would the Coastal Act and associated regulations wield the power, or would the anti faction with its more restrictive demands?

Despite the late hour the supervisors allowed us an opportunity to respond to the opposition's testimony. Bob led off answering a number of questions raised by the opposition as well as rebutting some of their assertions. With regard to the "so-called Town Meeting" that Hale had spent so much time discrediting, Bob pointed out that we neither sponsored nor organized that meeting. That was the doing of the GECAG. They invited us to appear and discuss our project. They, not we, called for the vote. With regard to the charge by Adams that the State Parks Superintendent had approved of our project because "…the Berlincourts had told him of strong citizens' approval," Bob noted that that was hearsay and did not comprise evidence. The official evidence from State Parks is their letter of approval of our project. (Moreover, as already noted, Margie and I had never had any contact with State Parks Superintendent Picard.) In response to Pjerrou's attack against the settlement agreement, Bob remarked that both the County and we had entered into it of our own free will. We could not force the County to sign it nor could they force us to sign it. Bob countered Pjerrou's claims that our house would do great damage to the view from Cuffey's Cove by noting the great distance from there to our parcel as well as the fact that 14 much-closer Elk structures were already much more visible than our house would be from that view point. Finally Bob demolished Pjerrou's claim that a house at the Berrigan-mandated site would not be seen by visitors to the coast.

In response to questions raised by Doctor Adams regarding landscape irrigation, maintenance, and replacement, Sara Geddes pointed out that the answers were to be found on the landscape plans she had prepared for our project. I then showed some viewgraphs depicted a few oceanfront homes, which had recently been approved by the County, and which are of much greater visual prominence than ours would be. I included some remarks about standardization of camera and lens in photographic comparisons of visual impact in an effort to establish technical rigor aimed at countering the confusion Adams had generated in her attempt to discredit our photomontages. In Margie's concluding remarks she simply expressed puzzlement over why the opposition had regarded us, and our project, with such hostility.

The time had come for the Supervisors to rule on our application. This time the composition of the Board was more favorable to our cause, but nothing could be taken for granted. After all, they rebuffed our initial settlement demand. Their procedure would be similar to what had taken place at our previous Board hearing. From their elevated perches, each Supervisor would speak for a few minutes discussing various issues and providing a rationale for his or her decision. It was a little reminiscent of the Congressional hearings we'd attended back in Washington, except that there, politicians were always running for office, and their hearing comments were more likely to consist of election campaign rhetoric than rational consideration of the issues under debate. To their credit, the Mendocino County Supervisors focused on the issues this day.

Supervisor Peterson spoke first, evidently because our parcel was situated in his district. It was almost as if he was reading from a transcript of his comments at our hearing three years earlier. Perhaps he was, for a transcript of the earlier hearing was part of our lawsuit's administrative record, and, although we'd had to pay for its preparation, the County had free access to it. Peterson began by noting the beauty and rarity of promontories such as ours, which accounted for the strong emotions regarding it on both sides. Then he expressed his view that, no matter what decision the Board made, it would be appealed to its ultimate conclusion by whoever disagreed with the Board's decision. To his anti-faction constituents, who had expressed anger and betrayal over the settlement agreement, he was saying in effect that that agreement was actually of little consequence. (And indeed that would prove to be the case.) Peterson then commented that,

> "This decision on all of our parts, certainly in my term as a supervisor, will probably be the pinnacle of subjective decisions that I have the great good fortune in getting to make, because we're talking about subordinate to the character of the setting, whatever the Hell that means, in a situation like this."

I would have been happy to define it for him! Still ignoring professional testimony that the southeastern location would make our house more prominent from both the highway and the State Park view point, Peterson expressed his continued preference for the southeastern site that had been proposed by Berrigan. Surprisingly, he granted that, "Mr. Berlincourt is also correct in saying that in ten years, wherever they build it, it's going to have an effective tree screen around it." Now there was a significant concession. However, his vote would later indicate his unwillingness to grant us those ten years to achieve concealment. Finally, Peterson again argued that whoever owns property like ours owns the views from every square inch of it, even if they have to get up from the living room couch to get those views. A more conciliatory County position had been voiced by Planning and Building Services Department Director, Ray Hall, on 2-22-96 acting as Coastal Permit Administrator at a hearing on the Coastal Development Permit application of Peter and Patricia Clark for their project south of Point Arena. In that case views from the residence were also at issue, and Hall stated that, "… the applicant has some right, if that's the correct word, to some view of the ocean from this oceanfront lot."

In any event, Peterson expressed his opposition to both Plans 3 and 4. One of our concerns had been that there might be a tendency for other Supervisors to go along with positions adopted by a Supervisor in whose district the project under consideration is located so as to receive similar courtesy in return. Such goody trading is of course rampant among members of Congress. So we were relieved when Supervisor Delbar spoke next and pledged support for both of our plans. He said that he had listened to the professional testimony, and he disagreed with Peterson, saying a house in a swale is certainly subordinate. Delbar's opinion on ocean views from our house was in agreement with that of Hall regarding the Clark residence. Delbar also stated his preference that our house not be located close to the highway. Finally, he congratulated us on having done the best that could be done under the circumstances.

Supervisor Campbell began her comments by congratulating Peterson for his service on the Board, which was to conclude in 70 days. And she commended him for having formed the GECAG to foster community participation in local development issues. She then expressed appreciation for the clarification provided in answer to questions she'd raised on landscaping and water service. Significantly, she mentioned that in some reapplications that had come before the Board nothing in them had changed, but "In this case I feel that the applicant has truly listened to the concerns of the people that have made their concerns public." She found Bob's listing of changes we'd made helpful in that regard, and she liked our use of natural materials. At this point she cast her vote in support of Version 4. Then, addressing Mary Pjerrou, she remarked,

> "I also want to say to Mary, I'm feeling somewhat the same as
> you, and I'm glad you've come in as long as you did, because
> your comments are very important, but take care of yourself."

(Well, it's Mendocino County after all! It's a very informal place, and a perennial protestor like Pjerrou would certainly be well known to the supervisors.)

Supervisor Shoemaker was the model of brevity as he stated his agreement with the Staff and State Parks recommendation in favor of Plan 4.

Chairman Pinches was more talkative, and he expressed his support for property rights, and granted that, "…the Berlincourts can criticize the process. It cost them a lot of money." But as he saw it, our proposed house would give us most of what we wanted and would conform with most of the concerns both for people at the parks and on the highway. He considered the view from a parcel as a very important part of property rights. As if following his script from our earlier hearing, he remarked that, if our property had such extreme value for public benefit, then why hadn't State Parks picked it up when they had the opportunity? In the end he favored both Plans 3 and 4.

At this juncture Supervisor Shoemaker offered a motion in favor of adopting Plan 4, and it was seconded by Supervisor Delbar. The final vote was four to one in favor, with Supervisor Peterson dissenting. With that, supervisor Pinches thanked all who came the long distance to participate. And he added, "And also I'd like to congratulate the Berlincourts, and their family. Welcome to being residents of Mendocino County." I was speechless, but Margie managed to say, "Thank you very much." Whereupon Peterson chimed in, "This is a normal Mendocino County experience." That was followed by some tension-relieving laughter. But I could have gladly wrung his goddamned neck! He and the anti faction had stolen four years from our retirement and had cost us $200,000 in legal fees. Moreover, in the meantime, construction costs had skyrocketed. Zotter approached Margie and said something to the effect that, "Well we got it through," almost as if he'd been on our side all along, and he wondered why she wasn't smiling. She responded, " Because it isn't over yet."

But at least we had a 4 to 1 vote by the County Supervisors, and we had acceptance by State Parks in addition. That would handicap the inevitable appeal to the Coastal Commission. The Commission just might be reluctant to overturn such a favorable County vote together with an endorsement from State Parks.

CHAPTER 17

ANTI FACTION APPEAL TO THE COASTAL COMMISSION

The Board of Supervisors' favorable vote on our project on 10-26-98 had the same effect on the anti faction that a good whack with a broomstick has on a hornets' nest. The counterattack was immediate and intense. Protest letters began reaching the California Coastal Commission even before an appeal had been filed, and, within about two weeks, a total of 24 were received. The Mendocino County Notice of Final Action on our case reached the Commission on 11-2-98. The anti faction had the next ten days in which to file their appeal, but they weren't taking any chances. They filed on 11-4-98. The listed appellants were Doctor Hillary Adams and Roanne Withers of Mendocino County Coast Watch, and Ron Guenther of the Sierra Club Mendocino/Lake Group (although the appeal did not bear Guenther's signature). That appeal was the final straw that put an end to our willingness to donate our northern beach property to the state. We had earlier been spurned on that offer as well as our offer of a no-development deed restriction on our five-acre parcel. Obviously our opponents were more intent on stopping us completely than seeking a win-win solution.

Among the protest letters to the Coastal Commission was one from Rabbi Margaret Holub. That, together with Reverend Schaeffer's earlier letter to the Mendocino County Supervisors, comprised indictment by both Jewish and Christian theologians (but, happily, we were spared indictment by the Pope's emissary in Elk). On 11-5-98 *The Mendocino Beacon* published a "Letter to the Editor" by Loraine Toth, which stated in part;

> "Those who purport to believe in, for example, inviolate property rights as an American Right, and threaten others with physical, or economic harm for exercising their right to freedom of speech, should hang their hypocritical heads in shame. They are thugs."

There could be no doubt that this was aimed at us, although we could recall no instance of having threatened anyone with "physical or economic harm." Either the editor had forbidden use of our names, or Toth feared a lawsuit if she named us. But we never entertained the thought of suing any of the anti faction. There was nothing to be gained by that.

Again the anti faction initiated a petition, and again it was prominently displayed in the Elk Store, and again customers were urged to sign it. A total of 89 Elk residents and 104 visitors did so. But the petition cost Elk Store proprietor Ben MacMillan his biggest account. Sam Haynes, the new owner of the Harbor House, an elegant local bed-and-breakfast inn and restaurant, was shopping at the Elk Store. When he approached the checkout counter, MacMillan asked him to sign the petition. That was a red cape to a bull of a conservative like Sam, and he simply put down his groceries and left, never again to shop at the Elk Store so long as MacMillan owned it. Evidently, Sam didn't agree with the assertion by Doctor Hillary Adams that our house would threaten the livelihoods of Elk bed-and-breakfast inns.

Again we wrote to our steadfast supporters. We were apologetic for continuing to call upon them, but it was important that the Coastal Commission not get the impression that there was only one side to our case in Elk. Our friends kindly provided 11 letters of support and a favorable petition with 32 signatures of local residents. In nearly all instances the letters of support concentrated on the compliance of our project with the County regulations and avoided mention of the opposition, but Ken Anton, a geologist and Libertarian, couldn't resist a jab at the anti faction. On 11-30-98 he wrote the following to the Coastal Commission:

> "After four years of watching this fiasco unfold while other visible development in town goes without protest, it is my opinion that the opponents to this project are attacking the Berlincourts solely because of personal dislike and are abusing the County and Coastal Commission process to obtain some sort of sick personal gratification. I have heard some opponents expressing concern about having a Veteran live in town (there is a strong anti-military sentiment in Elk), but that might only be the beginning of social engineering prejudices here."

Now, what were the stated reasons for the Adams-Withers-Guenther appeal of our project? The first was an assertion that other sites on the parcel offered "better protection of the public's visual resources." The second attacked the height of our proposed structure, incorrectly claiming that it would be 20 feet high. The third claimed that, "even with a drilled pier foundation system," we did not have adequate setback from the bluff edge. The fourth called for additional landscaping to screen the building immediately.

Adams and Pjerrou, subsequently wrote lengthy letters to Coastal Commission Staff Planner Jo Ginsberg expanding on those objections. Pjerrou's 11-18-98 letter consisted of five pages of single-spaced fine print. It contained at least 17 erroneous claims. Only one is worth mentioning here, viz., that the "...attitude of the community [was] firm but friendly." Well, if the attitude we'd been experiencing was "friendly," I'm grateful we were spared their hostile attitude! Among the 84 pages of attachments to Pjerrou's letter were copies of our conditional settlement agreement, our lawsuit petition No. 74134, the 1995 anti-faction petition against our original application, 20 pages of 1995 letters that had been written in opposition to our original application, and four incendiary 1995 articles from *The Mendocino Beacon* on our original application. The 1995 materials were of course not pertinent to our 1998 reapplication.

Doctor Hillary Adams' 11-16-98 letter to Jo Ginsberg was also single spaced, and a half page longer than Pjerrous.' It contained at least 18 false claims. Several indicate either her unfamiliarity with, or, alternatively, her inability to comprehend the meaning of, the County regulations, which, after all, are not rocket science. Interestingly, Doctor Adams did a lot of research on our real estate activity, even going so far as providing maps and purchase prices of our holdings (one of which we no longer owned) as attachments to her letter. Her purpose was to establish that we were "developers!" For the anti faction, there could be no more-derogatory appellation. Adams' triumphant tone in announcing that revelation brought to mind Hungarian linguist Zoltan Karpathy's declaration in "My Fair Lady." As Professor Higgins described it, "with a voice too eager and a smile too broad" Karpathy announced triumphantly that Eliza Doolittle was born "Hungarian, not only Hungarian, but of royal blood!" We composed paragraph by paragraph rebuttals to the Pjerrou and Adams letters which we were prepared to provide to Ginsberg. However, she expressed no interest in local politics and seemed savvy enough to see through the pettiness of the Pjerrou and Adams letters, and so we refrained from pressing our rebuttals on her.

In the appeal process, the Coastal Commission Staff conducts a *de novo* review. In effect they ignore the County findings and rulings and go back to square one, examining all of the evidence to arrive at the facts and their own determination of whether or not the project conforms to the County Local Coastal Plan. Then they make a recommendation. If they determine that the appeal does not raise a "substantial issue" the appeal does not even go to a hearing before the Commission. If staff believes the appeal does raise a substantial Issue, then the Commission may either agree or disagree. If the Commission agrees, then the case will be heard by the Commission, and the appeal will either be upheld or denied. If the Commission disagrees, the appeal is in effect denied.

On 11-23-99 we received a telephone call from Coastal Commission Staff Planner, Jo Ginsberg. She informed us that she planned a site visit eight days later on 12-1-98. She told us to have a mock-up of the house with metal scaffolding in place on our parcel for her visit. She referred us to a local (Little River) builder, Steve Hale, who had erected such mock-ups satisfactorily for her in the past. We were already acquainted with Steve and knew that he was not related to our opponent, Judith Hale, and so we were comfortable about approaching him. But the timing was far from ideal. By the Wednesday before Thanksgiving we had secured Hale's agreement to perform the task. He suggested that for a little extra he could provide some mock evergreen trees to simulate vegetative screening as well. We accepted his suggestion. Later we would part with $3,000 for his services.

On Sunday, 11-29-98, Margie and I departed standby on an early jet from Washington to San Francisco (my sixteenth transcontinental round trip of this quest), and it was a very bumpy ride. On Monday, in light rain, Hale and his crew delivered the scaffolding to the site. Then on Tuesday morning, beneath overcast skies, they set up the scaffolding outlining the main features of the house.

Ginsberg, a tiny thirtyish woman, arrived right on schedule at 2:45 PM, and with her was her supervisor, Robert Merrill, around forty and of average build. They were all business, no small talk, and busied themselves checking out the mock-up and the site in general. Throughout, Merrill took numerous photographs. Next, with Steve accompanying them, they visited the burner-ring view point at the State Park to the north. While there, they witnessed the raising of the mock trees (which were really quite pitiful). From there they proceeded north to the Cuffey's Cove view point (two miles by road from our parcel, 1.6 miles as the crow flies). Next they drove south of our parcel to a location on Highway One, which would provide the closest public view of our house. According to Steve that view proved to be of greatest concern to them. (Plan 3 would actually have been better from that perspective, but that was water over the dam.) Back on our parcel, Merrill asked about the Berrigan-mandated site to the southeast, and we explained that it would be much closer to the Highway One public view point which he had just visited. Because Ginsberg and Merrill had agreed to meet with us later on 12-3-98 at their Coastal Commission office in San Francisco, we would have an opportunity to provide more background on that issue at that time. After Ginsberg and Merrill had departed Steve told us that, from what he had overheard, our prospects looked good. However, in our presence they'd expressed no opinions whatsoever.

On 12-3-98 we met with Ginsberg and Merrill at 10 AM at Coastal Commission headquarters in downtown San Francisco. Because they had no memory of receiving the copy of our 69-page "Reapplication Addendum" that we had sent to them eight months earlier we provided them with another. They were also unaware of State Parks' endorsement of our project this time around, and so we provided them with a copy of Superintendent Picard's letter. Ginsberg and Merrill were, of course, well aware of the opposition letters, petition, and telephone calls they'd received from Elk, and, of course, all the contents of the County file on our case would soon be at their disposal. But they claimed to have no interest in Elk politics nor the lawsuit associated with our case. It was clear that their principal concerns centered on visual matters and related mitigation measures, not on the height and setback issues also raised by the appeal. Accordingly, with reference to our "Reapplication Addendum" we focused on the virtues of the swale site as having minimum impact on public views, noting though that the northern bluff edge site would have provided us with far superior ocean views. Quizzed about the Berrigan-mandated site, we showed them a photomontage depicting a view from Highway One of a house at the center of it. If situated so close to the highway, it would dominate the scene and block public views to the ocean. Fortunately, this proved to be a major concern to Coastal Commission Staff. We addressed mitigation measures by showing our landscaping plans and showing photos of tall, dense, and vigorous evergreens growing on nearby points north and south of ours.

Because of statutory time limits the Commission would normally have heard our case in December, but Commission Staff had not received the County files in time for a proper review. It was therefore necessary for the Commission to open our hearing at their San Francisco meeting on 12-9-98 and "continue" it (postpone it) to the next month's meeting, which would be in Los Angeles. We were a little apprehensive about this procedure, and so we requested Jeff Speich to represent us at the 12-9-98 hearing. Had there been any move to put our case to a vote that day, Jeff was to intercede on our behalf, citing the fact that no Staff Report had yet been issued. The hearings began at 9 AM, and it was 7 PM by the time the Commission addressed our case. Happily, the continuation went smoothly. In hindsight, we had wasted Jeff's time (and our money).

Good news reached us on 12-15-98! On that date Ginsberg informed Bob Schlosser by telephone that her Staff Report would be supportive of our Coastal Development Permit application. However, it would recommend special conditions requiring "non-reflective" windows, no outside lights on the northern end of the house, and greatly increased landscape screening, all of which were acceptable to us. Ginsberg had also telephoned Sara Geddes to discuss the added landscaping requirements.

Ginsberg's Staff Report was issued on 12-18-98, and, while it was supportive, it was not as strong an endorsement as we would have liked. With regard to whether or not the appeal raised a substantial issue, the report stated:

> "Commission Staff believes the appeal of the development, as
> approved by the County, raises a substantial issue of whether the
> residence, located in a designated Highly Scenic Area, would
> be sited and designed to protect coastal views in the manner
> required by the policies of the LCP [Local Coastal Plan]. The site
> is visible from a number of public areas, and, as approved by
> the County, the project will have significant adverse impacts on
> visual resources. Commission Staff thus believes the project, as
> approved by the County, raises a substantial issue with regard to
> conformance with the visual and scenic policies of the County's
> LCP…"

But, fortunately the Staff recommendation *de novo* on our project was much more supportive. It read:

> "The Staff recommends that the Commission approve with
> conditions the coastal development permit for the proposed
> project on the basis that, as conditioned by the Commission, it
> is consistent with the County's certified LCP and with the public

access and public recreation policies of the Coastal Act. Staff believes the current project, as approved by the County, is inconsistent with the visual and scenic resource policies of the LCP. However, Staff believes that if certain special conditions are attached to the permit, the project will be consistent with the County's LCP. These conditions include additional design restrictions and requiring additional landscaping that will result in better screening of views of the development from the town of Elk, the State Park, and Highway One..."

On cursory reading these two recommendations might seem to be contradictory, but they're not, for the Staff Report simply asserts that our project deserved approval only with the additional special conditions that Commission Staff had specified. Most importantly, the Staff Report later states:

"If the house were sited to the east, it would be much more visible from Highway One than it currently is, especially from vantage points adjacent or close to the parcel, and the development would block views of the ocean as well...Thus the Commission finds that the proposed location of the proposed house, in the swale in the southwestern portion of the site is the site that best protects views to and along the scenic coastal area..."

So much for Berrigan's eastern site. May it *requiescat in pace*! We can't imagine that our opponents ever really wanted that site built on. More likely it was simply a ploy to try to discourage us from building at all.

One disturbing aspect of the Coastal Commission Staff Report was the inclusion of 20 pages of anti-faction letters written in 1995 in opposition to our original application as well as copies of four incendiary 1995 articles from *The Mendocino Beacon* opposing our original application. Those items had been included as enclosures with Pjerrou's 1998 letter of opposition in an obviously deliberate attempt to poison our 1998 case with anti-faction venom from our 1995 case. In so doing, Pjerrou presented Coastal Commission Staff with a dilemma, and we were more than a little concerned about how they might handle it.

Now what of the special conditions mandated in the Coastal Commission Staff Report? They cover four-and-a-half pages single-spaced. One-and-a-half pages have to do with landscape screening. Whereas the County had required 66 trees and shrubs, the Coastal Commission required 200, as well as annual reports for five years. (We mailed the last of our annual landscaping reports on 11-30-05. By then we had planted 401 trees and about 40 shrubs.)

Several of the remaining special conditions were repetitions of those required by the County, and several were new. The Coastal Commissioners themselves would soon add others and would require that many of the special conditions be placed as deed restrictions on our property. Over all, the special conditions were much more onerous than a typical homeowner would tolerate. Indeed, if government were to be as intrusive in all cases of new construction, there would surely be open revolt. But would-be California-coastal-zone residents are too few in number to mount such a rebellion effectively. In our case, we were simply so overjoyed to see some light at the end of the tunnel that we weren't going to make a fuss about the special conditions. Our focus now was entirely on the upcoming hearing of our case by the California Coastal Commission. It was scheduled for 1-14-99 in Los Angeles. Whereas things had moved glacially slowly in Mendocino County, the Coastal Commission's pace was rapid.

CHAPTER 18

CALIFORNIA COASTAL COMMISSION HEARING

On 1-12-99 Margie and I boarded a jet at Washington Dulles Airport bound for Los Angeles (my seventeenth transcontinental round trip on our quest for a Coastal Development Permit). Two days later the California Coastal Commission would make a determination on the appeal of our Coastal Development Permit application. Landing in Los Angeles was like old times. We'd lived in the suburbs of the City of Angels for fifteen years and had many happy memories from our time there. As the plane touched down on the runway it passed one of my old haunts, the building that had been the proud Headquarters of North American Aviation, the company that blazed the trail to the moon, its divisions now scattered among other corporate entities by the vagaries of high-technology industrial ferment. The airport terminal building also brought back memories, memories of myriad departures to faraway places, for business trips, scientific conferences, and vacation trips. It was like a homecoming. It seemed appropriate that the ultimate hearing in our battle to return to California should be in Los Angeles. And the omens were good!

But we weren't taking anything for granted. We'd arrived early in Los Angeles so we could stake out the Olympic Collection Conference Center and sit through a whole day of Coastal Commission sessions prior to our own hearing. That way we could observe how the Commission operated and sense the tone of their deliberations. It wasn't reassuring, primarily because of the extent and complexity of the issues the Commissioners faced. That accounts for the multiplicity of lawsuits the Commission has faced. In fact, Item 9 on the first day's agenda consisted of a report from the Deputy Attorney General on ten of those lawsuits.

Of the twelve voting Commissioners, four are appointed by the Governor of California, four are appointed by the California Senate Rules Committee, and four are appointed by the California Assembly Speaker. Six of them are "public members" appointed at large, and six are local elected officials, one from each of six coastal districts. In the Conference Center they occupied the high table on a raised platform above both their staff and the audience. The Commission dealt with an enormous multitude of disputes backed by mountains of bureaucratic paperwork. Speakers, both for and against, were allowed three to five minutes to state their cases. Had all of the Commissioners diligently reviewed all of that paperwork, or were some merely rubber stamps for the staff recommendations, or were others simply voting their political convictions? Those questions would not be answered, but there would soon be a decision on our case.

The next morning Margie and I were joined by Bob Schlosser and Jeff Speich well before the start of the session. Our plan was for Margie and me to yield our allocated times to Bob, who would be the primary speaker. Jeff stood by to deal with legal issues if they arose. We were on the alert for the appellants, Doctor Hillary Adams, Roanne Withers, and Ron Guenther, but, to our delight, they didn't appear. Apparently their anti-development zeal was exceeded by their aversion to spending money and effort to travel the "vast" distance from Elk to Los Angeles.

At 9:19 AM Chairman Sara J. Wan opened the hearing on the appeal of our project. A shortage of travel funds had precluded the presence of Ginsberg and Merrill, and so Steven Scholl, Deputy Executive Director of the Commission, rose to provide the staff background. He began with this disclaimer:

> "First a couple words about the staff report, which is fairly lengthy, as you undoubtedly noticed. We did include in that a large amount of correspondence, and that included some correspondence from opponents of the project who had submitted items regarding a previous site proposed in 1995, and I just wanted to explain that, because if you look in Exhibit number 19, which is some 60 pages long, a good portion of that is letters regarding a little different project proposal from 1995. Obviously that's not the subject of this hearing here. The only reason we included it is that the opponent included that with their correspondence, and we wanted to make absolutely sure we didn't leave anything out that was part of the record."

Obviously, the commission staff had seen through Pjerrou's tactic and wanted to be certain that the Commissioners were not influenced by it either.

Chairman Wan then moved right along. Scarcely pausing for any response, she declared,

> "Since staff is recommending that we find substantial issue, are there three or more commissioners who wish to object to the finding of substantial issue? Seeing none, we can just move directly into the - we can find substantial issue and move directly into the hearing."

With that she denied us any opportunity to argue the substantial-issue matter, whereas, according to the Commission's procedural rules we should have been allowed

215

three minutes to argue that point. But Jeff wisely concluded that it was the better part of politics not to make an issue if it.

Scholl then continued, pretty much echoing what was in the Staff Report. It was evident that he had been well prepared to make his presentation. In order to illustrate the points he was making, he showed a number of slides of photos taken by Merrill from the various public view points. The scaffolding was scarcely visible in some and not visible at all in others. He was highly effective in making the salient points, viz.; that the area was highly scenic; that "there is really no part of the site where construction could occur that wouldn't be visible from some public place;" that the challenge is to minimize the impact on the view; that the proposed site is pulled far to the south to minimize views from Cuffey's Cove and the State Park; and that the more eastern site proposed by the County in 1995 would have placed the house close to Highway One, where it would be quite prominent. He reiterated the Staff recommendation for approval, stating that that recommendation was based on a special condition for substantially more landscape screening than the County had specified, and another special condition requiring no exterior lighting of the structure that's visible from the north, i.e., from the community of Elk. Finally, citing the favorable geotechnical report on our site, Scholl dismissed the appellants' setback complaint.

One of the Commissioners then stated that, as he read the record, the applicants had sued the County after denial of an earlier application, and that had resulted in a conditional settlement agreement. Why he had raised this point was not clear, but Scholl concurred. Chairman Wan then called for comments from our side, noting that we would be allowed a total of 15 minutes. Jeff responded first, confirming that a lawsuit had been filed to preserve our rights, and that, while that was pending, we had entered into a conditional settlement agreement to reapply. He noted that the design had been modified; that we had done an analysis of alternative siting to determine the location for minimum visibility; and that our siting choice had been confirmed by County Staff, by a 4 to 1 vote of the County Supervisors, and by Commission Staff.

Margie and I then yielded our time to Bob. A portion of his remarks follows:

> "...The new project differs from the old project in that we've moved it to the point on the property that's the lowest elevation on the property and that's the farthest distance away from all the public viewpoints from which it can be seen. We've also located in on the southern part of the property, so...no part of the project will be visible from the beach at Greenwood State Beach. Having revised the project in this way, we took it to the... State Parks Department, who's our most affected neighbor, and their letter's in the file that you guys have there that the State Parks Department recommended approval of our project, and, in addition, they commended us for working with them to try to

mitigate their concerns as to the visual impact of the project. The County staff analyzed the different options for siting the project, and the County Staff concluded that the place that we're locating the project now is going to be the least visible of all the alternative sites on the property. Mendocino County Board of Supervisors, as Mr. Speich indicated, voted 4 to 1 in favor of our project, and Bob Merrill and Jo Ginsberg, both of the Coastal Commission Staff viewed the scaffolding that you saw up on the site from all the different affected viewpoints, and they concluded that the siting that we've chosen for the house now is the best site on the property where we can locate a single family residence, so, therefore, in summary, there's four public bodies that have reviewed the project this time around. All four of them have independently reviewed the information, and all four of them are recommending to the Commission that the project be approved..."

A careful reader will note that Bob had made four highly-significant points that had not been mentioned by the two preceding speakers.

Now, to interject, at some point during the proceedings an individual sitting behind us had struck up a conversation with Jeff. He was highly sun-tanned and had long flowing sun-bleached hair. He looked like a typical California beach hippie, although perhaps a little older, maybe early forties. His card (a beach hippie with a card?) revealed that he was Mark Massara, a lawyer and Director, Sierra Club Coastal Programs. Well, so the appellants were represented after all! And if you google Massara, you'll find that he founded the Surfing Attorney's Association. You'll also find that he's famous for his role in a Clean Water Act case in San Francisco Federal District Court against Louisiana-Pacific and Simpson Paper, two Companies operating pulp mills in northern California. It turned into one of the largest Clean Water Act cases ever prosecuted. Had we known that at the time, we'd have "had an awful fright!" He just looked like a damn hippie. Never, never underestimate your adversaries. Well, Massara made it clear that he represented the appellants and asked if we were willing to accept the more stringent landscape screening special conditions recommended by Commission Staff. We informed him that we had already agreed to that, and, in turn, he let us know that he was not going to be obstructive. Thus the rug was pulled out from under appellants Adams, Withers, and Guenther!

It's interesting to speculate about that. The Sierra Club has a multitude of disparate Groups like the Mendocino/Lake Group scattered throughout the United States. They can be a lot of loose cannons, and they can muddle into matters where the Headquarters of the Sierra Club might prefer not to tread. I suspect that at Sierra Club Headquarters they choose their battles pretty carefully. In our case, Guenther's name and his stated

Sierra Club affiliation on the appeal implied the full force of the Sierra Club. Yet, Guenther had not signed the appeal, either because he hadn't cleared it ahead of time with Headquarters and was just bluffing, or because Adams and Withers had been in such a hurry to file the appeal that they didn't wait for his signature. In any event, Massara had reviewed our case and decided not to intervene. We were most grateful for that.

But to return to the hearing, Commissioner Tuttle asked Bob to explain the rationale used in siting our proposed house. This again gave Bob an opportunity to explain the pros and cons of the various possible sites in a systematic manner. A few questions then followed having to do with the Geotechnical Report and the availability of water. Then Commissioner Reilly asked why the applicants had found the eastern site proposed by the County in 1995 to be unacceptable. Bob explained that with 11 acres nobody would want to build close to the highway. He added that a house at the eastern site would require a lot of cut and fill, would be highly visible from the highway, and would block public views to the ocean. He didn't mention that it would also decimate our ocean views.

Then, the tiresome question of our parcel's access to water was raised yet again, this time by Commissioner Reilly. He began by asserting, "This is a critical water short area as I understand it." (That's debatable, because the Elk County Water District actually conducts a thriving business selling excess water that is trucked to distant water-starved areas of the County). Reilly then launched into a long line of questioning that was again reminiscent of the water-rights wars of the old west. From the nature of his questions it was clear that he'd been prompted, if not by de Vall or Peterson, then by de Vall's 1995 letter of protest that had been included as one of the attachments to Pjerrou's 1998 letter to the Commission. That issue had of course been put to bed by Acker's testimony and letter of evidence at the Board of Supervisors' hearing. But Commissioner Reilly wouldn't let go. Indeed, it appeared he was going to be obstructive, but evidently Chairman Wan had tired of the water issue, for she interceded to call on Mark Massara for his testimony. The latter's words follow:

> "Madame Chair, good morning. I'm Mark Massara. I'm representing Mendocino Coast Watch and Sierra Club Mendocino/Lake Group, appellants in this matter. Staff and the applicant have already described that this is another one of those spectacular north coast parcels located on a rocky headland with incredible views in every direction south of the town of Elk and adjacent to a state beach. The property itself is so spectacular that any development located nearly anywhere on the parcel will have impact, viewshed impact, and given this constraint and the nature of the parcel, we're supporting Staff and Staff's recommendations regarding the detailed landscaping and lighting prohibitions. I think that Staff has done

an admirable job in this case in requiring mature landscaping and an enormous number of trees and screening that with any luck will minimize viewshed impact from this project, and so with that we're supporting Staff. Thank you."

Thank you Mark Massara, Esq. Surf on! Can you imagine how Adams, Withers, and Guenther would have reacted to Massara's representation of their appeal?

At this juncture, Jeff made the point that in the original case the Coastal Permit Administrator had mandated the eastern site without ever having been on the parcel, whereas the present site selection was the result of a thorough analysis of all possible sites aimed at minimizing visual impact.

With that Chairman Wan closed the public hearing and turned first to the staff and then to the Commissioners for comments. Commissioner Nava responded by suggesting that there be a special condition or a deed restriction whereby the applicants assume responsibility in the event of bluff failure in the future, meaning no shoreline protective devices. Other Commissioners weighed in on the issue agreeing that in the event of accelerated bluff retreat the applicants must not be allowed to build shoreline protective devices or sea walls, but rather accept the risk and responsibility either to move or remove the house. Language to that effect had been developed for recent cases, and Chairman Wan suggested that Staff develop language for our concurrence while other matters were being addressed.

With regard to the special condition requiring that there be no night lighting whatsoever on the north-facing sides of the structure, Commissioner Reilly suggested an addition to provide that the lighting plan must meet the approval of the Executive Director. He also suggested a modification with regard to water service, suggesting that the applicants demonstrate that they have water service from the local water district prior to permit issue, rather than prior to occupancy, as had been required by the County.

Chairman Wan then turned briefly to other agenda items to allow us time to negotiate deed restriction language with Commission Staff. That task proved to be relatively straightforward. When Chairman Wan returned to our case, she promptly asked for a motion. Commissioner Nancy Fleming (Mayor of Eureka, who lived in a cottage on Indian Island in Humbolt Bay and with her husband was co-owner/operator of the "Nancy Stout" tugboat) moved for approval of our project, with a yes vote for all of the amendments. The motion was seconded by Commissioner Mary Herron. Whereupon Chairman Wan remarked, "Moved by Commissioner Fleming, seconded by Commissioner Herron. Any objection to a unanimous role call? Seeing none, so ordered."

We had done it! The final vote was 9 to 0 in our favor with three Commissioners temporarily out of their seats, evidently attending to what they considered to be "more important" matters.

Nearly four-and-a-half years after our original application was filed we had our approval! So in the end the convoluted process we had endured had finally produced the right result. Perhaps Winston Churchill was right when he commented that, "You can always count on Americans to do the right thing - after they've tried everything else."

Our team retired to the patio outside the conference center for a celebration, and we were joined briefly by Steven Scholl, who stopped by to congratulate us. I recorded the event on film and returned to the meeting room to photograph that scene as well. (And of course I used high-speed black-and-white film so as not to create any flash disturbance.) Then, expressing our heartiest thanks to Bob and Jeff, we left for the airport to fly to Dallas to spend several days with our daughter, son-in-law, and grandsons before flying home to Virginia. It would be a happy time.

But not so fast! True, we had an approval, but we didn't yet have a Coastal Development Permit. That would follow only after satisfactory filing and recording of the deed restrictions. But that should take only a couple of weeks, right? Don't be too sure.

CHAPTER 19

A FINAL PROBLEM AND A FINAL IRONY

The Coastal Commission approval of our project was duly reported in Charlie Acker's Elk column and in a separate article in the 1-21-99 issue of *The Mendocino Beacon*. Both were factual and non-judgmental. The highly contentious part of our efforts to build our dream house on the California coast was now at an end (or so we thought). It hadn't been a walk in the park, but now all of that was behind us. What remained was to complete the bureaucratic paperwork, badger Bob and Mike to complete the detailed working drawings for our house, solicit bids, and sit back and watch the house go up.

On 1-22-99 the Coastal Commission mailed us, not a permit, but a "Notice of Intention to Issue Permit." It listed the standard and special conditions and indicated which of the latter were to be incorporated into deed restrictions on our property. At the bottom of the original cover page was a place for our signatures to acknowledge that we had received and understood all of the conditions. We signed and promptly returned that form to the Commission. Along with the "Notice of Intent to Issue Permit," we received forms on which we were to enter our deed restrictions along with other information. We were then to return those forms (notarized), along with a current title insurance policy, to the Coastal Commission Legal Department for review. After obtaining their approval we were to have the deed restrictions recorded by Mendocino County. The County was then to send the original of the recorded deed restrictions to the Coastal Commission. Only then would the Commission finally issue our Coastal Development Permit. Well, we were impatient, and, as you can imagine, Rome wasn't built in a day. Indeed, it took a full four months from the date the Commissioners approved our permit application until, on 5-15-99, the permit was in our hands. I'll spare you the negatives of the Coastal Commission's and County's bureaucratic delays, slights, indignities, and complications that we had to endure along the way, and just mention one good Samaritan, a civil servant who was truly helpful in the best traditions of the civil service, viz., Jeff Staben of the Coastal Commission Legal Department.

What of the deed restrictions themselves? They covered two-and-a-half pages single-spaced and are listed here in abbreviated form:

1. Any additional development on the parcel requires another permit (i.e., like "return to start" on a board game).

2. The guest quarters shall be without kitchen and shall not be separately rented.

3. The owner understands that the site may be subject to extraordinary geologic and erosion hazard and the owner assumes the risk from such hazard.

4. The owner waives any claims of liability against the California Coastal Commission for any damage arising from the permitted project.

5. The owner agrees to indemnify and hold harmless the California Coastal Commission against any and all claims arising out of any work performed in connection with the permitted project.

6. The owner agrees that any adverse impacts to property caused by the permitted project shall be fully the responsibility of the applicant.

7. The owner shall not construct any bluff or shoreline protective devices to protect any improvement on the site that is threatened by natural hazards.

8. The owner shall remove the house and its foundations if bluff retreat reaches the point where the structure is threatened. If portions of the improvements fall to the beach, the owner shall remove all recoverable debris from the beach and ocean and dispose of the material at an approved disposal site. The owner shall bear all costs of removal.

We had objected only to the use of the word "extraordinary" in the third of those restrictions. It brands our parcel with an adverse descriptive term not justified in light of our favorable Geotechnical Report. At such time as our property might go on the market, that word could scare away potential buyers. However, that's standard language for the Commission, and negotiating its removal was not practical. Note that Items 4, 5, and 6 were designed to protect the Commission from any liability whatsoever with respect to our project.

A Final Problem And A Final Irony

With our Coastal Development Permit firmly in hand we wrote to Ron Zumbrun and Jeff Speich expressing our most grateful appreciation for their outstanding and effective efforts on our behalf, stating that there was no doubt in our minds that, given the climate in Mendocino County and the State of California, we could never have realized our rights without their legal expertise and wise counsel. And with that we authorized them to take the necessary legal action to end our lawsuit. Actually, we had bittersweet feelings regarding the end of our lawsuit. We'd grown quite attached to it, for there was comfort in knowing that we had legal recourse. And there was satisfaction in knowing that it caused the Mendocino County and State Parks bureaucracies to squirm at least a little, even if not commensurate with their just desserts. The "Notice of Entry of Dismissal" for our lawsuit was endorsed and filed by the Mendocino County Superior Court of California on 6-24-99, three years and three months after our complaint was filed.

As it turned out we needn't have been in a hurry to get our permit. Building was booming on the coast, and Bob and Mike were up to their eyeballs in projects. As a result, there was slow progress on the final working drawings for our house. Needless to say, we leaned hard on Bob and Mike to try to hurry them along.

In the meantime, we continued to hear of the activities of Doctor Hillary Adams. While Adams and Roanne Withers had been actively contesting our application, they were also contesting an application for a Coastal Development Permit application submitted by Bob and Luanne Smiley, who have since become fast friends, she a medical doctor, and he a retired career naval aviator and lawyer. They sought to build a house high on a mountainside on their 182-acre parcel east of Highway One a few miles south of Elk. Despite active opposition from Doctor Hillary Adams and the other usual suspects, the County approved the Smiley project. Their case, like ours, was appealed to the Coastal Commission, but in this instance the Commission upheld the appeal, thereby denying the project. The Smileys subsequently sued the Commission and prevailed. Their story, like ours, is long and tortuous, and I hope they might someday tell it as I'm telling ours. Together our stories illustrate the capricious nature of the permitting process and how vicious the anti faction can be.

And so in June of 1999, when we were told that Doctor Hillary Adams had been thrown by her horse and sustained one (or was it two?) broken ankles, we found it difficult to be sympathetic, especially because it was said that the horse had been shot. The word among property-rights advocates in Elk was that they shot the wrong one. But, that view was evidently not shared by the Mendocino Coast Audubon Society, the California Native Plant Society, the Mendocino Land Trust, and the Mendocino Area Parks Society. Indeed, as reported in the 4-12-01 issue of the *Fort Bragg Advocate News*, those organizations honored Doctor Hillary Adams nearly two years later with their Environmental Achievement Award consisting of a signed poster by Ken Michaelsen, a gift certificate from Gallery Bookshop, and recognition certificates from Congressman Mike Thompson, State Senator Wesley Chesbro, and State Assemblywoman Virginia Strom-Martin.

223

We were to hear still more of the activities of Doctor Hillary Adams. On 8-9-99 we received a telephone call from Roger Sternberg, Executive Director of the Mendocino Land Trust, a private non-profit conservation organization that acquires land from willing sellers for public benefit. He had been approached by Doctor Hillary Adams with regard to our Elk properties and wondered if we might be willing to sell them. He mentioned that the State of California had made $7 million available over the previous two years and was currently allocating $5.5 million. Expressing appreciation for his call, I explained that the final working drawings for our project were being prepared, that we were intent upon proceeding with construction, and that, in fact, just a month earlier we had put our Virginia house up for sale. Further, I mentioned that, had it not been for Doctor Hillary Adams and her cohorts, our house would already be in place, and there would be a no-development deed restriction on our adjacent five-acre parcel. Unfortunately, the legal fees we incurred in securing a permit, and the increased building costs resulting from the delay, meant that we could no longer consider a no-development deed restriction on that parcel. On the other hand, had Sternberg called us six years earlier, who knows, we might have been spared our little unpleasantness. But we took it as a positive sign that Doctor Hillary Adams was attempting to work through the Mendocino Land Trust. It was as if she'd been ideologically rehabilitated. Well, not really. Her attacks on coastal development continued unabated.

Two months later, on 10-9-99, we signed a sales contract on our Virginia house, and we were able to set the closing date in the first week of the new millennium, thereby avoiding the unpleasant and near-impossible task of dealing with partial-year income tax forms from two different states. But we had to have a place to live in California while our house was under construction, and so, on 12-7-99, I left on still another transcontinental round trip, this time to seek a rental. I was fortunate to find a two-story house south of Fort Bragg on an acre of land and within walking distance of an oceanfront park. It was a little like two houses in one, with a kitchen, living area, bedroom (or two), and bath on each floor. The upper floor had a large stone fireplace and nice ocean views, and so we would spend most of our time upstairs. I took pictures of the rental, inside and out, so Margie would be able to see what I had committed us to. On the same trip I met with our architects to deal with countless details of the working drawings, and I checked out the Stocklin Iron Works in Santa Rosa, which would later fabricate the spiral stairs for our new home. Then, because I was flying standby, my return flight took me to Baltimore, from which I made my way home.

On 1-7-00, having closed on our Virginia house sale, and having donated our beloved 1984 Audi 5000 wagon to charity, we departed the Washington, DC, area bound for California in our 1993 Volkswagen Passat. It was a little reminiscent of our 1955 trip from Washington, DC, to Los Angeles via 1953 Nash Ambassador. There would again be a change of lifestyle, and we looked forward to a new adventure with great anticipation. We arrived in Fort Bragg a day early, but after dark, after a harrowing drive in a fierce rainstorm over the mountains on Route 128. Fortunately, there was a key under the doormat. To my delight, Margie liked the rental. We would spend two happy years there.

On 3-22-00 we entered into a contract to sell our 5-acre Albion parcel, which had been on the market for several years. The sale couldn't have come at a better time, for it simplified the financing of our new home. Three days later, some ten months after our Coastal Development Permit had been issued, Bob informed us that the working drawings for our house were finally complete and would go out to bid in another two days. Then on 3-28-00, on our behalf, Bob filed an application for a Building Permit at the Fort Bragg office of the Mendocino County Department of Planning and building Services. (Don't confuse a Building Permit with a Coastal Development Permit. In order for the former to be issued, you must already possess the latter.)

Unfortunately, a problem soon developed. When County Planner Rick Miller checked with the Coastal Commission in Eureka, they had no record of our coastal Development Permit. That Commission office had been established just a few months earlier, and, although Robert Merrill had been transferred there from San Francisco, our permit evidently had not. But it couldn't be located at the Commission's San Francisco office either. Fortunately, we had a copy of the original that we had signed and had sent back to the Commission on 5-16-99. That proved acceptable.

On 4-13-00, after carefully checking over our final working plans, Rick Miller informed Bob Schlosser that he'd found changes from the plans that had been approved by the Coastal Commission and that he thought we were trying to slip some things past him, and that he was going to inform the Coastal Commission. Bob confirmed that we had relocated the water storage tanks (which would be underground and hence not visible to the public in any event), had reduced the window area by 35 square feet on publicly visible sides of the house, and had changed from redwood siding to cedar siding, all of which we considered to be non-substantive changes. Informed of these changes, Merrill determined that we would have to submit a Coastal Development Permit Amendment Application with a check for $200. But he assured us that Staff would deem our changes to be "Immaterial," and, if our application reached him by 5-8-00, he would place the matter on the consent calendar for the next Commission meeting that was to take place in Santa Rosa on 5-10-00. We met his deadline by delivering it to him in person in Eureka. Getting there turned out to be a delightful four-hour drive north through the Redwoods. Merrill informed us that the CCC almost routinely approves immaterial changes, but that "interested parties" are given ten days to respond, and that, if any did, the issue would be placed before the Commission at their June meeting. I have no idea how many of the anti faction might have been informed. This was another chance for them to take a shot at us, but fortunately they didn't! And so, with clearance from the Commission on 5-24-00, County Planner Rick Miller passed our plans to the County Building Department for their plan check. That was accomplished in two days. Evidently the pace is much faster in that department. Building people tend to be action oriented, planners more contemplative. The next step was to pay the school tax that's levied on new home construction. We drove to the Mendocino Unified School District administration building in Mendocino and parted with $5,709.

All that remained was to select a builder, who would then secure the Building Permit by paying a $2,153.21 fee to the County. We received three bids, and on 6-6-00 we selected Pacific Construction, a partnership of Richard Stumpf and Cutler Crowell. Richard would serve as on-site construction supervisor for our house. Construction took a full 18 months, much longer than we'd hoped, but it was worth the wait. Overall, Pacific Construction did an excellent job. The many skilled workmen were remarkable in their ability to carry on despite the often-harsh weather. Several worked with their magnificent dogs nearby, assuring us a warm, tail-wagging welcome whenever we visited the building site.

But this account isn't intended to describe the building process. Rather, its focus is on the conflict between scenic preservation and property rights, and, of course, the related bureaucratic processes of securing permission to build. By all rights this account should then be complete at this point. Unfortunately, it's not. There just happened to be a final problem, and it reopened our contentious interactions with County planners and our more salutary interactions with Coastal Commission planners. The difficulty had to do with getting electric power to our house. In hindsight, in view of the intensive and prolonged scrutiny to which our project had been subjected, it seemed inconceivable that we could encounter such last-minute difficulties.

To understand the nature of the problem, it's helpful to review the process which brought electric power to the Crahan property, the ocean-front parcel immediately to the south of our property. On 3-26-98, a mere ten days prior to our second application for a Coastal Development Permit, Ray Hall, acting as Coastal Permit Administrator, had approved for the Crahan project an overhead power line identical to the one we had proposed in our reapplication. A line of poles already ran along the western side of Highway One. The poles carried telephone cables. The plan in both cases was to replace the short telephone poles with taller dual-use poles, which would continue to carry the telephone cables at the original height, while supporting electric power lines at their tops. That was quickly accomplished for the Crahan project, bringing electric power 777 feet closer to our project. The County Staff Report for the Crahan project, written by Supervising Planner, Linda Ruffing, acting as Project Coordinator, had stated:

> "The costs associated with undergrounding the electrical service
> for 777 feet on the parcel would exceed $25,000. Staff does not
> believe the visual impact of the higher poles warrants the cost
> associated with placement underground."

Clearly, in approving the Crahan project the Coastal Development Administrator (Ray Hall) agreed that the visual impact of the higher poles did not justify the exorbitant cost of undergrounding.

A FINAL PROBLEM AND A FINAL IRONY

When Pacific Gas and Electric engineers completed their similar design for our power-line extension they submitted it routinely to the PG&E Land Agent, Larry Badgley, for review. A meticulously professional land agent, he noted that nowhere in our Coastal Development Permit did it mention connection to the electric power grid, let alone the means of connection. Our position was that it was clearly called out on our plans, which had been thoroughly reviewed and approved by the County and the Coastal Commission. But Badgley was paid to keep PG&E out of trouble, and he wasn't going to run any risk that the company that paid his salary might get into trouble for erecting an unauthorized power line extension. So on 2-26-01 he sent copies of the PG&E plan for our power line extension to both the County and to the Coastal Commission and asked if it would be necessary to apply for a Coastal Development Permit. How's that for asking for trouble? Jurisdictional problems arose immediately regarding whether the County or the Coastal Commission would deal with the issue, and it took four long months of four-way negotiations to settle the matter! In the end the ball ended up in the County's court. And you guessed it. The County lacked the same compassion for our pocketbook that they had accorded Mrs. Crahan's. Moreover, because our extension would be about 50% longer than hers, the cost differential for undergrounding would come to nearly $40,000 in our case. The fact that our power-line extension approach had always been in our plans and had been thoroughly discussed with the County Project Coordinator made no difference. Well, we were in trouble, and, again, we were not getting equal protection of the law.

Rather than attempt to meet the problem head on, we decided to slow down a bit and think about creative solutions. At the time, we were visiting our building site daily keeping an eye on construction progress, and at the end of each visit we drove eastward on our newly-installed driveway toward Highway One. We always enjoyed the view toward the mountains over on RD Beacon's property east of the highway. One day, Margie happened to notice a number of power poles on those mountainsides and realized that a possible solution to our electric power dilemma had been right before our eyes all along. We promptly called for an appointment with RD, and, comfortably seated in his mountaintop bar, asked if we might purchase a power-line easement across his property. He didn't even want money, merely dinner at the Little River Inn. It just happened that for some time he'd wanted to get power down to where his driveway meets Highway One, and so our footing the bill to get it there was just fine with him. But he still could have soaked us for the easement and didn't. We couldn't have asked for a better neighbor. And so the three of us enjoyed a delicious dinner at the Little River Inn.

Pacific Gas and Electric quickly designed a 1,200 foot extension from east to west with four poles, the last one close to the east side of Highway One opposite our driveway and close to RD's. From there we'd have to drill under the highway so the line could run underground beside our driveway to our house. And it obeyed all the regulations, which were less stringent east of the highway. But the County (Frank Lynch, Ray Hall, Frank Zotter) didn't like it, and said we'd have to apply for another Coastal Development Permit with little prospect for success unless we went underground all the way. Might there have been just a little residual resentment over our lawsuit? But we knew that we were on firm ground and in accord with the regulations. So we decided to reactivate correspondence between Jeff Speich and Frank Zotter. In our view the County was in violation of Item 13 of our conditional settlement agreement, the one that says,

> "Upon issuance of a coastal development permit with conditions
> subjectively acceptable to the Berlincourts, the Berlincourts shall
> dismiss the Berlincourt lawsuit with prejudice."

Without electricity our permit was sure as hell not "subjectively acceptable," and, unfortunately, our legal pen pals that had managed to construct our conditional settlement agreement couldn't seem to make any progress on this electrical impasse. In the end it took Bob Merrill, by then an outsider to the controversy, to resolve the conflict. He trotted out Coastal Act language that explained the situation to the County in language they could understand. On 8-1-01 we received a friendly letter from Frank Lynch authorizing us to proceed with our power line extension. It read in part,

> "I'm glad we could reach agreement with this and apologize for
> the time wasted while the Coastal Commission and the County
> sorted out who had permit authority."

We were touched. In retrospect, maybe Frank Lynch wasn't so bad after all, just in with a bad crowd. And Merrill? We can't thank him enough for his helpful intervention.

On 12-4-01 we moved into our new home, still not connected to the electric power grid. That would take yet another month, a California Department of Transportation encroachment permit to drill under the highway, and a total outlay of approximately $38,000. Never mind, a propane-powered auxiliary electric generator was noisily powering our house in the interim. And on that first night in our new home the sunset over the ocean was unforgettable!

But, just as there was a final problem there was also a final irony. Living on this magnificent parcel for the past four years, we've explored many more of its nooks and crannies. And we recently came upon a discovery, which, had we known of it earlier, might have greatly simplified our quest for our coastal development permit. What we discovered were additional patches of Castilleja Mendocinensis or Mendocino Paintbrush, which you'll recall had been designated as "rare and endangered" in Dr. McBride's Botanical Report. These paintbrush patches are so located that, under County practice, development of the southeastern building site mandated by Berrigan would have been prohibited. It's not surprising that they hadn't been reported in Dr. McBride's botanical survey, given the dense vegetation that impedes access to that area. Of course there's also a possibility that these paintbrush patches could have been established by windborne or bird-borne seed sometime during the twelve years since that survey. It follows that rare-and-endangered-species restrictions on development may favor *either* side in a dispute over development. It's all a roll of the dice.

However, as is amply clear from our experience, that's only one of the many capricious factors that determine the fate of anyone so reckless as to attempt to build on the California coast. No, of course, it shouldn't be like that, but, until the California Coastal Act is properly reformed, it will be. In the meantime, if you want to live dangerously, try applying for a Coastal Development Permit in Mendocino County!

EPILOGUE

As already recounted in this book, during the course of our six-year quest for a permit, four other nearby oceanfront homes were granted speedy permits, virtually free of scenic exactions. Those four homes and ours have now all been completed for several years, and so it's possible in hindsight to compare their visual impacts as a basis for judging both the California Coastal Act itself and its implementation in Mendocino County. That would of course be best accomplished by actually viewing the houses from their nearest public view points. Next best would be a comparison based on photos taken from the nearest public view points, each taken with the same camera and lens so as to assure an accurate and unbiased comparison. Such photos, all taken with the same 35 mm camera and 20 mm lens appear in figures 6 through 10. Figure 6 shows the Duarte home viewed from the boundary of Jug Handle State Reserve, its closest public view point, which is 103 feet south of the house. Figure 7 shows the MacIver home viewed from the boundary of Van Damme State Park, its closest public view point, which is 64 feet south of the house. Figure 8 shows the Crahan home viewed from Highway One, its closest public view point, which is 109 feet east of the house. Figure 9 shows the Spires home viewed from Highway One, its closest public view point, which is 50 feet east of the house. Figure 10 shows our home viewed from the Highway-One turnout, its closest public view point, which is some 800 feet southeast of the house. That our home has the least visual impact is not surprising in view of the much-closer proximities of the other houses to their public view points (and the facts that two of the other houses are larger and three are taller than our home). It's also noteworthy that all four of those other houses obstruct broad expanses of public views to the ocean. That's why there's so little evidence of the ocean in Figures 6 through 9.

Because the view of our home from the upper level of Greenwood State Beach was a highly contentious issue in our case, I include a photo of our home (Figure 11) taken from the State Park burner-ring view point approximately one-half mile to the north of our parcel. It was taken with the same 35 mm camera equipped with a 20 mm lens, and It depicts the after-construction scene that we simulated earlier on our 20" x 30" photomontage. It's only with some difficulty that our home can be seen at all at the scale of Figure 11. It was of course more-easily seen on our 20" x 30" photomontage held at arm's length, and, equivalently, when actually viewed from the burner-ring view point one-half mile distant. Our home is also more-easily seen in Figure 12, a photo taken from the upper-level picnic area of Greenwood State Beach with a telephoto lens. That telephoto lens makes it appear four times larger than in a 20 mm lens photo like Figure 11. Even with that degree of magnification, our home still appears relatively inconspicuous when compared with the other four houses in their 20 mm lens photos. Moreover, it's important to note that our home is not visible from the beach below, whereas, as is evident in Figure 5, the Duarte home is very highly visible from public view points on Pine Beach at distances as close as 150 feet.

Often during our quest for a permit, our adversaries also argued that our project would have highly adverse impact on the view from Cuffey's Cove 1.6 miles (as the crow flies) to the north. Pertinent to that issue is Figure 13, a photo taken from the Cuffey's Cove turnout. Most prominent are several brightly colored Elk structures about two inches from the left edge of the photo. In contrast, you might require a magnifying glass to discern our home and three neighboring homes that are ever-so-faintly visible clustered about 2.5 inches from the right edge of the photo. From this it's apparent that, rather than campaigning against our project, the anti faction could have benefited the view from Cuffey's Cove to a far greater extent simply by planting vegetative screens around their own structures and repainting them in dull, earth-tone colors.

Still another comparison of all the structures of concern here is possible using the superb aerial photographs that can be accessed on the internet at *www.californiacoastline.org*, courtesy of the California Coastal Records Project. An excellent photo of the village of Elk is also available there. The pertinent image numbers are as follows: Berlincourt 200503714, Crahan 11804, Duarte 11504 (brightest colored house; parkland is to the right of the house), MacIver 200503486 (parkland is to the right of the fence line), Spires 11807 (leftmost house), village of Elk 200503703.

And with that I rest my case, hoping that the telling of our story will help spur land-use reforms that bring about a more balanced, equitable, and harmonious relationship between scenic preservation and property rights, or in other words, a relationship fully consistent with the United States Constitution.

ACKNOWLEDGMENTS

I must first acknowledge those who opposed our building project, although I'd have happily done without them. But, without them, there'd have been no story. Their remarks, letters, and opinions, liberally quoted in this account, add perspective by representing the other side in the ongoing competition between scenic-preservation mandates and property rights. Likewise, their personal attacks provide interesting insight into human nature and shed light on the culture of Mendocino County.

I more happily acknowledge our far greater debt to all who helped us along the way! During a seemingly-endless eight-year relationship, from initial contact to move-in date, Bob Schlosser and Mike Leventhal, our highly-talented architects, stood by us through thick and thin, tolerated our deluge of changes, and still managed to design a masterpiece that enriches our lives every day. Our thanks are due Sara Geddes for tasteful and effective landscape screening plans and for her highly-professional advocacy on our behalf before the Board of Supervisors. We were exceptionally fortunate to have outstanding legal representation by Ron Zumbrun, Jeff Speich and Neal Lutterman. Without their untiring and highly professional efforts, we'd never have realized our legal rights. Our hearty thanks are due The Pacific Legal Foundation for the letter they sent to the Board of Supervisors in support of our cause. We also thank them for having introduced us to the Zumbrun and Findley Law Firm. For the outstanding construction of our dream home, highest praise and thanks are due Richard Stumpf, Cutler Crowell, and their highly-skilled crew, all of Pacific Construction.

We also thank our loyal supporters from the village of Elk and its environs. They provided advice and encouragement throughout. And they campaigned tirelessly on our behalf through five public hearings. Especially noteworthy were the efforts by Mac and Barbara McKnight, Dean and Rae Wisdom, John and Ruth Raffety, and RD Beacon. But essential contributions were made by all of the following: Leanore Almanrode, Kenneth and Kathryn Anton, Sallie Beacon, Mary Berry, Amy Bloyd, Dave Brotherton, Elaine Bryant, Jim Carr, Dan Clelland, Elizabeth Crahan, Darwin Christiansen, Lorene Christiansen, Martin Christiansen, Beth Corwin, Don Daniels, Anna Daniels, Ross Dinyari, Theodore and Anita Galletti, Stephen Garner, Michael Garrison, Robert and Joan Gates, Hildagard Graves, Bud Kamb, Richard and Karen Keehn, George Lawrence, Everett Liljeberg, Lars

Liljeberg, Ruth Liljeberg, Melvin and Jane Matson, Rebecca Matson, Robert and Sue Matson, William McKenzie, Lauren Miller, Parker Mills, Richard Mitchell, Richard Mitchell Jr., Sharon Mitchell, Sandra Moores, Ed and Kimi Olivera, Denise Pacheco, Bruce Raabe, Joan Robison, Larry Roderick, Dave and Audrey Skilton, Erna Smith, Kevin and Terry Smith, Patricia Smith, Jeff and Tricia Spires, Edwin Staneart, Dean and Helen Turner, Karl and Marliss Waidhofer, Martha Wilcox, Tom Wolsky, and Paul Young.

But, above all, my thanks to Margie, the love of my life, for helping to extricate me from the mess I got us into (and for allowing me to live to tell the tale)!

APPENDIX

The parties to this CONDITIONAL SETTLEMENT AGREEMENT) (agreement) are Ted G. Berlincourt and Marjorie A. Berlincourt (collectively, the Berlincourts), on the one hand, and the County of Mendocino (county) and Board of Supervisors of the county (board), on the other hand, who enter this agreement with respect to the following facts:

RECITALS

A. The Berlincourts are the record owners of approximately 11 acres of real property in the County of Mendocino, commonly known as 7000 South Highway One (the Berlincourt property) and more fully described in the document a copy of which is attached as Exhibit 1 hereto and incorporated by this reference.

B. In July of 1994, the Berlincourts applied to the county for approval of a coastal development permit (the Berlincourt application) for the development and construction of a single family residence on the Berlincourt property.

C. From the filing of their application until August 24, 1995, the Berlincourts and their representatives engaged in considerable dialogue with the county and its representatives relative to the Berlincourt application. As a result of this dialogue, the Berlincourt application was modified in several material respects.

D. On august 24, 1995, the coastal permit administrator for the county conducted a public hearing on the Berlincourt application as modified and denied the application. The coastal permit administrator issued his findings in support of his denial of the Berlincourt application on September 28, 1995.

Appendix

E. Following the denial of the Berlincourt application, the Berlincourts filed a timely appeal to the board seeking reversal of the coastal permit administrator's decision denying the Berlincourt application.

F. On November 13,1995, the board heard the appeal of the coastal permit administrator's denial of the application. At that hearing, on a 3-2 vote, the board rejected the Berlincourt's appeal of the coastal permit administrator's denial of the Berlincourt application.

G. On March 13, 1996, the Berlincourts filed in the Superior Court for the County of Mendocino their Verified Petition for Writ of Mandate (CCP # 1094.5), Damages (CCCP # 1095), and Complaint for Declaratory Relief, Monetary Compensation and Violation of Civil Rights, Action No. 74134 (the Berlincourt lawsuit), relative to the Berlincourt application. The county and the board were named as defendants and respondents in the Belrincourt lawsuit.

H. The Berlincourts continue in their desire to develop and construct the single family residence on the Berlincourt property and, to that end, intend to reapply for a coastal development permit. The reapplication includes two alternative proposed plans, Version 3 and Version 4, both of which differ from that set forth in the Berlincourt application. A copy of the reapplication is attached as Exhibit 2 hereto and incorporated herein by this reference.

I. It is the desire and intention of the parties to this agreement to settle and resolve the claims and causes of action alleged in the Berlincourt lawsuit. The settlement of the controversies existing between the Berlincourts , the county and the board is, however, expressly conditioned upon (1) issuance of a coastal development permit with conditions subjectively acceptable to the Berlincourts and (2) the right of the Berlincourts to withdraw the reapplication for any reason at any time prior to the issuance of an acceptable permit and to then prosecute the Berlincourt lawsuit. It is the further desire and intention of the parties that the reapplication shall not prejudice or affect in any way the Berlincourt's prosecution of the Berlincourt lawsuit in the event that action is subsequently prosecuted for any reason. It is the further desire and intention of the parties that this settlement shall not prejudice or affect in any way any rights, remedies, or causes of action the Berlincourts may have in the future with respect to the reapplication.

AGREEMENT OF THE PARTIES

It is agreed by the parties hereto as follows:

1. The parties acknowledge that the recitals set forth in Paragraphs A-I, inclusive, are true and correct.

2. Within 90 days of the date that this agreement is executed, the Berlincourts will file the reapplication with county's Department of Planning and Building Services (PBS). Concurrent with the filing of the reapplication, the Berlincourts will pay PBS the normal filing fee for a coastal development permit application.

3. Upon filing the reapplication with PBS, the reapplication shall be deemed complete.

4. PBS shall assign the reapplication to Frank Lynch as the project coordinator (the project coordinator).

5. The reapplication shall be evaluated initially by the project coordinator independently of the Berlincourt's prior application. Only after the reapplication is initiallly evaluated by the project coordinator may the project coordinator:

   a. have access to information existing in PBS's file or files related to such prior application except insofar as such information is included in the reapplication or is subsequently introduced by the Berlincourts, or

   b. discuss the reapplication with Gary Berrigan, Mary Stinson, or employees in PBS' Fort Bragg office including, but not limited to Linda Ruffing.

6. The project coordinator shall memorialize in writing and include in the reapplication file any discussion he may have in person or on the telephone with any person relevant or related to the reapplication. The project coordinator shall include in the reapplication file all evidence of communications bearing on the case, whether in person or by telephone, letter, facsimile, electronic mail, etc.

7. Prior to filing the reapplication, the Berlincourts and PBS will agree how the project defined in the reapplication will be described in any referral or public notice related to the project. Thereafter, PBS, county and board shall consistently describe the project as agreed.

8. Any referral or information relevant to the reapplication that is directed or communicated by the project coordinator to any member of the board shall be directed or communicated to every member of the board.

9. The project coordinator shall make all information in the reapplication file readily available to the Berlincourts or their designated representative. On request, the project

coordinator shall transmit to the Berlincourts via priority mail copies of all documents placed in the reapplication file.

10.   Upon determination that he is ready to prepare a staff report relative to the reapplication, the project coordinator shall:

a. give the Berlincourts and their representatives fifteen (15) days' notice in writing of his intention to prepare a staff report, and

b. direct to the Berlincourts and their representatives in writing any comments or concerns that the project coordinator may have relative to the reapplication so that the Berllincourts and/or their representatives may respond in writing to such comments or concerns.

Thereafter, the Berlincourts may submit to the project coordinator additional information relevant to the reapplication. Upon written request made within the 15-day notice period, the Berllincourts, or their representatives may request, and the project coordinator shall grant, up to an additional forty-five (45) days to submit any such additional information. In no event shall the project coordinator prepare the staff report before receiving and considering such additional information submitted by the Berlincourts and/or their representatives.

11. The reapplication shall not be heard by a coastal permit administrator. Instead, the reapplication shall be heard in the first instance by the board.

12. Except as expressly provided in the following paragraph, the parties shall not prosecute the Berlincourt lawsuit while reapplication is pending and shall take any and all action appropriate and necessary, including an application to the court in the Berlincourt lawsuit, to stay or hold such litigation in abeyance without prejudice to any party.

13. Upon issuance of a coastal development permit with conditions subjectively acceptable to the Berlincourts, the Berlincourts shall dismiss the Berlincourt lawsuit with prejudice. At any time prior to issuance of a coastal development permit with conditions subjectively acceptable to the Berlincourts, the Berlincourts may, for any reason, withdraw the reapplication and prosecute the Berlincourt lawsuit. Notwithstanding, the Berlincourts acknowledge that by entering into this agreement County has not agreed that it will issue a coastal development permit or that, if it issues such a permit, the permit will contain conditions subjectively acceptable to the Berlincourts.

14. In the event that the Berlincourt lawsuit is subsequently prosecuted for any reason by any party thereto, such litigation shall in no way be affected or prejudiced by the

reapplication including, but not limited to, any effect caused by any staff report prepared by the project coordinator or action taken by the board; in all respects, the Berlincourt lawsuit shall go forward as if no reapplication were made. Notwithstanding the foregoing, the Berlincourts will and do retain all rights, remedies and causes they may have in the future with respect to the reapplication independent of rights, remedies and causes of action they are asserting in the Berlincourt lawsuit and unaffected in any way by this agreement.

15. The purpose of this agreement is to settle claims which are denied and contested or are potential, and this agreement is the result of a compromise. Nothing contained herein shall be deemed as an admission by any party of any liability of any kind to any other party, all such liabilities being expressly denied.

16. The parties hereto agree to bear their own attorney's fees and costs incurred in connection with the Berlincourt lawsuit or the resolution of matters reflected in this agreement provided the Berlincourt lawsuit is not subsequently prosecuted.

17. The parties shall execute and deliver all documents and perform all further acts that may be reasonably necessary to effectuate the provisions of this agreement.

18. Except as stated herein, the convenants, agreements, representations, warranties, terms and conditions set forth in this agreement shall be binding upon, and inure to the benefit of, the successors and assigns of all parties hereto.

19. The parties hereto acknowledge and agree that each has been represented in negotiations for, and in the preparation of, this agreement by counsel of their own choosing. This agreement shall not be construed against the party preparing it, but shall be construed as if it were prepared jointly by counsel representing all of the parties hereto.

20. The terms of this agreement are intended by the parties as a final expression of their agreement and understanding with respect to such terms as are included in this agreement and may not be contradicted by any evidence of any prior or contemporaneous agreement. The parties further intend that this agreement constitutes the complete and exclusive statement of its terms and that no extrinsic evidence whatsoever may be introduced to vary its terms in any proceeding involving this agreement.

21. Each party acknowledges that neither party, nor agent or attorney for any other party, has made a promise, representation or warranty whatsoever not contained herein concerning the subject matter hereof to induce such party to execute this agreement.

22. This agreement may be executed in several counterparts, and all such executed counterparts shall constitute one agreement, binding on all parties hereto, notwithstanding all of the parties hereto are not signatories to the original or to the same counterpart.

23. This agreement is effective when all parties have signed it.

24. This agreement may be modified, but only if the modification is in writing and signed by all of the parties to this agreement.

25. Each party hereto recognizes and acknowledges that this agreement is not intended to and shall not release any of the parties hereto from any liability or damages, if any, caused by, or arising out of, the failure or refusal to perform any or all of the acts required on their respective parts to be done, as per the terms and conditions of this agreement. In the event of any breach of this agreement, the party aggrieved shall be entitled to recover from the party who breaches, in addition to any other relief provided by law, such reasonable attorney's fees and costs as may be incurred by the non-breaching party in enforcing this agreement.